THE
GREATER
RESET

THE
GREATER
RESET

Reclaiming Personal Sovereignty
Under Natural Law

MICHAEL D. GREANEY
&
DAWN K. BROHAWN

TAN Books
Gastonia, North Carolina

Cover design by David Ferris—www.davidferrisdesign.com

Cover image: Rebuild the world concept image © Francesco Scatena/Shutterstock

Library of Congress Control Number: 2021951930

ISBN: 978-1-5051-2259-6
Kindle ISBN: 978-1-5051-2260-2
ePUB ISBN: 978-1-5051-2261-9

Published in the United States by
TAN Books
PO Box 269
Gastonia, NC 28052
www.TANBooks.com

Printed in the United States of America

To John Moorehouse

Contents

Introduction

"Old things, but in a new way."

—Pope Benedict XV,
Ad Beatissimi Apostolorum, § 25

The year 2020 marked an unprecedented moment in history. For most people across the globe, "normal" economic and social life came to a near standstill. An unseen enemy, exploiting the weaknesses within an interconnected and interdependent system, crept in and, uncontained for several months, spread across borders and began to ravage the world's populations, economies, and societies.

By March 11, 2020, the COVID-19 global pandemic had officially arrived.[1] Human nature and human institutions, faith and reason, were about to be tested.

It is against this backdrop that Dr. Klaus Schwab and Thierry Malleret published their book *COVID-19: The Great Reset*[2] in early July 2020. This was at a time during the global pandemic when few medical scientists or political leaders considered it realistic for a vaccine to be manufactured

---

[1]   On March 11, 2020, the World Health Organization officially declared COVID-19 a pandemic. Kathy Katella, "Our Pandemic Year—A COVID-19 Timeline," *Yale Medicine*, March 9, 2021, https://www.yalemedicine.org/news/covid-timeline.

[2]   Klaus Schwab and Thierry Malleret, *COVID-19: The Great Reset* (Geneva, Switzerland: Forum Publishing, 2020).

and distributed in time and in sufficient quantities to every country to halt the spread of the coronavirus.

Highlighting the perils to human life and the economy posed by COVID-19, Schwab and Malleret analyzed the "systemic pandemics" of poverty, racism, and war. They observed how these ancient evils have been heightened and accelerated not only by the virus but by the fear, anger, and misinformation transmitted virally via the internet. For our very survival, the authors warned, people and nations of the world need to change course. As Schwab and Malleret observed, "We are at a crossroads. . . . One path will take us to a better world: more inclusive, more equitable and more respectful of Mother Nature. The other will take us to a world that resembles the one we just left behind—but worse and constantly dogged by nasty surprises. We must therefore get it right. The looming challenges could be more consequential than we have chosen to imagine, but our capacity to reset could also be greater than we had previously dared to hope."[3]

The Great Reset: New Vision or Old Errors?

Why has the "Great Reset" provoked such widespread concern and even outrage among religious and conservative commentators? How could His Eminence Gerhardt Cardinal Müller characterize it as a virtual totalitarian blueprint[4]

---

[3]   Ibid., 4.

[4]   Edward Pentin, "'Great Reset' Plan Parallels Some of Pope's Initiatives—But There's a Crucial Difference," *National Catholic Register*, February 4, 2021, https://www.ncregister.com/news /great-reset-plan-parallels-some-of-pope-s-initiatives-but-there-s

and find himself in substantial agreement with, for example, Thomas DiLorenzo of the "anarcho-capitalist" group LewRockwell.com, who declared, "'The Great Reset' is the latest deceptive euphemism for totalitarian socialism that is being promoted by yet another group of wealthy corporate elitists who think they can centrally plan the entire world economy."[5]

What called forth this reaction? What assumptions and principles underpin Schwab and Malleret's proposed macro and microeconomic reforms? How would they affect national and global policies, laws, and institutions—as well as every person on earth?

The answers to these questions had been formulated at an international conference several months before the book was written and before the pandemic had gripped the world. On January 21–24, 2020, the World Economic Forum (WEF) had convened for five days in Davos, Switzerland, for its fiftieth anniversary. It brought together a select body of the world's elite—60 heads of state, 250 ministers, 1,000 CEOs, 800 vice presidents of global companies, 300 young leaders, and 450 representatives of non-governmental organizations, global institutions, the media, and academia.

The theme of the 2020 conference was "Stakeholders for a Cohesive and Sustainable World." Its stated purpose was

---

-a-crucial-difference.

[5]   Thomas DiLorenzo, "The Great Nonsense of 'The Great Reset,'" LewRockwell.com, March 27, 2021, https://www.lewrockwell.com/2021/03/thomas-dilorenzo/the-great-nonsense-of-the-great-reset/.

to discuss "the main challenges of global society, their para-doxes and possible solutions."[6]

These "possible solutions" had been incubating over ten years as products of the WEF's Global Redesign Initiative (GRI). Schwab describes the GRI as "a wide-reaching review of the institutions and practices of global governance and the management of the global economy aimed at determining how the world should restructure the international system to better tackle the multiple challenges of globalization."[7]

Interestingly, Klaus Schwab, an engineer and economist by training, launched the World Economic Forum in 1971. It was founded to promote the "stakeholder concept" as the new and dominant global model for creating a better capitalism. This would replace traditional shareholder capitalism and advance environmentally sound economic and social development.[8]

What, however, is "stakeholder capitalism"? Schwab defines stakeholder capitalism as a system in which companies must serve not only shareholders but *all* stakeholders to achieve long-term growth and prosperity.[9] As part of their approach,

6 "At the Age of 50, Is Davos Going Through a Mid-Life Crisis?" World Economic Forum, accessed August 13, 2021, https://www.weforum.org/agenda/2020/02/is-davos-going-through-a-midlife-crisis/.

7 Klaus Schwab, "Foreword," *The World Economic Forum: A Partner in Shaping History, The First 40 Years* (Geneva, Switzerland: The World Economic Forum, 2010).

8 "A Platform for Impact," World Economic Forum Institutional Brochure, accessed August 16, 2021, http://www3.weforum.org/docs/WEF_Institutional_Brochure_2019.pdf.

9 "About Klaus Schwab," World Economic Forum, accessed August 17, 2021, https://www.weforum.org/about/klaus-schwab.

the WEF's manifesto declares "that companies should pay their fair share of taxes, show zero tolerance for corruption, uphold human rights throughout their global supply chains, and advocate for a competitive level playing field."[10]

Unfortunately, even with the best of intentions, we can design solutions that do not work or that end up causing greater harm than the original problems. To understand the implications of Schwab's "stakeholder capitalism," the WEF's proposals, and why these have aroused such deep suspicion and alarm among many around the world, this book will examine the flaws and inadequacies of the Keynesian framework within which *The Great Reset* bases its analyses and solutions.

Concentrated Power and Wealth: A Threat to Lives and Livelihoods

In *The Great Reset,* a follow-up to the January 2020 conference in Davos, Schwab and Malleret spotlight the dramatic widening of the wealth gap around the world. During 2020, most people in the United States saw their incomes fall and savings evaporate due to job loss and business closures. At the same time, a tiny number saw their share of wealth and power increase, largely due to the dramatic rebound in the stock market during 2020.

An Oxfam report entitled "Public Good or Private Wealth" presented at the 2019 WEF Conference stated that 2,200 billionaires worldwide saw their wealth grow by 12 percent

---

[10] "The Davos Manifesto," The World Economic Forum, accessed August 13, 2021, https://www.weforum.org/the-davos-manifesto.

while the poorest half saw its wealth fall by 11 percent.[11] A joint report issued in September 2020 by Americans for Tax Fairness and the Institute for Policy Studies (based on data from *Forbes*) found that:

- America's 643 billionaires gained $845 billion in the first six months of the pandemic.
- Total net worth of the nation's billionaires rose from $2.95 trillion to $3.8 trillion.
- Amazon's Jeff Bezos was the biggest winner, adding $73.2 billion in net worth.
- Meanwhile, there were over 50 million jobs lost, with nearly 14 million still unemployed.[12]

Schwab and Malleret point out the inadequacies of the present measures of economic health, such as Gross Domestic Product (GDP), which hide gross imbalances in wealth and income among individual citizens: "It is not only the overall size of the economy that matters but also the distribution of gains and the progressive evolution of access to opportunity. With income inequality more marked than ever in many countries and technological developments driving further polarization, total GDP or averages such as GDP per capita are becoming less and less useful as true indicators of individuals' quality of life. Wealth inequality is a significant

---

11   Dylan Matthews, "Are 26 Billionaires Worth More Than Half the Planet?" *Vox*, January 22, 2019, https://www.vox.com/future-perfect/2019/1/22/18192774/oxfam-inequality-report-2019-davos-wealth.

12   Keith Griffith, "Rich Get Richer," *Daily Mail*, September 18, 2020, https://www.dailymail.co.uk/news/article-8747619/US-billionaires-gained-845-BILLION-six-months-pandemic.html.

dimension of today's dynamic of inequality and should be more systematically tracked."[13]

Their book highlights inequality of income, wealth, opportunity, and risk as key drivers of violence, crime, and social upheaval. They note that the COVID-19 pandemic has not been the "great leveler" as some have asserted. On the contrary, the pandemic has been a "great unequalizer," compounding inequalities in income, wealth, and opportunity.[14]

The First Step toward a Cure

The pandemic has opened an opportunity to shift from our present path toward economic collapse, political and social upheaval, and irreparable environmental destruction. Schwab asserts that humanity must seize the moment to create a more just, inclusive, and sustainable system. The irony of the Great Reset, however, is that it undermines its own objectives of reducing inequality and conflict and increasing equal opportunity.

Whether intentional or not, the solutions offered in *The Great Reset* would further erode the dignity and empowerment of every human person. These include such redistributive measures as:

- universal basic income,
- a mandatory global tax on corporations,
- increasing the economic power of government,
- unlimited monetization of government debt by central banks,

---

[13]   Klaus Schwab and Thierry Malleret, *COVID-19: The Great Reset* (Geneva, Switzerland: World Economic Forum, 2020), 59.
[14]   Ibid., 2.

- and the further undermining of private property in corporate equity.

The last point bears note. While never explicitly stating this as an objective,[15] the WEF has become associated with the phrase "You will own nothing, and you will be happy."[16] Technologists might point to a future where people are freed from the encumbrances of never-ending accumulation of material things in order to enjoy the convenience and mobility of services-on-demand. For many people, however, the idea of owning nothing and being subject to the whims of the government or an elite ownership class conjures visions of the Orwellian society of *Nineteen Eighty-Four*.

Perhaps the idea of "private property in corporate equity" means little to most people, as this is something few people experience. In examining the deeper meaning of "property" as a set of ownership rights and powers that are intrinsic to human nature, however, the danger of abolishing private property ("everyone will own everything; no one will own anything") becomes more apparent. This book, *The Greater Reset*, will examine how the popes and other natural law proponents understood the connection between property and human dignity, power, participation, and freedom.

---

[15] "Fact check: The World Economic Forum does not have a stated goal to have people own nothing by 2030," *Reuters*, February 25, 2021, https://www.reuters.com/article/uk-factcheck-wef/fact-check-the-world-economic-forum-does-not-have-a-stated-goal-to-have-people-own-nothing-by-2030-idUSKBN2AP2T0.

[16] David Ansara interview with author Douglas Kruger, "You will OWN NOTHING and you will be HAPPY," Centre for Risk Analysis, February 12, 2021, https://youtu.be/60MzTlrOCXQ.

Is there a conspiracy at work between the WEF and its cohorts? One point is undeniable and can be attributed to all sides of the debate. Illustrative of the "moral omission" of both capitalism and socialism, Schwab and Malleret's "Great Reset" neither offers a free market, non-redistributive way to equal opportunity nor allows access to acquire sufficient productive capital to generate an independent income and control over one's own future. Thus, the Great Reset fails to empower economically every person; instead, it concentrates power in the government and in a private elite.

We face an inescapable question: If our present paradigms of monopolistic capitalism and collectivist socialism (and admixtures such as the Great Reset) have failed to offer sound principles for creating universally enabling, unifying, and sustainable solutions, is it time for a new paradigm?

We then need to ask if there are new ideas that would promote the dignity and the economic and social sovereignty of each human person—under the ultimate sovereignty of the Author of all creation, human nature, and absolute values. Do these new ideas offer a way of uniting a growing constituency for free markets and private property, as well as making the State economically dependent on the citizens, rather than vice versa?

Simply put, we do not view the "Great Reset" as a true reset or fundamental system correction at all. It is merely a twenty-first-century rehash of the same old corrupting, power-concentrating systems of both collectivist socialism and individualistic capitalism. And these systems led us to the present moral, social, political, and economic crisis we now face—an outgrowth of the "New Things" of socialism and modernism that emerged two hundred years ago.

In accepting the existence of certain universal truths and of an Absolute Source of those universal truths by reason or faith, we need the humility to acknowledge that we as individuals cannot perceive or understand truth in its totality. We are not God: omniscient, omnipresent, eternal, and perfect. By acting together in our shared search for the truth and with respect for each other (regardless of our personal differences), however, we can perfect and build upon our understanding of such absolutes as truth and justice.

By acting in accordance with those absolute values or principles, we can continue to reform our human systems to enable each of us to exercise our natural rights and develop our unique potentials. We may not know perfect truth and justice, but we can witness and experience the consequences of violating those absolutes both individually and as a society.

Promoting the Dignity of Every Person

On April 17, 2020, not long after the start of the lockdown in the United States, the Center for Economic and Social Justice (CESJ), an interfaith, grassroots think tank based outside of Washington, DC, published an article, "Universalizing Capital Ownership: How Article 17 of the Universal Declaration of Human Rights Can Renew the Post-Pandemic Economy."[17] Characterizing the COVID-19 pandemic as a

---

17   "Universalizing Capital Ownership," CESJ, accessed August 16, 2021, https://www.cesj.org/just-third-way-feature/universalizing-capital-ownership-how-article-17-of-the-universal-declaration-of-human-rights-can-renew-the-post-pandemic-economy/.

global war, the article called for united effort on the scale of World War II. Only a rapid mobilization of global resources and scientific expertise, with the concerted effort of leaders and citizens, could end the threat worldwide.

Witnessing the devastation to human lives, the economy, and the social order wrought by the pandemic, CESJ proposed a strategy for rebuilding the economy at the local, national, and global levels. What made CESJ's proposal unique was its basis in the dignity and empowerment of the human person, not a private or governmental elite.

Starting with universal values and moral principles as expressed in the Catholic Church's social encyclicals and other sources, it asked, "How can we rebuild the economy in a way that would empower every person from birth to death?" The answer lies in Article 17 of the Universal Declaration of Human Rights: "(1) Every person has the right to own property individually as well as in association with others. (2) No one shall be arbitrarily deprived of his property."

The question of *how* each person can acquire productive capital in which to exercise his or her own property rights was answered in §1 of the 1776 Virginia Declaration of Rights (removed by Thomas Jefferson in the Declaration of Independence). This asserted that every person has the rights "to life, liberty, *with the means* of acquiring and possessing property, and pursuing and obtaining happiness and safety."

Unlike the WEF's Great Reset, CESJ based its Just Third Way of Economic Personalism on natural law principles of economic justice within a personalist framework for reforming the money and tax systems. This would shift the use of the central bank from monetizing government debt to applying sound free market principles of business and banking. The proposal would ensure that all new money and credit would be created solely for private sector growth, backed by marketable goods and services (not government debt), and tied to a stable standard of value.

CESJ's proposal characterized money and credit as "social tools" (rather than as commodities) created by human beings to facilitate the production, exchange, and consumption of marketable goods and services. Based on the "feasibility" requirements of standard capital finance, it outlined a new role for commercial banks, central banks, and insurance companies.

Rather than serving only the already-wealthy, these powerful institutions could now provide equal access to every citizen to the financial means of acquiring shares of productive capital in profitable companies. Insured capital loans could be repaid by the new assets' future stream of pre-tax corporate profits. Once the loans were repaid, each citizen would own and control shares of new capital, providing them an independent source of income.

The book before you, *The Greater Reset*, asks: Must we simply accept a world where systemic poverty, racism, and war are inevitable, unavoidable, and irreparable? Or can we turn the present crisis into an opportunity to "reset" the system back to universal principles and absolute values of natural law? Can we then apply those principles to build upon the new possibilities, discoveries, and advances of the twenty-first century?

Are concentrated power and ownership inevitable? Not if we go back to the correct starting point of society—the dignity and empowerment of each human person.

Restoring Human Dignity
and Healing the World

What do we mean by the "*Greater* Reset?"

We mean returning to eternal truths embedded in human nature. Guided by these truths, each of us can organize with others to build the world anew, armed with the gift of reason, committed to pursuing justice, and inspired by the spirit of *caritas*. Through acts of social justice, as called for by Pope Pius XI, we can reform our social institutions to promote the dignity, freedom, and full development of every human person as a sovereign being and steward of creation.

This book will explore the essential social institutions that hold the key to liberating every human being. In examining Louis Kelso and Mortimer Adler's simple formulation of the system principles of economic justice as guided and corrected by the virtue of social justice, we will then explore how Kelso's concepts of money and credit relate directly to the idea of "participatory justice."

Louis Kelso's system of "future savings," asset-backed money, and capital credit loan insurance as a substitute for past savings-based forms of collateral—possibly combined with something like R. Buckminster Fuller's idea for a twenty-first-century monetary standard based on the kilowatt-hour[18]—suggests an innovative but justice-based way of universalizing equal access for every individual, from birth to death, to acquire ever-advancing technology.

In this way, the machines and artificial intelligence that now threaten the livelihoods of many working people could

---

[18] Described in Fuller's book, *Critical Path* (New York: St. Martin's Press, 1981).

be owned and controlled not just by a fraction of humanity but by every human person, with equal access to "the means of acquiring and possessing property." As an economically empowered citizen-owner, each of us could be liberated by our technologies from the necessity of economic toil, providing time to develop virtue, our personal good, and the common good.

By "common good," we mean the institutional environment within which every human being as a "political animal" ordinarily exercises rights and becomes more fully human, or virtuous. The common good must not be confused with common *goods*, those things owned by the community as a matter of expedience or convenience, such as roads, bridges, even public parks, and so on. Rather, the common good consists of that vast network of institutions—that is, social structures or habits—that provides our social environment.

Furthermore, from the pro-life perspective, such a justice-based economic development framework for the common good would virtually eliminate economic rationalizations for abortion. As respect for the dignity and rights of each person is reinforced within a life-enhancing economic environment, respect for the lives of the unborn will grow throughout the general society.

The purpose of this book is not to prove or disprove that there is a conspiracy at work, either in the WEF or with Schwab's "Great Reset." Rather, this book will reveal the historical roots of the errors in principles and applications of what Schwab and others propose. *The Greater Reset* will argue that the WEF's proposals would shape basic institutions, laws, and policies in ways that lead to totalitarianism and the accelerating destruction of human life.

This book will also demonstrate how Schwab's (and the WEF's) plans, whether intentional or not, build power and wealth into the State and/or into a tiny private elite, and not—as called for in the social teachings of the Church—in every human person. This book will delineate the moral, economic, and political implications of private property in the twenty-first century. Stated simply, "Own or be owned."

Our world is still struggling to bring the COVID-19 pandemic to an end. Similarly, the battle against the age-old pandemics of systemic poverty, racism, and war rages on.

CHAPTER I

The Great Inversion

1.1. Role Reversal

Why is there a growing chorus of global leaders today calling for a "Great Reset" while more and more citizens angrily denounce it? What is happening with the world that so many people would even consider changing virtually every aspect of society? What has led us to this moment of crisis—and truth—for all of humanity?

For much of human existence, life for most people has been filled with toil, want, disease, and war. There has never been a time in history when everyone enjoyed equal dignity, freedom, and opportunity, with equal access to the means to live a good life.

Instead, what we have had during the best times is hope that life would improve—or continue to improve—for everyone. However, when enough people lose hope for a better future, chaos and destruction are sure to follow. Societies start turning to dictators, demagogues, capitalism, socialism, Great Resets, and so on to restore order.

How did this state of affairs arise when incredible technological and medical advances are being made daily and
the potential exists for everyone on earth to lead a good life?
One simple answer is that we put ourselves and our own creations in the place of God and made something other than
the good of every human person the goal of life.

The Great Inversion

In *God and Intelligence in Modern Philosophy* (1925), his
doctoral thesis published nearly a century ago, Venerable
Fulton J. Sheen examined how the basis of modern society—both civil (State) and religious (Church)—had shifted
from reason to faith. While this might sound ideal to those
who believe in God, results have proved otherwise for people
of all faiths and philosophies, not to mention non-believers.

In his study, Sheen noted that there has been what we can
call a Great Inversion in the order of creation. This has completely overturned the meaning and purpose of life. God's
role and man's have been reversed, turning God into man's
servant. A distorted supernature has replaced nature. Of
course, when we use the term "supernatural" in this book,
we are using it in its literal sense as that which is above nature
and human nature—that is, *über*-natural or divine. We do
not mean the popular notion of vampires, ghosts, and so on.

Distinguishing nature from supernature (and *vice versa*)
is vital, even though both are integral and complementary
parts of reality. Confusing them, ignoring one in favor of the
other, or absorbing one into the other effectively nullifies or
even abolishes a significant part of reality.

Jesus Himself noted that natural and supernatural matters should be kept in their proper place. When He stated that what belongs to Caesar—this world—should be given to Caesar and what belongs to God should be given to God, He was giving commonsense guidelines for keeping matters in the right order.[1]

At the same time, Jesus also reminded us that while the natural and the supernatural orders each have their own rules—so to speak—they necessarily go together, each one completing and fulfilling the other. As He said, man does not live by natural things ("bread") alone but by the spirit—the "Word of God"—as well.[2]

Unfortunately, however, because much modern thought attempts to impose supernature on nature or absorb nature into supernature, the meaning and purpose of life has been changed. Instead of every human being becoming more fully human—that is, virtuous—we have created a system in which man becomes God.

With self-deification, the goal is to gain enough power to impose one's personal vision on others. This will establish "the Kingdom of God on Earth," the "consistently recurring objective of American messianic movements."[3]

---

[1]   See Matt. 22:15–22; Mark 12:13–17; Luke 20:20–26.

[2]   See Matt. 4:4.

[3]   Adam Morris, *American Messiahs: False Prophets of a Damned Nation* (New York: W.W. Norton and Company, 2019), 6–7, 256. This was also the theme of "the (First) Great Awakening," a wildly enthusiastic religious revival that swept through New England in the mid-eighteenth century. Ibid., 17, 50, 72–73, 82, 134–35; Chris Jennings, *Paradise Now: The Story of American Utopianism* (New York: Random House, 2016), xii, 38, 295; J. D. Dickey,

As Sheen noted, such an approach ultimately seeks to create a terrestrial and temporal paradise in which the abstract concept of "humanity" replaces the supreme (highest) actuality of God. Individual human beings, and even God, are relegated to second or third place, and eventually no place at all. As Sheen concluded:

> There is "an alteration in the seat of authority." It is a transfer of the seat of authority from God to man, and a transfer of the measure from God to man. "The earth of things, long thrown into the shadow by the glories of the upper ether, must resume its rights."[4]
>
> "In the beginning God made man to His own image and likeness."
>
> In the twentieth century man makes God to his own image and likeness.[5]

Despite the grimness of his conclusion, Sheen did give a little hope. At least by the first quarter of the twentieth century, not everyone had succumbed to the urge to play God or had

American Demagogue: The Great Awakening and the Rise and Fall of Populism (New York: Pegasus Books, 2019); William G. Mc-Loughlin, *Revivals, Awakening and Reform* (Chicago, Illinois: University of Chicago Press, 1978), 8, 18, 19, 20, 158–59, 171–78, 182. Seeking the Kingdom of God on Earth was not restricted to movements in the United States, as Msgr. Ronald Knox noted in *Enthusiasm* (1950) and Dr. Julian Strube of Heidelberg University reveals in his work.

4   William James, *Pragmatism: A New Name for Some Old Ways of Thinking* (New York: Longmans, Green and Co., 1907), 123. [Note in text.]

5   Fulton J. Sheen, *God and Intelligence in Modern Philosophy* (New York: IBE Press, 2009), 320.

yielded to the temptation to restore the temporal paradise through the power of deified collective man.

According to G. K. Chesterton in his introduction to Sheen's book, there remained at least one bastion of common sense against the flood of irrationality: the Catholic Church. As Chesterton wrote, "In this book, as in the modern world generally, the Catholic Church comes forward as the one and only real champion of Reason."[6]

Despite the complexity of *God and Intelligence*, Sheen's main point is very simple. The modern world is suffering from an abandonment of reason and common sense. Tremendous problems have been caused by discarding basic and universal truths of human existence, as well as rational methodologies for determining what is "true." As Sheen said, "There are many who, not lacking either wisdom or penetration, find such a 'kingdom of God' no more than a travesty, and who, through their love of truth, cannot listen to these prophets. The wisdom of the ages and the epitome of our experience is given in the simple truth understood by the simple and forgotten by many a philosopher, that we are not 'God-makers but God-made.'"[7]

What Sheen observed about the inversion of the roles of God and man has ramifications far beyond the confines of academic studies or even religious belief. Confusing the natural and the supernatural means that we render to God what is man's and to man what is God's. Faith and reason become

---

[6]   Ibid., 9.
[7]   Ibid., 321.

separated, as are charity and justice, the intellect and the will, and the natural and the supernatural.

What should go together, each one completing and fulfilling the other, is put in opposition. The human intellect is split in two, changing the nature of truth and thus reality[8] as deemed necessary or expedient to gain some end.

Confusion does not end there. Since human beings are far from being gods, humanity, the collective—an abstraction created by man—becomes God. As the representative of the People (as opposed to mere people), the State, in the words of Thomas Hobbes, is transformed into a "Mortall God" that must be obeyed on earth as the immortal God is obeyed in heaven.[9]

This puts the presumed dignity of the collective or some elite before the actual dignity of the human person under God. The implicit totalitarianism inherent in the collectivist or elitist understanding of dignity has caused some to claim we are in the End Times, even though "of that day and hour no one knoweth."[10]

Solutions That Create Problems

While prophets of doom have often been wildly inaccurate, no one can deny that many things *are* seriously wrong in the world today. While the analyses of critical systemic problems may be largely correct, they have engendered a slew of

---

[8] "A proposition is true . . . when the corresponding state of affairs is the case." J(ózef) M(aria) Bocheński, *The Methods of Contemporary Thought* (New York: Harper and Row, Publishers, 1968), 6.

[9] Thomas Hobbes, *Leviathan*, II.xvii.

[10] Matt. 24:36.

ill-considered solutions, such as the Great Reset, universal basic income, stakeholder capitalism, inclusive capitalism, democratic socialism and capitalism, and similar proposals.

After even the most superficial examination, one point becomes clear about the various schemes. Taking Sheen's analysis into consideration, we realize that they are not solutions. Many of the proposals tend to be directed to the wrong goals, and the solutions fall short in one of two ways, often both.

Firstly, to establish God's (or, more accurately, collective man's) Kingdom on Earth, such proposals tend to focus primarily on meeting people's immediate material needs and not on enabling every human being to develop as a sovereign person and special creation of God.

Then there is the issue of funding these proposals. No feasible means is proposed to sustain these programs financially. Simply legislating against greed or mandating redistribution is not practical. "Soaking the rich" only works if there are rich people to "soak." Once their wealth has been redistributed and their value as persons ignored, they are as poor as everyone else.

Secondly, there is a glorification of the collective, and a consequent vast increase in State power. This erodes, and sometimes eliminates, respect for the dignity of the individual human person, as well as what it means to be a human being and the purpose of life itself.

Both misdirections can be characterized as elevating purely animal needs—the most immediate needs of mere survival—to the level of the most important needs—that of the meaning and purpose of life. Along with the inversion of the natural and the supernatural orders that Sheen noted, the economic order and the personal orders are reversed. Meeting material needs becomes the sole end of existence. If the desired or anticipated end of some program is to secure some material benefit, anything goes. The end justifies the means. This is pure moral relativism. Ignoring human personality, moral relativism relegates human life to the level of any other animal. That the Great Reset takes this for granted may be its most fundamental problem and profoundest error.

1.2. Modern Symptoms of the Decline

The Great Reset did not arise suddenly, but as a response to evils that are as real and pervasive as they are overwhelming. We must not think, however, that these problems—the wealth and income gap, involuntary immigration, joblessness, and so on—bad and immediate as they are, are particularly modern, or that they resulted from the COVID-19 pandemic.

Getting Back on Track

Many people cannot accept the possibility that some problems may have causes other than a hidden conspiracy, or that the cause may be irrelevant to developing a viable solution. A poorly designed system, for example, can mimic a conspiracy down to the smallest detail. Even so, many people will insist that the whole situation is intentional, a way deliberately designed by an elite to control others.

Rather than work to find solutions, such people will argue endlessly over who is responsible. Identifying and punishing the guilty becomes more important than solving the problem.

They fail to realize that if there really is a conspiracy or hidden cabal behind what is happening, the best solution is to make it difficult or impossible for the conspiracy to work.

Structuring the system to inhibit wrongdoing and encourage doing right is called "internal control." Internal control cannot stop all wrongdoing, but it can make it very difficult and the profit too small to bother with.

Ferreting out the guilty or the presumed guilty is a waste of time and resources when there is no clear evidence of wrongdoing. The commonsense—and socially just—approach is to make it difficult for anyone to profit by anything he might do contrary to the rights of others or the common good.

We do not have to agree why particular problems exist, just that they do. If we are truly interested in finding a solution, we cannot get diverted into side arguments or play the blame game. We must identify the problem.

Symptoms must be dealt with, and they must be dealt with effectively. At the same time, any action we take cannot contradict the reason for doing it in the first place. We need to discover the direct causes of the symptoms (not the motives of any conspirators) and present a possible solution that not only addresses the problem—once it has been identified—but considers the demands of individual human dignity along with "a decent respect to the opinions of mankind."[11]

Nevertheless, although all people are important and have the dignity that is due to their status as human persons, not all opinions are equal. Respecting other persons does not

---

[11]   Declaration of Independence.

mean upholding their opinions if the opinions are not worthy of respect. At the same time, we do not insult someone simply because we disagree with that person.

That being the case, we must prioritize problems—or symptoms—recognizing sometimes that a problem simply is not that important. Other times, even if a problem is of overriding importance, it may not be immediate. We can address it later. Then there are the problems that are not merely important but pressing. Those we must deal with immediately.

As a case in point, we may annoy some people by saying that the COVID-19 pandemic was not the main problem. Instead, it was a trigger that exposed serious weaknesses and problems in the social order that have been building up for at least two centuries. This gave an enormous impetus to proposals such as the Great Reset, vesting them with a suspicious sense of urgency that rightly or wrongly convinced many people that there was a conspiracy afoot.

The Problem of Über-Wealth

Whether the pandemic and the subsequent Great Reset is a conspiracy or the result of opportunism is irrelevant. The real problem is what to do about the situation—and the Great Reset is not the answer.

Take, for example, the fact that there is a tiny minority of über-wealthy people in the world—that is, people whose accumulated riches make ordinary millionaires look like *petite bourgeoisie.* A number of these ultra-rich grew enormously wealthier during the time when the global economy had virtually shut down. The subsequent, much-touted "recovery" has benefitted few ordinary people.[12]

What accounted for the wildly lopsided economic increases for the super-wealthy while most people, including middle-income wage earners, suffered some of the worst economic losses in a generation? Even during some of the slowest periods in the COVID-19 economy, speculative gains on the world's stock exchanges were skyrocketing. On June 27, 2008, the day the "bear market" was officially announced, the Dow Jones Industrial Average closed at 11,346.51. Thirteen years later, June 28, 2021,[13] the Dow closed at 34,283.27, a rise of 302.14 percent during a presumed economic downturn and a pandemic!

There is production, certainly, and at nearly the level before the pandemic began. Consumer demand, however, is being driven by withheld consumption during the pandemic, not by anything sustainable.[14]

As soon as current savings are depleted, we can expect to see consumer demand fall, triggering another recession or depression. This could be fatal, as the Keynesian countercyclical approach will not be able to rescue us as government credit has already been stretched to the limit and beyond.

---

[12] Gwynn Guilford and Sarah Chaney Cambon, "U.S. Economy's Rebound Is 'Without Historical Parallel'," *The Wall Street Journal*, June 3, 2021, A-1, A-8.

[13] June 27, 2021, was a Sunday and the market was closed.

[14] David J. Lynch, "Automation Sees a Boost As Employers Struggle to Hire," *The Washington Post*, May 20, 2021, A-1, A-20.

The Threats

While the pandemic and the various responses to it did not cause the problems, it certainly made them much more immediate and revealed their magnitude. Today's challenges are no different from what has in various forms always afflicted people, but—with or without a conspiracy—in many ways are almost cosmically greater in scope:

- The wealth and income gap
- Widespread poverty
- Destruction of the environment
- Conflict-driven immigration
- Excessive state power
- Decay of families

We cannot honestly say that the Great Reset is an overreaction to seemingly overwhelming problems. That would be to deny what is painfully obvious. We can, however, say that it is the *wrong* response—which naturally leads us to look at the *right* response.

1.3. How to Look at Problems

To do him justice, Klaus Schwab, architect of the Great Reset, does not directly target people as the source of today's problems. By ignoring the impact of concentrated power on the dignity, equal opportunity, and empowerment of every human person, however, his solutions would vastly increase the power of the State and that of a tiny elite.

Rather than institutionalizing the fundamental right of every person to become a self-sufficient owner of productive

capital, the Great Reset would further concentrate ownership, economic power, and thus political power. This would
lead to a system that can only be described as totalitarian.

Searching for the Guilty: A Waste of Time

It can come about almost as if by chance. When looking
into the immediate issues that afflict society today, people
are often tempted to seek scapegoats and blame unpopular
individuals or groups. The temptation is to convince ourselves that if only we could get rid of everyone we dislike
(e.g., the radicals, reactionaries, rich, poor, undesirables,
defectives, useless eaters, inferior races, Catholics, Jews,
Gypsies, straights, gays, the ungodly, or the too godly), all
will be well.

For some reason, however, it never seems to work out that
way. Once the undesirables have been purged, it inevitably
happens that the problems remain. It then becomes necessary to identify other individuals or groups who are stifling
progress or advancing too fast and eliminate *those* people;
the program is not working because *those* people are not trying hard enough or are working against it.

It comes as no surprise that radicals who guillotined reactionaries at the start of the Reign of Terror during the French
Revolution were later executed for insufficient revolutionary
fervor—and yet the problems remained. Many early socialists developed their theories because they believed the Revolution had failed or had not gone far enough and the world
needed more extreme change.

A Sense of Helplessness

A similar situation exists today. People complain about the wealth and income gap, widespread poverty, unemployment, and so on, making solutions such as the Great Reset sound very attractive.

Seeing that individual efforts are ineffective to correct such problems, however, they conclude some evil person, group, or institution must be responsible. Private property, the laws of economics, etc., must be wrong because they interfere with establishing and maintaining a perfect society in which everyone gets what he needs, and the reign of peace and justice is established. Although these problems relate to rights of private property private property and the inexorable laws of economics, they cannot be overcome by ignoring or rejecting those laws, as many adherents of socialism and the Great Reset seem to assume.

These problems emerge not because private property and the laws of economics are invalid or because of a conspiracy. They arise because private property and the laws of economics are not being applied properly. Instead, they create barriers to full participation by many within these social institutions rather than accessibility for everyone.

Money, Production, and Capital

Take, for example, something as fundamental and pervasive as money. Money is merely the term for how someone measures and exchanges what he or she produces for what someone else produces. Believe it or not, once you understand that simple fact, you understand the essence of money.

This leads to another issue, though: How do you produce? If solely by human labor, then most people can be productive. Everyone owns (or is supposed to own) his or her own labor, and most people can add their labor to the production process.

If, however, non-human things that we call "capital," tools that can be used to produce, are productive, then people who own capital tools can also be productive. That is because ownership—private property—entitles the owner to what is produced with the tools he owns.

When anybody can own labor, capital, or both, then anybody can be productive. Being productive, anyone can consume what he produces, or exchange some of what he produces to others for what they produce that he wants to consume. To the extent that everybody can be productive, everybody has access to money.

When Technology Displaces Labor

What happens, however, when capital becomes more productive than labor and not everyone has access to the money to acquire the labor-displacing capital? In that case, only those people with access to money can own capital and be productive, and only owners of capital can be productive and have access to money.

People whose labor cannot compete with capital become non-productive and must rely on some form of redistribution to be able to consume. Since only government has the power to redistribute on a large scale without destroying society, at least in the short term, the power of the State increases exponentially. As the productive power of the few accelerates and concentrates, the State increasingly redistributes income to sustain the many who cannot produce sufficiently to meet their own needs.

Obviously, there is a problem here. *But what?* If the problem is private property, money, or technology, is the solution to *abolish* ownership, exchange, and tools? Or do we need to change *how we use* ownership, exchange, and tools?

The Wrong Response

The Great Reset and similar proposals are a response to the fact that if only some people can use money to buy tools, you will have concentrated capital ownership, and only capital owners will be productive. If only capital owners can be productive, you will have a wealth and income gap.

Since that is the case—so proponents argue—we must redistribute what the few produce for the benefit of the many. This necessarily means an enormous growth in State power under the control of the super-rich, but the end justifies the means, right?

Ultimately, neither the State nor the super-rich who control the State can provide for everyone at the desired levels of material wellbeing, or at all. When people realize this truth, demands increase to eliminate the unfit, as well as surplus population, as every additional recipient of redistribution means that each recipient gets less.

Other people change from being your "fellow man" in solidarity to being potential or actual rivals in conflict. By taking as a given that a relatively few productive (or sufficiently productive) people can permanently support many unproductive people, the Great Reset unintentionally builds injustice and conflict into its system in the name of justice and peace.

1.4. A Personalist Analysis

As its name suggests, behind the Great Reset is the fixed belief that nothing less than a complete change in the economic system, fundamental institutions, and human nature itself can save the world. Without that, the situation is hopeless.

A Response to Helplessness

Many people see the inexorable and heartless laws of economics taking away all hope and grinding them into the dirt. That is why proposed solutions like socialism, the New Deal, the Great Society, the Great Reset, universal basic income, inclusive capitalism, democratic socialism, or any of the programs whose names are legion find receptive audiences. Nature is not working, or is working the wrong way, so change or bypass it.

Nevertheless, a situation is hopeless only if we assume we are helpless. We agree that nature operates according to its own rules, whether we are referring to persons—human beings—or things. Natural law is absolute, whether we are referring to the laws of physics that govern the material world or the general code of human behavior—that is, the natural moral law written in the heart of every human being.

No one can legitimately override natural rights, even with the best intentions. This is because exercising our natural rights is the normal way in which we become more fully human—that is, virtuous.

Consequently, if the system is poorly structured in a way that denies people exercise of their natural rights, we should not perpetuate that system or legitimize institutional barriers to equal access and opportunity. Instead, we should make certain that people's natural rights are secured and effectively exercised. They will then find it easier to become virtuous when they can be liberated and educated to pursue the meaning and purpose of their lives.

Polish Personalism

In *The Acting Person* (1969), Karol Józef Wojtyła (Pope Saint John Paul II) examined the question of the human being as a person—that is, something, or rather *someone*, with inherent rights who, by exercising natural rights, becomes more fully human. Wojtyła's personalism, as described in *The Acting Person* as well as essays and lectures, and, later, in his papal encyclicals, requires that all human beings have effective and material exercise of their natural rights simply because they are human beings and therefore persons. We are not allowed to abolish natural rights as the socialists do or pay meaningless lip service to them like the capitalists.

It is futile to try to change the absolutes of nature, including the natural law or human nature itself. Instead, we need to change the erroneous assumptions at the root of the problem. We need to make nature work for us rather than against us—that is the Great Problem with the Great Reset and similar proposals: not that it seeks the obvious good of material wellbeing but that it seeks to impose it by command. It ignores the essence of the human person that makes care for the wellbeing of others something good in the first place. It thereby denies personality and therefore humanity.

1.5. A Personalist Solution

The current world climate raises an important question: how do we make nature work for us instead of against us as we believe would happen with the Great Reset?

What Is Thomistic Personalism?

From the Abrahamic perspective, the world was made for the human person, not the other way around. Given that, our approach to the question of how to make nature work for us instead of against us must respect the dignity and sovereignty of each human person under God.

We therefore reject collectivism, as it is based on the sovereignty of an abstraction created by human beings. We also reject individualism, as it admits only the sovereignty of an elite and is blind to the dignity and sovereignty of every person. We believe the only acceptable option is personalism, specifically the Thomistic personalism of Pope Saint John Paul II.

Thomistic personalism refers to any school of thought, or intellectual movement, which focuses on the reality of each person's unique dignity and promotes the fundamental human rights of each human person within the framework of natural law and Aristotelian-Thomism.

Personalism recognizes the "political" (in the Aristotelian sense) nature of human beings, who as members of groups create institutions to support each person's wellbeing and dignity. As such, personalism rejects the idea that the State or any form of society or collective creates rights.

A fundamental principle of personalism is that rights are inherent in each human being. Personalism seeks the empowerment and full development of every person, not only to realize one's own human potential and individual good, but also to be liberated and educated to work for the good of others and for the common good. It offers principles for restructuring social, political, and economic institutions and laws toward that end.

A Practical Approach

Thomistic personalism is far more than a plan or proposal for economic reform. There are profound insights into the nature of existence to be found in a personalist approach to understanding man's relationship to God, to others, and even to one's self. There are mystical and religious discernments fundamental to understanding what it means to be human and a person. That is not what this book is about.

Instead, this book is about how people can build a better, if (because we are not God) imperfect, system that conforms to the principles of natural law. The goal is a social order that provides equal opportunity and access to the means for every person to satisfy their legitimate material and spiritual needs and wants.

This can be achieved by organizing and restructuring the institutions of the common good, our social structures or habits, through "acts of social justice." The goal of social justice is to ensure maximum feasible participation in what

Aristotle called "the life of the citizen in the State" (*politikos bios*) by as many people possible. *The Greater Reset* seeks to show how to make the world work for everyone, not just for a capitalist elite or a socialist collective.

Purely religious issues are not the focus of this book; those are matters of individual conscience and personal faith. Instead, this book will adhere to the principles of rendering to man what is man's and respecting religious freedom—a theme running through John Paul II's pontificate. Moreover, this book will pragmatically examine the assumptions behind the Great Reset and its goals from a natural law perspective, emphasizing the inherent rights of life, liberty, and private property. We will, in short, build the case for what we call "economic personalism."

Economic Personalism[15]

What is "economic personalism"? It is an economic system centered on the dignity and economic empowerment of each person.

Consistent with John Paul II's focus on "the acting person," economic personalism recognizes that life, dignity, and liberty require each person to have the power and independent means to support and sustain one's own life, dignity, and liberty by means of one's private property rights.

Socialism and capitalism concentrate economic power in a state bureaucracy or private sector elite, respectively.

---

[15] The more technical aspects of economic personalism are explained in Michael D. Greaney and Dawn K. Brohawn, *Economic Personalism: Property, Power and Justice for Every Person* (Arlington, Virginia: Justice University Press, 2020).

Proposals like the Great Reset abandon distinctions between socialism and capitalism, merging the two together into what Hilaire Belloc called the Servile State.

Still, the bottom line is the same, whether you call it democratic socialism, democratic capitalism, or the Kingdom of God on Earth. Exercise of natural rights is either abolished outright or rendered ineffective. Natural rights themselves, however, cannot be abolished, as they are inherent in human nature.

Participation Is Key

Inability to participate in or exercise natural rights creates what we can call the *non-acting* (i.e., passive) person in contrast to John Paul II's *acting* (or participating) person. Most people thereby become mere objects of the acts of others.

Ordinary people can thereby be rendered largely incapable of becoming virtuous unless they take extraordinary steps or make heroic efforts. A society that allows full participation only by the extraordinary or heroic individual cannot be considered just.

That is not to say each of us should not strive to be extraordinary and heroic when necessary. Structuring a society so that it only benefits its presumably superior members, however, clearly violates the ideal of a world that works for everyone.

In contrast, economic personalism seeks to diffuse economic power structurally by democratizing access to capital ownership for every person, ordinary and extraordinary alike. Specifically, economic personalism seeks to reduce the growth of State power and universalize access to money and credit.

In this way, people as full participants in the institutions of the common good will be able to become productive and contributing members of society. By gaining access to private property, money and credit, and similar institutions, people can become productive members of society instead of being limited to an existence as passive recipients of the productions and contributions of others. They will thereby gain the effective means to acquire and develop virtue by participating in society, becoming more fully persons.

CHAPTER 2

The Dictatorship of Money

2.1. What Is Wrong with the Great Reset?

N *on novum sub sole*—"Nothing new under the sun." These words from Ecclesiastes, possibly the grimmest book of the Old Testament, can be a wail of despair or, paradoxically, a rallying call of hope. If the situation is so bleak, how did people survive before? Is the Great Reset a sign of the End Times as some are hinting, or is it just the latest in a series of problems, the likes of which we have dealt with before, and survived, sometimes even thrived?

Good Intentions, Bad Results

It is a simple fact that civilization has progressed. Often it has not been by a straight route, and often with a tremendous amount of stumbling and straggling, even backsliding. Yet there has been progress.

Still, the world is not perfect, and never will be, despite the false optimism of some people. There are serious problems that get worse by the day, and with the 24/7 news cycle, seemingly by the hour. The wealth and income gap is increasing by leaps and bounds, and social and political instability are almost commonplace. As for the so-called "new normal," it often appears to resemble the old abnormal.

Nations throughout the world have reached a breaking point. National indebtedness has soared to unprecedented levels, endangering national sovereignty and even the survival of nation states.

To try and make the world work better for everyone—or even work at all—Klaus Schwab and the World Economic Forum (WEF) have proposed to "reset" the global economy. Presumably, this will allow everyone to lead a decent life, at least with respect to basic material needs, such as food, clothing, shelter, health, and education.

Other people and groups have presented similar proposals, sometimes differing only in rhetoric from Schwab's Great Reset, but the goal remains the same: the global economy, in their view, must be reorganized in such a way as to ensure that all people, especially the poorest of the poor, have their material needs met adequately in a world of peace and prosperity.

Even though the Great Reset may be well-intentioned, it not only misses the point but even goes in the opposite direction. Human beings are more than just creatures to be taken care of and treated benevolently. We should, and often must, strive for a decent material life for ourselves and others, but that is not the essence of existence.

According to Aristotle and Catholic teaching, the meaning and purpose of life is to become more fully human—that is, virtuous. *How* we meet our most basic material needs is just as important as simply meeting them—the end does not, and should never, justify the means. How we do something determines in many cases whether we are fulfilling or are able to fulfil our potential to become more fully human.

For example, even if we are starving, we may not take the food that is keeping alive someone else who is starving. Whether he chooses to sacrifice his life to save ours and give us what he has of his own free will is another matter. Taking away his choice or his life, however, is never virtuous regardless of the anticipated benefit to ourselves.

Thus, it is vitally important that people have some way of meeting their basic material human needs without inflicting harm on themselves, on others, or on the system. Doing things in any way contrary to what it means to be human, that violates our capacity to become virtuous, defeats its own purpose. We do not become more fully human by becoming anything other than human. It is even worse when we force non-humanity on others by making it difficult or impossible for them to become virtuous.

We find it significant, then, that Schwab speaks of changing human nature to conform to his vision of a better world in which everyone has his material needs met.[1] The Great Reset may work for "progress, people and planet"[2] (there is certainly nothing wrong with that!), but it does so in a way that works against people becoming more fully human and fulfilling the meaning and purpose of life.

---

[1]   Klaus Schwab with Nicholas Davis, *Shaping the Future of the Fourth Industrial Revolution: A Guide to Building a Better World* (New York: Currency, 2018), 155–91.

[2]   Klaus Schwab with Peter Vanham, *Stakeholder Capitalism: A Global Economy that Works for Progress, People and Planet* (Hoboken, New Jersey: John Wiley and Sons, Inc., 2021).

We need, therefore, to take the Great Reset, universal basic income (UBI), and similar proposals for what they are. They are efforts to try and improve the world, but are directed to limited or even harmful goals, or use inappropriate or ineffective means to reach those goals.

Ignoring the Problems

Essentially, the Great Reset is an attempt to make the world work without addressing any of the underlying problems that cause it not to work in the first place. This is important, for as the scientific aphorism goes, "form follows function."

Thus, our social institutions will reflect our assumptions as to why they exist. A society that is oriented toward full human development and educating people to become responsible adults and citizens, capable of taking care of themselves, will have a profoundly different institutional form than one dedicated to taking care of people as permanent dependents—that is, children or slaves.

However people define the meaning and purpose of life for themselves, the institutions of the common good will be directed to that end. If the goal of life is only to have material needs taken care of, then the world will be arranged as a giant nursery. Everyone will presumably get what he needs (as determined by others) as a UBI or other form of redistribution unless he happens to annoy the babysitter in some fashion.

That is why we question not the intent but the ends and means of the Great Reset, UBI, and similar proposals. They are directed to institute ways to take care of people by controlling them, not to help them develop more fully as human beings by taking care of themselves. Our task as adult, fully participating members of society, however, is not to attack or tear down such efforts. Instead, we need to determine what went wrong and fix it. Then we can develop and present better alternatives that respect the fullness of human dignity and that are directed toward ends compatible with human nature and our mission in life.

There is, nevertheless, an even more important issue involved. Some people claim that the Great Reset completely ignores God and religion.[3] At least one authority describes the proposal as a set of "theological-political visions linked to liberation theology."[4]

A Few Critical Omissions

Obviously, omitting God is critically important, but we will not address it directly. For the purposes of this book, we acknowledge an Absolute Source of all creation and thus of the natural law written in the heart of every human being by that Source. Failure to acknowledge God and the natural law is a serious omission from the Great Reset, but it is outside the scope of this work.

As essential as we believe it to be for personal salvation, mandating a particular faith or philosophy will not create a better world. A theocracy or an established church is rarely, if ever, a good idea.[5] While the civil power may not dictate any

---

[3]   Edward Pentin, "'Great Reset' Plan Parallels Some of Pope's Initiatives—But There's a Crucial Difference," *National Catholic Register*, February 4, 2021.

[4]   Ibid.

[5]   Heinrich A. Rommen, *The State in Catholic Thought: A Treatise in*

specific belief system, however, we believe that to safeguard the rights of every individual, society must unify around a universal set of moral values that originate from a transcendent Source of creation and of the natural law.

If people act in a manner consistent with human nature and the just application of the natural law in human positive law, neither the State nor any other civil authority (regardless how rich or powerful) should have anything to say about religion, regardless of someone's faith, or lack thereof. In 1863, Pope Pius IX explained the true meaning of the *extra Ecclesiam nulla salus* doctrine, "outside the Church there is no salvation," as it applies external to the Church and in civil society: "There are, of course, those who are struggling with invincible ignorance about our most holy religion. Sincerely observing the natural law and its precepts inscribed by God on all hearts and ready to obey God, they live honest lives and are able to attain eternal life by the efficacious virtue of divine light and grace. Because God knows, searches and clearly understands the minds, hearts, thoughts, and nature of all, his supreme kindness and clemency do not permit anyone at all who is not guilty of deliberate sin to suffer eternal punishments."[6]

Making himself even plainer, His Holiness concluded by saying, "God forbid that the children of the Catholic Church should ever in any way be unfriendly to those who are not at all united to us by the same bonds of faith and love. On the

---

Political Philosophy (St. Louis, Missouri: B. Herder Book Company, 1947), 586–612.

[6]   *Quanto Conficiamur*, § 7.

contrary, let them be eager always to attend to their needs with all the kind services of Christian charity."[7]

The implication is clear. Knowledge of God's existence and of the natural law completed and fulfilled by the supernatural law must influence and guide our civil relations with other people and society but must not necessarily be prescribed under civil law. As far as civil life is concerned, God and the natural law give general norms only.[8]

That is the true sense of Pope Pius XI's 1925 encyclical, *Quas Primas*, "On the Feast of Christ the King." It is not a mandate for a theocracy or a divine right kingship as the only legitimate form of government, as some have maintained. Instead, in sharp contrast to the ultrasupernaturalists who demand their faith-based understanding of divine law as the rule for civil society, *Quas Primas* is a declaration that society must be based on natural law.

As far as civil society is concerned, specific applications of religion and law should be determined by people themselves according to circumstances and preferences, as long as what is proposed or done conforms to general principles of religion and morality, and harms no one.

That being said, we have to acknowledge that not only does the Great Reset ignore God and religion, it also removes the human person from God's dominion. By redefining or ignoring fundamental rights such as life, liberty, and private property (clear violations of human dignity), Schwab makes a serious

---

[7]   Ibid., § 9.

[8]   Heinrich A. Rommen, *The Natural Law: A Study in Legal and Social History and Philosophy* (Indianapolis, Indiana: Liberty Fund, Inc., 1998), 16, 59.

mistake. He would, in effect, establish what Fulton Sheen called a "religion without God," even if that is not his intent.

Natural rights define us as persons and are the basis of personalism. Dismissing them is not consistent with what it means to be a human person. Therefore, the Great Reset proposal fails to live up to the intentions of its promoters on several grounds, particularly in its underlying assumptions. Specifically, the Great Reset fails in these ways:

- It is directed exclusively to material wellbeing, avoiding the issue that there is more to life; human beings are persons, not things.

- It ignores the fact that how material needs are met must be consistent with essential human nature and the meaning and purpose of life; by assuming that the end justifies the means, it proposes to override or redefine such fundamental human rights as liberty and private property, changing essential human nature and the natural law.

- It cuts off most people from full participation in society by viewing them strictly as consumers, not producers of wealth, thereby inhibiting or preventing them from becoming virtuous and developing to their fullest possible human potential.

- It assumes the feasibility, even inevitability, of an economic and monetary model, developed in its modern form by John Maynard Keynes, that has brought the world to the brink of economic, political, and social disaster.

- It leaves in place the current political and financial power structure, and by concentrating wealth seeks to assert total power over the destinies of all people by a very small political-economic elite.

Even though Schwab and other promoters of the Great Reset may have good intentions, the entire approach is fundamentally flawed. Measures may be necessary as short-term expedients—yes, something must be done immediately to safeguard human life—but are only barely tolerable in an emergency such as we currently face. They are not, and can never be, solutions.

2.2. The Role of Money

Pope Francis has repeatedly declared that the love of money is a serious problem in today's world. Although this is true, we understand this differently from His Holiness.

The Proper Use of Money

Francis looks exclusively at how wealthier people use their money. Apparently explaining his enthusiasm for the Great Reset, inclusive capitalism and so on, he believes the wealthy use their money properly when they provide employment for workers or give it directly to the poor.

Certainly, we agree those are noble uses of money. Both are essential in the present condition of society, notably the shambles of the global economy. Shocking as it might seem, however, neither job creation nor almsgiving is the best use of money. Both create a condition of dependency inconsistent with human dignity.[9]

This suggests that the proper use of money is primarily to assist all people to become individually productive, not to become wage, debt, charity, or welfare slaves.[10] People should be able to take care of themselves through their own efforts and not be a charge on private charity or public welfare.

The real problem with money is not that the rich are able to use it in ways that benefit only themselves but that the poor do not have access to the same opportunity and means to use it the same way. Jobs, charity, and welfare are not enough. What the poor need is not the money of the rich (except as a temporary helping hand when necessary) but a way to use their own money for themselves.

Nowhere is this more evident than in the assumption embodied in the Great Reset that limits most people to jobs and redistribution as their sole sources of income. Given that, as technology advances and displaces people from their jobs, the demand for redistribution can only increase.

The Rise of Über-Wealth

Although it seems as if advancing technology is the real problem, money and finance are central to the problems the Great Reset purports to solve, as well as to a comprehensive solution it misses. The displacement of labor (and thus income) by technology is self-evident. On the other hand, the misuse and manipulation of money—an institution or

---

9   Cf. *Quas Primas*, § 19.
10   *Rerum Novarum*, § 3.

social tool that should be accessible to everyone—is far more subtle, almost insidious in its operation.

The effects, however, are spectacularly evident over the last two hundred years in the rise of the phenomenon of "über-wealth." This received a huge boost with the Keynesian New Deal in the 1930s when government debt replaced private sector assets as the preferred backing of the currency, what could be called "legal counterfeiting."

Creation of über-wealth accelerated dramatically beginning in the 1970s when the US dollar, the *de facto* global reserve currency, was taken off the gold standard and allowed to float. Freed from the necessity of maintaining a fixed value for the currency, the only consideration limiting the amount of money that could be created was political expedience and the ability of the already-wealthy to absorb the massive influx of cash into the economy.

Money as a Social Tool

Simply put, Keynesian monetary theory is designed to concentrate wealth, a fact that Keynes made clear throughout his *General Theory*. To understand why this is bad and anti-human, we must first understand money. As noted in the introduction, the essence of money is that it is how I exchange what I produce for what you produce. Money is a "social tool."

We produce to be able to consume. Of course, if we want to exchange our respective productions, we must have a common unit of measure, and it must be stable. That is so our medium of exchange remains the same value when we use it as when we obtained it.

Further, there should be no artificial or external interference in exchanges, such as artificially restricting how much of the medium is available. Worst of all is when some authority changes how we value or measure our medium of exchange and thus the value of what we are exchanging. As Louis Kelso explained:

> Money is not a part of the visible sector of the economy. People do not consume money. Money is not a physical factor of production, but rather a yardstick for measuring economic input, economic outtake and the relative values of the real goods and services of the economic world. Money provides a method of measuring obligations, rights, powers and privileges. It provides a means whereby certain individuals can accumulate claims against others, or against the economy as a whole, or against many economies. It is a system of symbols that many economists substitute for the visible sector and its productive enterprises, goods and services, thereby losing sight of the fact that a monetary system is a part only of the invisible sector of the economy, and that its adequacy can only be measured by its effect upon the visible sector.[11]

As John Paul II noted in *Centesimus Annus*, the currency should be stable, meaning it should always have the same

---

[11]   Louis O. Kelso and Patricia Hetter, *Two-Factor Theory: The Economics of Reality* (New York: Random House, 1967), 54–55.

value.[12] There is a very good reason for this, and it makes perfect sense once we understand Kelso's points. That is, you cannot change the unit of measure of value at will, nor limit how much or what you can measure.

A Flexible Standard?

Unfortunately, Keynesian monetary theory takes an ever-changing value of the currency—the unit of measure—for granted. As far as Keynes was concerned, the government has not merely the right but the duty to change the standard of value at will.

A flexible standard, however, is not a standard at all, but a weapon by means of which the economic elite and the government—those whom the Great Reset would keep in charge of the economy—maintain and extend their power over the rest of us. As Keynes asserted in the opening passages of his *Treatise on Money* (1930), the work he intended as his magnum opus (before it was shredded by Friedrich von Hayek[13]), "The State . . . claims the right to re-edit the dictionary. This right is claimed by all modern States and has been so claimed for some four thousand years at least. It is when this stage in the evolution of money has been reached that Knapp's Chartalism—the doctrine that money is peculiarly a creation of the State—is fully realized."[14]

---

[12] *Centesimus Annus*, §§ 19, 48.

[13] F. A. Hayek, "Reflection on the Pure Theory of Money of Mr. J. M. Keynes," *Economica*, 11, S. 270–95 (1931).

[14] John Maynard Keynes, *A Treatise on Money, Volume I: The Pure Theory of Money* (New York: Harcourt, Brace and Company, 1930), 4.

In other words, the State—or those who control the State—can change the value of money, even the definition of it, at will. Just as bad, consistent with Georg Friedrich Knapp's chartalism, money should not be backed by anything other than government debt. When the economy needs more money, the government issues more debt. When there is too much money, the government taxes it away.[15] Needless to say, there never seems to be "too much money" in the economy.

Money Manipulation

When money was backed by actual assets and pegged to a fixed standard of value, there was a natural limit to how much anyone could accumulate, set by the amount that anyone could produce. Once money was backed by government debt, however, the sky was the limit, for money did not represent production but rather the creation of money by fiat—essentially "legal counterfeiting"—and transfers of purchasing power and wealth.

That is why John Paul II and Kelso insisted on the need for a stable currency in a just economy. If I work for a week and am paid forty dollars, each dollar is worth an hour of my time, assuming a standard forty-hour work week. If the government doubles the amount of money in the meantime, the value of my money is cut in half.

---

[15]   Georg Friedrich Knapp, *Die Baurenbefreiung und der Ursprung der Landarbeiter* (1887); *Grundherrschaft und Rittergut* (1897); and *Die Staatliche Theorie des Geldes* (1905). An abridged version of this last was translated into English as *The State Theory of Money* (London: Macmillan and Co., 1924).

As a result, the bread that cost me one dollar in one-hour dollars last week, now costs me two dollars in half-hour dollars—the price does not change in real terms—but I buy it with one-hour dollars. My cost of living just doubled in real terms. Wealth has been transferred from the bread-consumer to the bread-maker.

Keynes called this loss-making by the poor and profit-taking by the rich "forced savings." When government inflates the currency, poor people pay more and get less, while rich people pay less and get more. In this way, the poor finance new capital acquisition by the rich.[16]

Inflation Harms the Poor

Keynesian dogma declares that inflation benefits debtors and harms creditors. People therefore conclude that it pays them to borrow money for consumption, to be paid back with cheaper, inflated money, or not at all.

All money, however, is a debt owed by the issuer of the money. When government backs new money with its own debt—which is standard Keynesian monetary policy—it creates money out of nothing by assuming a liability it repays with inflated money. The more money a government creates backed with its own debt, the more wealth it transfers from the poor to the government, and from the government to the rich.

People whose assets (if any) are in the form of money or quantified in terms of money, such as savings, wages, welfare, and charity, are creditors of the debtor government. They

---

[16]   John Maynard Keynes, *The General Theory of Employment, Interest, and Money* (1936), II.7.iv, IV.14.i, V.21.i, VI.22.vi.

are therefore harmed by inflation because what they have loses value every time the government creates more money backed with its own debt. Wages, welfare, and charity no longer buy what they did before.

Owners of productive capital, however—the rich—benefit greatly from inflation. Their assets are not generally in the form of cash or quantified in monetary terms. Instead, what capital owners have is *measured* in monetary terms, which is something entirely different.

So, while many consumers have vast debt, inflation does not benefit them—period. Most consumers get into debt because their wages do not cover living expenses in the first place. Inflation only benefits creditors who can pay their debts. It ruins those who cannot pay or who are on "fixed incomes."

This would not be the case if money had a stable value. Keynesian monetary theory, however, absolutely requires that money be *unstable* in value to concentrate wealth and prevent ordinary people from being able to save to get ahead. Making something like the Great Reset seem attractive, even logical, the poor remain trapped permanently in a condition of dependency on the State and the economic elite.

2.3. The Cockeyed World of Keynesian Economics

Of all the assumptions underlying the Great Reset and virtually the entire global economy today, the most damaging (apart from ignoring or dismissing God and religion) is the unquestioned acceptance of the economics of John Maynard Keynes. As we will see in the last chapter, many (if not all) of the problems the Great Reset intends to fix could be solved by implementing a more rational economic and financial system, one more consistent with reality and human dignity.

Two Bad Assumptions

Why is Keynesian economics such a great problem? There are two reasons that in combination have wreaked havoc on the global economy.

Firstly, Keynesian economics, along with the other mainstream schools of economics (Monetarist/Chicago and Austrian), embodies a flawed and inadequate understanding of money. This is the belief that money determines economic activity. You must cut consumption and save before you can invest and engage in productive activity. Money must therefore exist prior to production, distribution, and consumption.

The truth, however, is that money comes from production, not the other way around. What Keynes and Schwab missed is that you can save for investment by increasing production in the future instead of decreasing consumption in the past.

At this point, we need to make something clear. When we say that you can "save" by increasing production in the future, we do *not* mean increasing production in the future or the here-and-now for the sole purpose of accumulating wealth.

We hold with Adam Smith's first principle of economics that the only reason to produce anything is for consumption. To produce for any other reason leads directly to waste, fraud, consumerism, environmental damage, and countless other evils.

Our point is that instead of assuming with Keynes that huge accumulations of unconsumed production are a public benefit, they are actually a curse. When all production is intended for consumption, and only for consumption—and "saving for a rainy day" (deferring consumption) is simply a timing difference, not a repurposing—production and consumption can be in balance. Capital owners will find it more profitable in both the short and long run to produce only what customers want and need and do so in the most efficient and environmentally sound manner possible.

Secondly, Keynesian economics assumes that labor, the human factor of production, is the only real factor of production. Capital, the non-human factor of production, only provides the environment within which labor can be effective and is not a true factor of production.

Under Keynesian logic, labor is therefore the only means apart from redistribution and charity by which most people can gain income. In reality, capital produces goods and services the same as does labor, and thus is as fully a factor of production as labor.

Keynesian understandings of money and labor combine to form a system in which concentrated wealth is not merely an unquestioned fact—it is considered a positive good for humanity. This has resulted in a very inhuman global economy that the Great Reset, while intending the exact opposite, would preserve and expand.

A Worship of Wealth

Admittedly, on the surface it all seems very logical. In 1919, Keynes published the book that established his reputation as the world's greatest economist. He accomplished this feat by telling the wealthy and powerful what they wanted to hear. Thus, Keynes moved them in his direction, a direction in which they were already headed.

The book was titled *The Economic Consequences of the Peace*, and it contained a single sentence that provides the key to understanding the economic system that has held most of the world in financial thralldom for nearly a century. As Keynes declared in chapter 2 of his book, "The immense accumulations of fixed capital which, to the great benefit of mankind, were built up during the half century before the war, could never have come about in a Society where wealth was divided equitably."[17]

Consistent with his assumption that money determines economic activity, Keynes claimed that the only way to pay for productive machinery or any other non-human factor (capital) is to consume less than you produce, accumulate the surplus in the form of money, then buy the capital. This necessarily implies that if the world is to progress, there must be people who can afford to cut consumption and save enough to buy the increasingly expensive technology so that other people can have wage system jobs.

In his other book, *General Theory of Employment, Interest, and Money*, Keynes defined saving as "the excess of income

---

[17]   John Maynard Keynes, *The Economic Consequences of the Peace* (1919), 2.iii.

over expenditure on consumption."[18] As he then explained, this means that the only way to save is to reduce consumption below the level of income and accumulate the surplus production in the form of money savings.

Consequently, if you want to finance new capital (invest) so you can produce, you must first produce more than you consume, which begs the question as to where the original production came from in the first place! Production for non-consumption—waste—and wasteful consumption (consumerism) are, along with irrationality and illogic, built into the Keynesian system.

Systemic Contradictions

Another difficulty with Keynes's illogic is that to turn surplus production into money to finance new capital, customers must be found to purchase unwanted products. By economic and financial sleight-of-hand, this turns unwanted surplus production into wanted, non-surplus production that is consumed instead of saved by the poor, generating the profits—savings for the rich—to pay for more new capital.

Customers for the previously surplus production pay for it with consumer credit that mortgages their future income, keeping them poor. In this way, new money created to assist consumers out of temporary difficulties finds its way permanently into the coffers of the wealthy.

The wealthy then use the infusion of new money obtained from the sale of wasteful products to finance more wasteful

---

[18]   Keynes, *The General Theory of Employment, Interest, and Money,* II.6.ii.

products, accelerating the transfer of wealth from the poor to the rich. The poor are trapped in an endless cycle of debt.

That is not all. There is a serious problem with Keynes's assumption that capital only provides the environment within which labor can be productive. As technology advances and becomes more and more expensive, it does not create a need for more human labor, but for less. At a certain point, the number of jobs does not increase, but decreases.

At the same time, it becomes impossible for average people to save to purchase the technology that is taking their jobs. Most people become trapped permanently in a vicious circle of dependency caused by a lack of productivity capacity.

The Wrong Solution

To do Schwab and his confreres justice, the Great Reset is intended to fix this problem. Seeing that "creating jobs" is an economic and political self-delusion, the idea behind the Great Reset is to change the definition of what it means to be a stakeholder in a productive enterprise so that people no longer need pointless (and probably non-existent) jobs.

To implement the Reset, the concept of "stakeholder" would be expanded to include people who do not have a defined ownership stake in the business but who would be granted an equal opportunity with purported owners to receive income from profits instead of from wages.

This, naturally enough, would be legally required, increasing State power to be able to compel payment of profits to non-owners. By granting more power to the State, rights would be taken away from owners and given to non-owners to impose equality, or at least equitability of results. Private property and freedom of association (liberty) would be nullified, and human nature would be changed in its essence.

Nullified, that is, for most people. To keep the Keynesian system running, wealth must become concentrated in fewer and fewer hands. Further, if civilization is to advance, the wealthy must be exempt from the laws and even the system itself that binds others to a condition of permanent dependency.

As Keynes made clear, his ideal system is one in which most people own nothing, a few people own capital, and the State controls everything, distributing to all based on need. Not surprisingly, this is also the vision of Schwab with the "stakeholder capitalism" of the Great Reset. As he said, "We need a new, better global system: stakeholder capitalism. In this system, the interests of all stakeholders in the economy and society are taken on board, companies optimize for more than just short-term profits, and governments are the guardians of equality of opportunity, a level-playing field in competition, and a fair contribution of and distribution to all stakeholders with regards to the sustainability and inclusivity of the system."[19]

Ultimately, there is only one real difference between Keynes's system and the Great Reset. Where Keynes believed that everyone must have a job to have an income, the Great Reset maintains that everyone must just have an income. Where Keynes would leave people with the illusion that they are being productive and useful, the Great Reset would take that away.

---

[19]   Schwab and Vanham, *Stakeholder Capitalism*, 7.

A Few Bugs in the System

Schwab's proposal assumes, however, that the Keynesian system works as advertised. In reality, there are two major economic and financial flaws in Keynesian economics in addition to the logical flaws noted above, and thus in the Great Reset. These flaws include the misuse and manipulation of money in ways that concentrate wealth and the effect of technology in taking away income from non-owners.

As noted earlier, technology does not create jobs but destroys them. Schwab's Great Reset would sever non-owners from the fruits of ownership and the right of control, thereby effectively abolishing the natural right of private property. By taking away the power that private property confers on owners, abolishing it or rendering it meaningless also effectively abolishes liberty and seriously hampers people from becoming virtuous.

Contrary to Schwab's analysis, the real problem with technology is not that it is advancing. Instead, the real problem is that under the current system, most people do not have any way of owning the machines that are taking away their jobs, and thus eliminating their incomes. It is important to keep in mind that, modern myth notwithstanding,[20] the Luddites of the early nineteenth century were not protesting technology. They were protesting technology that put them out of work and deprived them of their livelihood.

---

[20] Kirkpatrick Sale, *Rebels Against the Future: The Luddites and Their War on the Industrial Revolution* (New York: Addison-Wesley Publishing Company, 1995).

Still, we must not attempt to change human nature as Schwab advocates to accommodate to technology or abolish technology to remain human as today's neo-Luddites insist, both being completely unrealistic. Instead, we must change the system of how new capital is financed and thus break the pattern of concentrated ownership; we must make technology and money serve people, not the other way around.

2.4. Über-Wealth vs. Ordinary Wealth

"The rich are different," said F. Scott Fitzgerald, to which Ernest Hemmingway did not really reply (although he should have), "Yes, they have more money." Unfortunately, Hemmingway's apocryphal riposte, while true—up to a point—is too limited. It does not acknowledge the almost surreal world of the super-rich that the near-global application of Keynesian economics has created and that the Great Reset would secure and bring to its inevitable conclusion.

A Despotic Economic Dictatorship

Before the rise of über-wealth, the rich were often able to evade the law or manipulate it to their advantage, at least in some measure.

Nevertheless, governments' survival and the rich person's ability to satisfy his desires still depended on the ability of ordinary citizens to be productive and keep an economy—and a country—running. With the rise of über-wealth and the erroneous belief that ultra-concentrated wealth is essential for economic development and political survival, the picture has changed.

Now, if one has enough money, rule of law, government, and even other people can easily become secondary or ignored altogether. We now face the establishment of a world of welfare slaves utterly dependent on the few who are incredibly rich for everything, even life itself—if they are permitted to live, a possibility that seems to become more remote with each passing day.

This vision of the future may strike the reader as hyperbole, but it most assuredly is not. Back in 1989, William Greider published a book, *Secrets of the Temple: How the Federal Reserve Runs the Country*. In hindsight, and with all due respect to Greider, it might have been more accurate to title the book *Secrets of the Boardroom: How the Financial and Political Elite Run the Federal Reserve—and the Rest of the World*.

Not that Greider was a voice crying in the wilderness. A host of other books chronicling the dangers of the financial monopoly, economic globalization, and the rise of the "corporatocracy" have warned us of the problem and presented demands for fundamental change in the world economy.

Titles include *The Creature from Jekyll Island* (Griffin), *Alternatives to Economic Globalization* (Cavanaugh and Mander), *Regime Change Begins at Home* (Derber), *The Divine Right of Capital* (Kelly), *When Corporations Rule the World* (Korten), and *Gangs of America* (Nace). Earlier generations gave us *Money Manipulation and Social Order* (Fahey), *Money! Questions and Answers* (Coughlin[21]), *Money Creators* (Coogan[22]),

---

[21]   This was the noted "Radio Priest," Father Charles Edward Coughlin.

[22]   Gertrude Coogan was Father Coughlin's economic advisor.

and what may be the progenitor of modern monetary conspiracy theory, *Coin's Financial School* (Harvey).

As with Schwab's Great Reset, none of these prophets of doom have identified the real danger or where change is truly needed. What they advocate is inevitably an increase in government power, not a return of power to ordinary people.

Greider himself seemed oblivious to Pius XI's encyclical, *Quadragesimo Anno*. Specifically, the plight of the ordinary person trapped in dependency by the corporatocracy and thus unable to "breathe against their will."[23]

Not to contradict Hemingway, then, but what the rich have is not more money but more access to money—and what money buys. They might not be different in what defines each of us as human persons, but the rich now inhabit a different world, and one that endangers the rest of us merely by existing and the way it functions. It is no longer merely that the super-rich have more money; they have it in ways that other people do not.

It is important to note that the rich are not a danger to us; rather, the different world they inhabit and the system they exploit is a danger. Chances are that many people would do exactly what the super-rich are doing now if placed in the same situation and as long as the institutions that the elite have manipulated remain uncorrected.

What, however, are the super-rich doing?

---

[23]   *Quadragesimo Anno*, § 106.

Owned by Their Own Wealth

In a supreme paradox, the people benefitting most from today's badly structured financial and monetary system generally have no idea what is really going on any more than do their handlers. These "handlers" are the wealth managers, "trustees and managing directors of invested funds," whom Pius XI called a "despotic economic dictatorship."

They think they know what they are doing, of course. As chronicled in such books as John Perkins's *Confessions of an Economic Hit Man* (2004), Bastian Obermayer's and Frederik Obermaier's *The Panama Papers* (2016), and Brooke Harrington's *Capital without Borders* (2016), insider and investigative accounts of the murky world of global finance give a frightening picture of how those who manage the wealth of the super-rich manipulate world events and hold themselves and their clients above the law.

Religious society is not exempt from this. Ministers of every faith can tell you how often rich donors try—and often succeed—to dictate practice and, on occasion, doctrine, and even who is allowed to be a member of that church, temple, or mosque. One wonders if there might have been a few philanthropists among the money changers Jesus drove out of the Temple.

Worship of Mammon

While details, attitudes, and opinions differ to some extent, there is a rather depressing monochrome tint to the whole picture. In common with Klaus Schwab of the Great Reset, all of them take the Keynesian economic paradigm for granted—especially the understanding of money.

As a rule, neither the super-rich nor their ostensible victims (particularly the nation states that are not able to collect tax revenue from the super-rich) see anything amiss in the fact of concentrated wealth. Per Keynesian doctrine, concentrated wealth is essential to economic development. The problem is who has and controls it, not that it exists.

Acting on Keynesian assumptions has had what can only be called inhuman consequences resulting from getting wealth and keeping it. The Great Reset would do nothing to fix this underlying problem.

Our task, then, is to determine what to do about such egregious misuse of the social tool called money. First, however, we need to understand where the problem originated.

2.5. The Origin and Preservation of Über-Wealth

Keynesian economics and the Great Reset not only assume concentrated wealth as a given but also consider concentrated wealth as essential for the survival of a technologically advanced civilization. Admittedly, Schwab appears to view highly concentrated wealth as a regrettable necessity where Keynes considered it a positive good, but the end is the same.

A Newer New Thing

Über-wealth did not appear as an economic, social, or political phenomenon until the last quarter of the twentieth century. This is due to one single fact: it was in the 1970s that the US dollar, the *de facto* global reserve currency, was taken off the gold standard and allowed to float.

As a result, the global monetary system became purely, instead of partially, Keynesian. In the European Union, the euro was the first currency to be instituted as Keynesian from the very beginning. In the United States, repeal of the Glass-Steagall Act that separated financial institutions by function and the subsequent consolidation of the financial services industry laid the groundwork for the Great Reset as the next logical step. There was no longer any brake or check on how much money could be created. The only question was how to get as much of it as possible in the shortest possible time.

At this point, we do not advocate for a return to the gold standard, except possibly as a last resort. What is needed is a fixed standard, regardless of what it is, and a monetary system that ties the amount of money in the system directly through private property to the amount of marketable goods and services in the economy.

That is where Keynes did incalculable damage by treating money as a commodity, the price and quantity of which can be changed at will by the State, instead of as a social tool to facilitate exchange. If money is a commodity, then the more of it you can get, the better—for you, anyway.

If money is a tool, however, then having more than you need to carry out transactions is waste. It is also unjust, as it prevents others from participating in economic life to the fullest.

That is why Aristotle's analysis of usury, along with the ancient prohibition in most faiths and philosophies, assumes that money *qua* money is a social tool. To treat it as a commodity having value in and of itself, or as a productive asset, is against nature and therefore wrong.

The Economic Hit Man

In his book *Confessions of an Economic Hit Man*, John Perkins describes the dirty tricks, even crimes, used to justify and carry out the creation of über-wealth. It is significant that nowhere in his account of his transformation from an economic hit man to someone with a conscience does he disagree with the goal of becoming rich, only with the ways in which it is done.

Perkins's account assumes as a matter of course that individuals and countries need money to become productive rather than the actual case that anyone with a feasible productive project can create money as needed to facilitate the transactions. He exhibits complete ignorance regarding the fact that money derives from production, not the other way around. He is also extremely vague on the process of money creation itself.[24]

You do not have to know how an internal combustion engine works to drive a car, however, or to get where you want to go. Perkins's observations are honest and accurate, even if his analysis is flawed. Even his writing is convincing—it is not good enough to be fiction.

Keynesianism works to institute and maintain non-owners in a state of permanent dependency on the wealthy elite and the State. The economic hit man strategy was and remains to create and maintain a dependency status binding

---

24   John Perkins, *Confessions of an Economic Hit Man* (San Francisco, California: Berrett-Koehler Publishers, Inc., 2004), 212-213.

less developed countries to the developed countries and, ultimately, the developed countries to the über-wealthy. The Great Reset is almost custom designed to complete this process and bring it to its logical conclusion: the complete dependency of everything and everyone on the financial elite.

We do not believe that this is the result of a conscious conspiracy, a point Perkins makes several times in his book.[25] Underlying Perkins's analysis, however, is the unconscious assumption that only existing wealth can be used to finance economic growth, and that is what really gives the wealthy and their managers power. Still, we concur with Perkins that the fundamental problem is not primarily evil people but a badly designed and implemented system driven by bad ideas.

The Panama Papers

Obermayer's and Obermaier's *The Panama Papers* reveals a vast international industry (if that is the right word) dedicated to assisting the rich and super-rich to hide money and avoid taxation. By means of incredibly complex networks of offshore shell corporations, trusts, foundations, beneficial ownership, front men, and agents, it is possible for those with enough money to avoid paying income or wealth taxes and to make intergenerational transfers without paying inheritance taxes or death duties.

Capital without Borders

Ultimately what happens, as the Danish investigative journalist Brooke Harrington explains in her book *Capital*

---

[25]   Ibid., xii. See also 156, 216–17.

without Borders, is that the wealth ends up owning the rich rather than the other way around. The gift of self to other persons and society becomes the sale of self into permanent bondage to the family fortune.[26] In this way, Keynesian economics exhibits a fatal progression that reaches its completion and logical end with the Great Reset:

- As technology advances and becomes more productive than human labor and more expensive than most people can afford with existing savings, small ownership disappears.
- Formerly independent small owners subsisting on profits become dependent workers for hire subsisting on wages.
- As technology continues to advance, wages are forced down and workers are ultimately displaced by automation. Government steps in and turns people formerly dependent on private sector employers into State dependents. Private sector employers are taxed to support direct welfare payments or job creation.
- Due to the erroneous Keynesian belief that existing accumulations of savings are essential to finance economic growth, tax policy becomes a trade-off between the need to finance private sector development and government spending.
- The tax base erodes at the same time government expenditures increase. Governments make up the dif-

---

26   Brooke Harrington, *Capital without Borders: Wealth Managers and the One Percent* (Cambridge, Massachusetts: Harvard University Press, 2016), 273–78.

ference by monetizing deficits—that is, issuing debt and creating new money backed by the debt.

- Monetizing deficits instead of taxing the rich (which would not be sufficient in any event, not to mention unjust to tax them differently from anyone else) allows the rich to not only retain their current wealth but also turn into super-rich by funneling the bulk of the new money into their coffers, directly and indirectly. This creates national super-debts that appear impossible to repay.

- To maintain the social welfare system, developed countries engage in neo-colonial economic policies that, by means of unrepayable loans, turn developing countries into permanent dependents of the developed countries.

- Individual governments become controlled by the super-rich, either directly, through the political process, or indirectly, by the perceived need for their accumulated wealth to finance economic growth.

- Members of super-rich families become controlled by their wealth managers, turning into slaves of their own money and servants of their servants.

In this way, the system operates to concentrate wealth and power in the hands of a few wealth managers of the super-rich. Propertyless people end up dependent on their governments, less developed countries end up dependent on fully developed countries, and the global economy ends up controlled by the managers of the super-rich. When due to a badly designed and misused system the world is awash in debt that to all appearances can never be paid, the stage is set for the imposition of global control by the super-rich by means of the Great Reset or something similar.

2.6. Why Not a Great Reset?

Ironically, critics of the modern global economic system—including Klaus Schwab and other advocates of a "new normal"—do not really have a problem with the system. Their issue is only with how the wealthy and their handlers manipulate the system to their own advantage and keep all the goodies for themselves.

Maintaining a Condition of Dependency

At the same time, wealth managers and their clients view themselves as public benefactors simply because they are wealthy! As Brooke Harrington reported, wealth managers "[see] themselves as playing a vital and very positive role" in economic development.[27] They come close to exhibiting hurt feelings when other people fail to realize this. As one of them stated, "Without our profession, there wouldn't be the large pools of capital available to fuel economic development. So many of us, if not all, see our work as primarily about helping people—not just our own clients, but more generally by helping maintain capital flows for investment and economic growth."[28]

This assertion could have been dictated by Keynes over a century ago. It hardly comes as a surprise that virtually no

---

27   Ibid., 257.
28   Ibid., 257–58.

one—whether Schwab and his Great Reset, the proponents of democratic capitalism or socialism, inclusive capitalism, or whatever—advocates breaking up and redistributing the capital accumulations (not that it could work as a solution).

What they demand instead is redistribution of the benefits of ownership and owners paying their "fair share" of taxes to support political and social programs. Whether greatly resetting, inclusively capitalizing, or democratically socializing, the one unbreakable rule in modern social reform, tantamount to a religious doctrine, is that ownership and thus control of capital, whether in the private sector or by the State, *must* be concentrated.

On the other hand, the Church calls for widespread ownership. Unfortunately, what Pope Leo XIII said in *Rerum Novarum* in 1891, and Pius XI said in *Quadragesimo Anno* in 1931, has been reinterpreted to mean redistribution of the benefits of ownership without actual ownership. Wealth must be concentrated. Questioning this is economic, social, political, and religious heresy, not to mention professional and social suicide.

Chesterbellocs and Catholic Workers

So pervasive has the doctrine of über-wealth become that it nullified two noted efforts protesting concentrated power and advocating widespread capital ownership: distributism and the Catholic Worker movement. G. K. Chesterton, Hilaire Belloc (the two of whom George Bernard Shaw pejoratively labeled "the Chesterbelloc"), Dorothy Day, and

Peter Maurin were strong advocates of expanded capital ownership and limited State power.

Many adherents and followers of Chesterton-Belloc and Day-Maurin, however, have largely, if not completely, abandoned advocacy of widespread ownership as traditionally meant. By that we mean the necessarily limited and socially determined exercise of the rights of private property, derived from the natural right to be an owner that is absolute and inherent in every single human being.

Some Catholic Workers these days seem to do little except condemn the wealthy for their wealth, the State for its stinginess with public benefits and failure to redistribute, and the rest of us for our lack of charity. A significant number of Catholic Workers and their supporters have gone to great lengths to prove that Day was really a socialist and a supporter of the very State power and control she excoriated.[29]

Chesterton and Belloc struggled from the very beginning with indifferent success to distinguish distributism from Fabian socialism. This was despite clearly defining distributism as "a policy of small distributed property."[30]

Clearly, without widespread ownership of capital as traditionally meant, and however good the intentions, only the State, the super-rich, or a combination of the two that Belloc called the Servile State will be in charge. Any or all of

---

[29] Harry Murray, "Dorothy Day, Welfare Reform, and Personal Responsibility," *St. John's Law Review* 73, no. 3, (Summer 1999): 789–804.

[30] G. K. Chesterton, *The Outline of Sanity*, vol. 5, Collected Works (San Francisco: Ignatius Press, 1987), 45.

those are going to be bad for anyone who is not a member of the ruling or controlling elite.

A Servile and Totalitarian State

From that perspective, the Great Reset is a stroke of genius if the goal is to preserve the Keynesian system. It comes across as a brilliant scheme to blend State power and private wealth in a unified effort to impose a condition of dependency (servility) on most of the people in the world.

Undoubtedly, the stakes are high. Without the Great Reset, we can look forward to an escalating conflict between a desperate and financially strapped public sector bureaucracy, and a paranoid and immensely wealthy private sector elite.

Economically and fiscally speaking, politics and finance— the real global superpowers—have reached the stage of mutually assured destruction. Within the current system, the political elite and the super-rich are going to have to come to terms or they will annihilate each other and drag the rest of us down to ruin in the ultimate "rich man's war, poor man's fight."

Warning shots have already been fired. Prior to the crackdown on the pro-democracy movement in Hong Kong, the former crown colony served as the principal conduit by means of which wealthy Chinese funneled money out of mainland China. This enabled the wealthy to hide profits and evade taxation.[31]

---

31 When China took over Hong Kong in 1997, it was useful for funneling vast amounts of foreign investment into China. After China began its Belt and Road Initiative and neo-colonial expansion program, the flow reversed as newly rich Chinese used Hong

This has put the "Belt and Road Initiative" at grave risk. Taking a page from the capitalist handbook, Chinese domestic economic growth and overseas expansion have been fueled by issuing massive debt to finance wasteful projects at home (e.g., the notorious "ghost cities") and engage in neo-colonialism.

This is particularly the case in Africa, where countries burdened with unserviceable debt they assumed due to the activities of capitalist economic hit men look vainly to Sino-socialism for redemption. What many in Africa are realizing too late is that they have been tossed from the Western capitalist frying pan into the Eastern socialist fire.

Making matters worse, the Chinese government has been forced to issue more debt to keep the economy going as profits are siphoned out of the country. A significant amount of this new money also ends up in the pockets of the wealthy and is sent out of the country to evade taxation.

In consequence, the Chinese economy is rapidly becoming a hollow shell, a pyramid scheme supported only by debt that is itself backed by other debt. Following the pattern of any pyramid scheme, the Chinese government has no choice but to keep expanding the amount of debt and hoping against hope that it will be able to recapture the money currently beyond its reach.

Cardinal Gerhard Müller, who has wondered "what 'image of humanity' is held by WEF members and those

Kong as the main conduit to shelter their wealth from taxation or confiscation. Natasha Khan and Yasufumi Saito, "Money Helps Explain Why China Values Hong Kong," *The Wall Street Journal*, October 23, 2019, A-18.

of other similar select groups," has "a decidedly jaundiced view" of the Great Reset and similar proposals, such as universal basic income.[32] He made this clear in remarks during an interview:

> Without directly referring to the initiative, he told the [*National Catholic*] *Register* Jan. 29 that two sides—"profiteering capitalism, big-tech giants of Western countries" and the "communism of the People's Republic of China"—are today "converging and merging into a unified capital-socialism," producing a "new colonialism" that the Pope has "often warned against."
>
> The goal, Cardinal Müller believes, "is absolute control of thought, speech and action."
>
> "The homogenized man can be steered more easily," he added. "The Orwellian world of *homo digitalis* has begun. Through mainstreaming, total conformity of the consciousness of the masses is to be achieved via the media."[33]

Like the wasteful projects and consumerism promoted by their capitalist brethren in the developed countries, nominally communist Chinese entrepreneurs have made enormous fortunes from the Belt and Road Initiative and expansion into undeveloped countries, as well as from Bitcoin mining. It might not be much of an exaggeration to say that every yuan of debt emitted by the Chinese government

---

32   Pentin, "'Great Reset' Plan Parallels Some of Pope's Initiatives."
33   Ibid.

has found its way as profit into the pockets of wealthy Chinese and out of China and into foreign tax havens via Hong Kong or Bitcoin transfers.

A Desperate Compromise

Objectively speaking, aside from the fact that any opposition to tyranny is a danger to a paranoid government, the pro-democracy movement in Hong Kong was never a real threat to China. Authorities, however, needed an excuse to take direct control of the "Special Administrative Region" to stop the financial hemorrhaging. The government has also started cracking down on Bitcoin mining, ostensibly due to concerns about pollution, but more likely to prevent anonymous[34] Bitcoin transfers out of the country.[35]

This gives the super-rich in the rest of the world a tremendous incentive to push for the Great Reset, UBI, inclusive capitalism, or something similar, and avoid direct confiscation by increasingly desperate nation states drowning in debt. Presumably by sacrificing a portion of their current income to fund the welfare system and relieve governments of the burden, the super-rich can keep all their existing wealth and most of their current income.

It comes as no surprise that Adolf Hitler got the backing of wealthy German industrialists by halting reparations

---

[34]   Bitcoin transfers are not untraceable, but anonymous. Auditors and authorities know where the money is but not necessarily who owns it. Ezra Galston, "Untraceable Bitcoin Is a Myth," *The Wall Street Journal*, June 17, 2021, A-15.

[35]   Gerry Shih, "Chinese Bitcoin Miners Are Breaking Ground in the U.S.," *The Washington Post*, June 18, 2021, A-1, A-24.

payments and promising they could keep their wealth if it benefitted the Reich. This worked while Hitler's plan of world conquest continued to go forward.

In the Great Reset, nation states would lose a measure of direct control over citizens by shifting the burden of social welfare to the super-rich. They would regain a semblance of the national sovereignty they have lost through the mounting burden of debt.

Similar to what happened in the late classical Roman Empire, the super-rich would lose their current near-total immunity from external financial demands on their fortunes by assuming direct responsibility for social welfare in lieu of direct taxation. They would gain a *de facto* sovereignty as near- or *quasi*-nation states through direct control of "stakeholders"; they would in this way become parallel or shadow governments as a new financial feudalism arose.

Except for the total disregard of the sovereignty of the individual human person under God, it seems like an ideal solution. The problem, however, is that the Great Reset cannot work. This is because all it really does is carry the current unworkable system (which it claims to replace) to its logical conclusion.

Keynesianism, socialism, capitalism, the Servile State—whatever you want to call it—is contrary to human nature and thus contradicts the natural law. It is anti-human at the most fundamental level. As the increasingly desperate world situation demonstrates, the Great Reset is based on bad assumptions and false principles. It cannot work.

That is the real issue. How do we make the world work (*really* work) for each person so that every child, woman, and man can fulfil his fullest human potential and grow in virtue?

2.7. Resetting the Reset

Most people agree that something must be done about the current world situation. But what? Perhaps not surprisingly, the answer in general is the same as it has been for thousands of years. If you do not want to reset and have government or an economic elite (often in history the same people) to control you, then you must have private property in capital and therefore power—over yourself and your own life, not over others. Political rights are meaningless without the economic rights to support them.

A Failure of Participative Justice

The problem is that as matters now stand under the Keynesian system and as proposed in the Great Reset, most people do not have access to the means to become capital owners—money and credit—and thus to participate fully in economic life. In today's world with its past savings assumption, the super-rich have a virtual monopoly over money and credit. Governments want to seize and control money and credit for their own purposes and have little interest in making it available to everyone.

The Great Reset does nothing to correct this problem. Instead of spreading out power, Schwab proposes to concentrate it even further by combining political and economic power in a single monolithic entity that is the Servile State in everything but name.

It is not the Servile State as Belloc envisioned it, a change due to the astounding advance of productive technology. Where Belloc was concerned with the injustice of forcing people to toil for their income (whether or not they wanted to), the aim today is to ensure that everyone has an income (whether or not they can work).

Nevertheless, people must both participate in economic life and work to become more fully human. We must be both producers and consumers. We cannot just be passive recipients of what others produce. Being a person means more than just existing. It means exercising rights, including economic rights, to become virtuous and thus more fully human.

More to Life than Animal Needs

Human dignity therefore demands a world in which people can meet all their human needs, not simply material needs. The Great Reset is designed to meet, just barely, people's material needs but not to enable every person to meet their higher human and spiritual needs.

Specifically, the Great Reset would continue to maintain unjust barriers that have crept into institutions—that is, our social habits and structures such as laws, customs, and traditions, that make up the common good and provide the environment within which people ordinarily carry out the tasks of living. Chief among the unjust barriers that the Great Reset would maintain are those within our institutions of money, credit, and banking. The unsound structuring of today's money, credit, and banking systems, along with gross inequality of citizen access to these essential institutions, drove this crisis in the first place. The question then becomes: What ought we to be doing?

We need to make it possible for everyone to have equal access to money and credit to acquire productive capital, the way the super-rich do now. By that, however, we do not mean letting other people expropriate the existing money and credit of the currently wealthy.

A Demand of Justice

What people own belongs to them by natural right. It would be unjust to take it from them, unless it can be proved in a court of law that what they have was obtained illegally. People—and that means *all* people, especially those whom we dislike or even hate intensely—must be presumed innocent until proven guilty.

What we want (demand, really) is the opportunity and access to the means to do what the rich are doing. That is, we want the chance to become wealthy ourselves, by ourselves, or at least capital self-sufficient on our own, without charity or redistribution.

The way to deal with the power wielded by the super-rich is not to confiscate and redistribute and put everyone under the care of the State. Instead, it is to take the personalist approach: vest everyone with the same power in microcosm. Ensure that the wealth of the super-rich remains nothing more than savings for them to consume, not a stranglehold on economic power and society.

Emancipation from the Slavery of Savings

To do that, we must first realize—and get academia and politics to come to the same realization—that neither the State nor the private sector need the wealth of the super-rich to keep the economy running. The simple fact is that it is better to finance private sector economic growth with future increases in production than with past reductions in consumption. We need to ensure as far as possible that as many people as possible own the new capital and participate in economic life. Currently in the United States and a number of other countries, this has been done in a limited way with the Employee Stock Ownership Plan (ESOP), but the ESOP can only be used for corporate employees and is not available to everyone.

If all new money is asset-backed and used in ways that create new owners or facilitate transactions by ordinary people, the super-rich will not be able to expand their wealth exponentially as at present. Today's ownership elite increase their wealth by reinvesting the unconsumed incomes generated by their capital. Under a more just structuring of global financial institutions, and without the constant creation of new money backed only by government debt (or in the case of many crypto currencies, nothing at all), the only thing the wealthy will be able to do with their wealth besides keeping what they have is spend it.

Given that it would take heroic effort to spend even a tithe of the vast fortunes in several lifetimes, no one need fear that they will be beggared—but they will no longer be able to use their wealth to control others; it will be "sterilized." Their power over others will be broken, all without committing a single injustice against anyone, and leaving people with their current accumulations intact.

As for the State, it is far better to turn as many people as possible into productive citizens and therefore taxpayers instead of unproductive "tax eaters." This sterilizes the wealth of the super-rich in the political arena by eliminating dependency on the few wealthy for tax revenue. The more people own capital financed with future increases in production, the more they can produce and derive an increasing proportion of their consumption income from that source.

As more people take care of their own needs through their own efforts, financial demands on the State will decrease and tax revenues will increase. Deficits will be replaced with budget surpluses that can be used to pay down today's enormous debt. Being backed with private sector hard assets instead of government debt, the currency will stabilize.

Organized religion will also benefit. With more independent believers able to contribute their time and money to their respective faiths, religious leaders will no longer be threatened with philanthropic blackmail or *de facto* establishment of private religions by the wealthy. Ministers will be able to focus on religious issues and, when necessary, be able to serve the poor instead of catering to the rich.

All in all, it should be obvious that collectivist socialism, individualistic capitalism, or their combination in the Servile State or the Great Reset do not respect human dignity or provide viable long-term solutions. Only a personalist economic system where every human being can acquire and possess private property in capital as well as consumer goods has the potential to assist all people to become virtuous.

2.8. Not What the Church Doctors Ordered

Many of the Great Reset's specific proposals may be essential in the short term to meet the most urgent human needs of survival and security. However, these temporary expedients are not solutions.

Redistribution, such as proposed under the Great Reset and universal basic income, is not financially or economically sound. Aside from its basic injustice when employed as a solution, it shifts sovereignty away from human persons and vests it in some abstraction, such as the capitalist elite or socialist collective. It thereby imposes a condition of permanent dependency on human persons.

The Demands of Human Dignity

A condition of permanent dependency—infancy, incompetence, or slavery—is inconsistent with the demands of human dignity. It can only be imposed for just cause after due process has been observed on a case-by-case basis. At no time does the end justify the means.

Natural rights are inherent in each human being and are, in fact, what define human beings as human persons. Ordinarily, human beings become virtuous by exercising their natural rights of life, liberty, and private property.[36]

---

[36]   Ibid.

Property is not the thing owned. It is the right to own, and the bundle of rights that define the exercise of the right. The right to be an owner is part of human nature itself.

That is why, under the description "the generic right of dominion" or "access," the Catholic Church recognizes that the right to private property is inherent, absolute, and exclusive. That is, the right to be an owner is without restriction, exception, or qualification in every human person, and owners may exclude all others from using what they own.

In contrast, the rights of ownership—that is, the bundle of rights that define how an owner may use what is owned—are necessarily limited, socially determined, and inclusive. In exercising their rights of ownership, owners must take others (including other stakeholders) into consideration. This is what the Catholic Church calls "the universal destination of all goods" or "use"—the concept of stewardship.

Denying persons their rights or permitting their exercise only as a grant from other persons or from some form of the collective prevents or inhibits people from becoming virtuous and implies they are not fully persons or persons at all.[37] This interferes with the meaning and purpose of life itself—which is to become more fully human.[38]

The question then becomes how and to what degree the proposed solutions inhibit people from reaching their full potential

---

[37]   "A good action essentially perfects the performing the action." Karol Wojtyła, "In Search of the Basis of Perfectionism in Ethics," *Person and Community: Selected Essays* (New York: Peter Lang, 2008), 45.

[38]   Wojtyła, "The Problem of the Theory of Morality," *Person and Community*, 155.

as human persons. In reality, these and other solutions—or at least elements of them—may be essential as expedients in the short term. Problems arise when they are imposed as permanent, long-term solutions, as in the Great Reset.

As Klaus Schwab stated in his book *Stakeholder Capitalism* (2021), the guiding principle at the heart of the Great Reset is "each stakeholder contributes what it can in stakeholder capitalism and receives what it needs."[39]

Thus, the principle of the Great Reset/stakeholder capitalism appears to be a restatement of the fundamental principle of the scientific socialism (communism) of Karl Marx and Friedrich Engels. That is, "from each according to his ability, to each according to his needs."[40]

Redefining Humanity

Since natural law is based on human nature, redefining its principles effectively redefines what it means to be human. The meaning and purpose of life shifts from becoming more fully human to ensuring an acceptable quality of life.

Democratic socialism and inclusive capitalism do not appear to differ materially from stakeholder capitalism, and therefore the same criticisms apply. Universal basic income (UBI), the idea that everyone should get a basic income regardless of one's economic input, is not itself a complete proposal, nor does

---

[39]   Klaus Schwab, *Stakeholder Capitalism: A Global Economy that Works for Progress, People and Planet* (Hoboken, New Jersey: John Wiley and Sons, Inc., 2021), 193.

[40]   Karl Marx, *Critique of the Gotha Program* (Peking, China: Foreign Languages Press, 1972), 17.

it pretend to be. It appears instead to be one of the elements proposed within Schwab's stakeholder capitalism.

Objectively, UBI is redistribution. As such, it increases consumption without a corresponding increase in production. Whether funded out of direct taxation, charitable contributions, or increases in debt, UBI (like the Great Reset itself) effectively punishes productive activity and rewards unproductive activity. This throws an economy out of balance and prevents people from becoming more fully human—virtuous.

Many of the problems that the Great Reset and stakeholder capitalism seek to solve stem from the inability of most people to be productive. This, in turn, is due primarily to the fact that technology has been advancing rapidly for the past 250 years or so, while human labor has stayed essentially the same since Adam and Eve.

This is because ownership of the new technology became concentrated in the hands of the few who had access to money and credit. This meant either the accumulated ("past") savings, which was negligible, or "future savings" made available through the commercial, mercantile, and central banking system—which made all the difference.

The Purpose of Production

Contrary to what seems to be the rationale behind the Great Reset, human beings naturally want to be useful and productive. This is part of the nature of what it means to be a human person. As Karol Józef Wojtyła (John Paul II) explained:

We are by nature creators, not just consumers. We are creators because we think. And because our thought (our rational nature) is also the basis of our personalities, one could say that we are creators because we are persons. Creativity is realized in action. When we act in a manner proper to a person, we always create something: we create something either outside ourselves in the surrounding world or within ourselves—or outside and within ourselves at the same time. Creating as derived from thinking is so characteristic of a person that it is always an infallible sign of a person, a proof of a person's existence or presence.[41]

In addition, production is not due solely to the human factor (labor) alone. Production is the result of both human and non-human factors. Great Reset proponents fail to acknowledge this or admit that if people cannot be productive with labor alone, some way must be found for them to own the technology that is displacing them. Instead, the advocates for the Great Reset make one or all these five fatal errors:

- Sovereignty and thus natural rights to life, liberty and private property are not inherent or effective in every actual human person, but only in an abstraction such as a capitalist elite or a socialist collective.
- Private property in capital is irrelevant if the fruits of ownership such as income and control can be taken from owners to be "equitably" distributed among non-owning stakeholders (i.e., where the enjoyment of the fruits of ownership does not depend on ownership).

---

[41] Wojtyła, "Thomistic Personalism," *Person and Community*, 171.

- People do not need to have production power if they have consumption power (i.e., the power to consume is more important than the power to produce).
- Only past savings can be used to finance new capital formation (i.e., the only way to increase production is by reducing consumption).
- Human labor alone is productive; technology and land at best only enhance human labor.

At first glance, these errors do not appear to have anything in common. On reflection, however, we see that they all share a certain orientation away from the human person, but there is no necessary correlation among them; for example, what does reliance on past savings have to do with the idea that labor alone is productive?[42]

If the good of actual human persons is not ultimately the goal of any proposal, act, law, institution, system, or anything else, then it may not be as good as claimed, or good at all. It may be anti-human and contrary to nature, even as adherents for proposals such as the Great Reset and similar programs cite nature, the environment, Mother Earth, and humanity itself in justification.

That is why, for example, both individualism, which exalts the presumably special human being above everything else, and collectivism, which glorifies the abstraction of humanity, are not consistent with human nature. Individualism

---

[42] The labor theory of value is a shift away from the human person because the capacity for labor is inherent in each human as a fact of *being*, while the capacity for ownership of capital is inherent in each human as a right of *personality*.

ignores human beings' social nature, while collectivism ignores individuality, both of which are essential parts of human personality.

The Human Person and Society

Sovereignty resides in human persons who possess an individual and social nature as members of society, not just in extraordinary individuals alone or in humanity. The whole of society exists for the good of every person. If this is not understood, protected, maintained, and integrated into daily life and all institutions, then the common good is both individually and socially unjust, and human dignity is offended.

A society that is individually and socially just—that is oriented to the good of each human person and is therefore structured virtuously—is one that respects the dignity of everyone and does so by adhering or conforming to certain principles. These are the principles of participation, distribution, and feedback, or correction.

That is, every system must be structured virtuously for every human person. Social structures are not themselves virtuous or vicious. They are structures of virtue (or vice). They can, and do, encourage or discourage people from becoming and remaining virtuous.

To be structured virtuously, a system, as well as the entire common good, must give equal access to the opportunity and means to participate in social life. There must be distribution of rewards and punishments according to each one's inputs or contribution to specific endeavors, institutions, or all of society.

Finally, there must be some means of correcting a system when it does not function in a just manner. These principles apply to all institutions and systems within the common good and are themselves the virtues of participative justice, distributive justice, and social justice, which will be defined later.

The Human Person under God

At this point, we want to examine the natural and thus inherent sovereignty of the human person. In the modern age, we must carefully and clearly distinguish the natural sovereignty of every human person from the assumed (or usurped) or delegated sovereignty of some particular individual, group, or even humanity as a whole.

The fact that every human person is by nature sovereign under God leads to certain conclusions. First and foremost, personal sovereignty cannot be taken away or denied without implying that those from whom it was taken are not human.

An assumption of natural personal sovereignty is built into the orthodox sects of the Abrahamic faiths: Judaism, Christianity, and Islam, as well as pagan Aristotelian philosophy. It is an integral part of what Aquinas called "the analogy of being."[43] "Analogy of being" is a complicated way of saying that all human beings are as human, and are human in the same way, as all other humans. It means that every human being has the "same"[44] capacity to become virtuous or vicious through the exercise of natural rights.

---

43   Wojtyła, "In Search of the Basis of Perfectionism in Ethics," *Person and Community*, 47.

44   The correct term is "analogously complete." For our purposes, however, we will say "same," with the caution that it does not

Every human being therefore has equal natural rights to life, liberty, and private property. This necessarily implies that every human being also has the related—and equally natural—rights to:

- participate in the institutions of society,
- receive rewards or punishments according to his inputs,
- and organize and correct institutions when they are flawed or not functioning properly or within acceptable parameters.

Human dignity and thus sovereignty is the basis of liberal democracy, which raises a difficulty today: what do we mean by "liberal democracy"? Not surprisingly, our understanding of "liberal democracy" depends on how we understand human dignity and sovereignty.

The Three Types of Liberal Democracy

To the collectivist, liberal democracy means that humanity, an abstraction or idea created by human beings, is sovereign. Consequently, whoever speaks for the collective (or has the power to assert the claim) is sovereign on behalf of the People. Individual human beings are only persons with rights if those in charge of the collective permit it.

To the individualist, liberal democracy means that certain individuals, an elite, are more human, or fully human, and thus have effective rights. Most individualists will agree

---

mean "identical," which would tend to collectivism and the belief that human beings are interchangeable copies of one another.

that all human beings have rights, but only an elite (also an abstraction created by human beings) has the capacity or ability to exercise them. Some extreme forms of individualism claim that the elite are the only ones with rights.

To the personalist, liberal democracy means that every individual human being is sovereign with the natural rights of life, liberty, and private property, and their related natural rights of participation, distribution, and feedback, or correction. As Fulton Sheen explained, "[Liberalism] can be used in three senses: (a) As a philosophy which believes in the progressive achievement of civil social, political, economic and religious liberties within the framework of a moral law. (b) As an attitude which denies all standards extrinsic to man himself, measures freedom as a physical power rather than moral power and identifies progress by the height of the pile of discarded moral and religious traditions. (c) As an ideology generally identified with the doctrine of *laissez faire*."[45]

Sheen's sense (a) is the personalist type of liberalism, (b) is collectivist, while (c) is individualist. As can be seen, collectivism and individualism both put sovereignty into an abstraction—that is, into an idea created by human beings for human beings, not by God. God creates human beings, not ideas that have no existence apart from the human mind.

There is a long and complicated philosophical argument Aquinas used to explain why God by His very nature, only deals in concrete actualities, not abstractions.[46] For our purposes, however, we only need to know that God is concerned with

---

45   Fulton J. Sheen, *Communism and the Conscience of the West* (New York: The Bobbs-Merrill Company, 1948), 7–8.

46   Ia, q. 14, a. 11.

people, not abstractions in any form.[47] God only cares about human creations when human beings use them for good or evil. Their creation, structuring, and use are human concerns.

God made man to live in society but did not dictate any particulars. The natural law, the general code of human behavior, gives general norms only. It is our task to apply them to create and maintain structures of virtue to assist people in becoming more fully human.[48]

That is the problem of human sovereignty. How do we structure our institutions and laws to allow maximum freedom to pursue virtue without interfering with others' pursuit of virtue?

Given human nature, some form of personalist liberal democracy that respects the dignity of every human being would appear to be optimal—which raises another question. If personalism is so obviously consistent with human nature and thus the natural law,[49] while collectivism and individualism are not, how did the Great Reset and similar proposals ever develop, much less become so popular?

---

[47] "Only man, the human person, and not society in any form is endowed with reason and a morally free will." *Divini Redemptoris*, § 29.

[48] Heinrich A. Rommen, *The Natural Law: A Study in Legal and Social History and Philosophy* (Indianapolis, Indiana: Liberty Fund, Inc., 1998), 14, 209, 227, 235.

[49] Wojtyła, "Human Nature as the Basis of Ethical Formation," *Person and Community*, 181–85.

CHAPTER 3

The Kingdom of God on Earth

3.1. The Democratic Religion

Proposals like the Great Reset are nothing new. In 1905, Monsignor Robert Hugh Benson wrote in a letter to his mother, "I have an idea for a book so vast and tremendous that I daren't think about it. Have you ever heard of Saint Simon? Well, mix up Saint Simon, Russia breaking loose, Napoleon, Evan Roberts, the Pope, and Antichrist; and see if any idea suggests itself. But I'm afraid it is too big. I should like to form a syndicate on it, but that it is an idea, I have no doubt at all."[1]

Benson was referring to his apocalyptic satire *Lord of the World*, a masterful—if in hindsight barely fictional—vision of a future world that has completely surrendered to socialism and modernism. In Benson's day, it was what the socialists and modernists had dreamed of for nearly a century. Bring God down from heaven, set up divine man in God's place, and create the terrestrial paradise, the Kingdom of God on Earth.

---

[1] Robert Hugh Benson, December 16, 1905, quoted in C. C. Martindale, *Life of Monsignor Robert Hugh Benson* (Longmans, Green and Co., 1916), II.65–66.

Defining Socialism and Modernism

What, however, do we mean by socialism and modernism? First, it must be clearly understood that in this book terms, including natural law, are given their natural law meaning as used within the Aristotelian-Thomist framework and applied in Catholic social teaching. That is, the natural law (the general code of human behavior) is based on God's nature, self-realized in His intellect. It is therefore discernible by human reason (*lex ratio*)[2]—not faith nor opinion, even majority opinion (*lex voluntas*).[3]

Socialism, while best summarized by Karl Marx as the abolition of private property in capital,[4] distorts the whole of the natural law, not just property. It can be stated broadly as any philosophy or political theory (or anything else) that shifts sovereignty—and thus natural rights, dignity, and personality—from the human person to the collective or some form of society.[5]

In "Catholic language," *modernism* has a specific meaning. It refers to a movement that claims to update religious belief and practice and bring organized religion in general, and the Catholic Church in particular, into the modern world.

---

[2]   Mortimer J. Adler, *How to Think About God: A Guide for the Twentieth Century Pagan* (New York: Collier Books, 1980), 22–26.

[3]   Karol Wojtyła, "On the Directive or Subservient Role of Reason in Ethics," *Person and Community: Selected Essays* (New York: Peter Lang, 2008), 57; "Human Nature as the Basis of Ethical Formation," 97.

[4]   Karl Marx and Friedrich Engels, *The Communist Manifesto* (London: Penguin Books, 1967), 96.

[5]   Cf. *Divini Redemptoris*, § 29.

In reality, modernism does nothing of the sort and cannot be considered modern in any meaningful sense. It revives ancient and outdated theories disproved and discredited centuries ago, then imposes a distorted understanding of the supernatural order onto the natural order. In this way, the natural order is absorbed into or abolished by someone's garbled, even corrupt version of the supernatural order.

Its present meaning is perhaps best understood as "theological relativism" (to coin a term), which is only modern because so many people today have succumbed to it. Under the possibly more descriptive labels of "enthusiasm" and "ultrasupernaturalism," Monsignor Ronald Arbuthnott Knox characterized modernism as "an excess of charity [that] threatens unity."[6]

We can therefore understand modernism as the theology of socialism, the Democratic Religion. Where socialism remakes God by distorting the natural law, modernism does the same thing by twisting the supernatural law. It attempts to usher in a new age of universal love that proceeds from the Gospel.

Modernism—ultrasupernaturalism—endeavors to do this by transcending Christ's literal meaning. It abolishes the precepts of the natural law, particularly justice, in favor of the supernatural law pertaining to faith and charity. In ultrasupernaturalism, as Fulton Sheen—not by coincidence a student of Knox—pointed out, in an excess of charity, we invert the natural and the supernatural, becoming creators of God instead of God's creations.[7]

---

[6]   Ronald Knox, *Enthusiasm: A Chapter in the History of Religion* (New York: Oxford University Press, 1961), 1.

[7]   Fulton J. Sheen, *God and Intelligence in Modern Philosophy* (New

In the ultrasupernaturalist framework, instead of the supernatural virtues fulfilling and completing the natural virtues, faith and charity replace reason and justice, respectively. This inserts contradictions into the belief system and violates the first principle of reason. The natural order and supernatural order become opposed to one another; for example, justice (the premier natural virtue) and charity (the premier supernatural virtue) are put into conflict.

In a sense, socialism and modernism are the same thing from different angles, the former external to Christianity, the latter internal. Socialism undermines Christianity from the outside, while modernism bores at it from within. As G. K. Chesterton put it, "This error then had many forms; but especially, like nearly every error, a fiercer one which was outside the Church and attacking the Church, and a subtler one, which was inside the Church and corrupting the Church. There has never been a time when the Church was not torn between that invasion and that treason."[8]

The effect of these "attacks" has been to shift worship away from an understanding of God based on reason guided and illuminated by faith to one based solely on faith or opinion that often contradicts what is discerned by reason. Doctrines are accepted or discarded because they are useful or inconvenient, not because they are true or false, respectively. Truth no longer reflects reality, what *is*, but a personal vision or

York: IBE Press, 2009), 320–21.

8   G. K. Chesterton, *Saint Thomas Aquinas: "The Dumb Ox"* (New York: Image Books, 1956), 108.

myth of what *should be*.[9] Truth, as one commentator asserts,
now goes beyond reality.[10]

For example, to the ultrasupernaturalist, it is ultimately
unimportant if Jesus is a historical Person. What matters is
whatever opinions someone attributes to Him. Consistency
with logic, empirical evidence, or the Gospels is irrelevant.[11]
As Sheen explained, "What is important is the subjective
effect he has on the mind of the believer. This is what in
recent years has been known as Modernism."[12]

---

[9]   This contradicts the understanding of myth as analyzed by Mircea
        Eliade: that myth, properly understood, embodies a fundamental
        truth. See Mircea Eliade, *Myth and Reality* (New York: Harper-
        Collins, 1968); also Henri Frankfort, *Before Philosophy: The Intel-
        lectual Adventure of Ancient Man* (London: Penguin Books, 1951).
        It is closer to Joseph Campbell's concept of God as a metaphor
        and myth as discernment of a transcendent self, "putting you in
        touch with the mystery that's the ground of your own being." Jo-
        seph Campbell, *The Hero's Journey* (2000).

[10]   Joseph Pearce, "Truth Beyond Reality," Institute of Catholic Cul-
        ture, accessed August 4, 2021, https://instituteofcatholicculture
        .org/events/truth-beyond-reality. The notion that truth can go
        beyond reality contradicts a fundamental principle of reason. In
        a 1982 interview with Bill Moyers when asked, "What is truth?"
        Mortimer Adler responded, "Truth consists in the agreement of
        what we think and what is in the world, what is real." *Six Great
        Ideas, I. Truth*, https://www.youtube.com/watch?v=-aa_r6iwk_A,
        1:36-1:48, accessed August 6, 2021; cf. J(ózef) M(aria) Bocheńs-
        ki, *The Methods of Contemporary Thought* (New York: Harper and
        Row, Publishers, 1968).

[11]   In this regard, Sheen noted the influence of Immanuel Kant in the
        eighteenth century, but there were also the contributors to *Essays
        and Reviews* (1860) and *Lux Mundi* (1889) that explained away
        supernatural events in the Gospels and treated Jesus as a purely
        human teacher.

[12]   Fulton J. Sheen, *Religion Without God* (Garden City, New York:
        Garden City Books, 1954), 170.

In essence, ultrasupernaturalism is a new idea of religion itself, one in which, as Sheen noted more than once, "we are not God-made but God-makers."[13] Since the natural law and natural rights are based on God's nature, and assuming man creates God, formerly inalienable rights of life, liberty, and private property become changeable by whoever has the power to force his will on others. Natural law itself changes from an absolute to a matter of opinion. As Sheen explained, "Two conclusions emerge. (1) There is a growing tendency in contemporary philosophy to present a religion without God. This is done either by denying God altogether, which is rare, or else by emptying the God-idea of all traditional content and identifying it with anything as vague as a 'nisus' and as vaporous as 'society divinized.' (2) As a substitute for religion in terms of God and man, the majority of philosophers of religion offer a religion in terms of value or friendliness of the universe."[14]

Thus, the connection between socialism—especially as a religion in opposition to Christianity—and modernism is not accidental. As Chesterton remarked, "Apparently anything can be called Socialism. . . . If it means anything, it seems to mean Modernism; in the sociological as distinct from the theological sense. In both senses, it is generally a euphemism for muddle-headedness."[15]

In both modernism and socialism, there is a shift from reason illuminated and directed by faith, and from justice

---

[13]   Ibid., 17.

[14]   Ibid., 82.

[15]   G. K. Chesterton, "There Was a Socialist," *G.K.'s Weekly*, May 10, 1930; cf. *Ubi Arcano*, § 61.

fulfilled and guided by charity, to faith and charity alone. This results in self-directed faith based on personal opinion (what Chesterton called "the Inner Light"[16]) and charity without justice[17] that merely projects one's ego onto others or society at large.

In natural law terms, this is the chief error of modernism, or theological relativism, and of socialism, which is applied moral relativism. It is the foundation of all heresies in any faith and philosophy, not just Christianity: *the shift of sovereignty away from human persons created by God and to abstractions created by man.* What makes this so incredibly subtle is that moral and theological relativists can be superficially orthodox Jews, Christians, Muslims, and even pagans, but for the wrong reasons!

Instead of accepting an article of faith because it is taught by an accepted authority and is consistent with or does not contradict reason, the theological relativist (ultrasupernaturalist) of any faith or philosophy accepts something because it agrees with his opinion, which may or may not be consistent with reason. To the ultrasupernaturalist, something is "true" because he believes it; he does not believe it because it is true.

Benson's Prophetic Non-Prophecy

A world gone mad by putting earth in the place of heaven (socialism or moral relativism) and man in the place of

---

[16]   G. K. Chesterton, *Orthodoxy: The Romance of Faith* (New York: Image Books, 1990), 76.

[17]   This is not true charity. As Saint Augustine said, charity is not a substitute for justice withheld.

God (modernism or theological relativism) was the theme
of Benson's *Lord of the World*. In common with the Great
Reset, the problem was that attaining the Kingdom of God
on Earth would, in Benson's opinion, require such fundamental changes in humanity as to deny nature, and (not
surprisingly) the Creator of nature. As Sheen explained a
generation later in his doctoral thesis, *God and Intelligence in
Modern Philosophy* (1925), modernism and socialism invert
the whole of reality:

> Putting the whole philosophy in a formula which
>   expresses a perversion of the traditional notions: —
> Mind is confused with Being.
> Grace is confused with Nature.
> Man is confused with God.
> . . . In the twentieth century man makes God to his
>   own image and likeness.[18]

In short, as Chesterton noted in his introduction to Sheen's
book, "They begin by bowing down to man as the image of
God; and then forget the God and bow down to the graven
image."[19] As Sheen later remarked, the seemingly inevitable
result of efforts to create a heaven on earth is a living hell.[20]

Admittedly, this is not how many people today understand *Lord of the World*, the best known of Benson's "sen-
sational novels." Possibly because he was able to gauge the

---

18   Fulton J. Sheen, *God and Intelligence in Modern Philosophy*, 320.
      See also Sheen's follow-up, *Religion Without God* (1927).
19   Ibid., 11.
20   Fulton J. Sheen, *Philosophies at War* (New York: Charles Scribner
      and Sons, 1943), 94–95.

likely result of certain trends in Edwardian society accurately, it has been reinterpreted as prophecy. Being considered a prophet instead of a satirist annoyed Benson considerably.

Benson's real achievement in *Lord of the World* was not his alleged inventiveness or presumed prophecy. Rather, it was the way he wove all the secular dogmas and doctrines that the intellectuals and upper classes of Edwardian England believed good about the world and bad about religion into a tapestry that turned all their assumptions upside down.

Yet even then, Benson's feat was not his originality. Ultimately, his satirical social and religious commentary consisted of heeding warnings from the popes and applying an extremely exaggerated version of what could happen due to ignoring principles of natural law and Catholic teaching. Rome had been explicit about the danger since 1832, when Pope Gregory XVI issued *Mirari Vos*, the first social encyclical.

Therein lies a tale that in some ways is more fantastic, even more shocking, than *Lord of the World* and what many see as its final realization in the Great Reset.

The Beginning of the Quarrel

The new world that emerged in the wake of the French Revolution and the Napoleonic Wars was one with which large numbers of people were disillusioned. Old ways had been replaced by a system that seemed inadequate at best, anti-human at worst. It was as if the world had changed completely, almost overnight.

That was not really the case. The French Revolution— embodying a pale imitation, even distortion, of the principles of the American Revolution twenty years before—exposed serious weaknesses in many fundamental institutions that had been building up for some time, particularly in State and Church. Society had been under increasing strain in many areas, especially from the Financial and Industrial Revolutions.

With the reinvention of commercial or mercantile banking in the fourteenth century, and the invention of central banking with the establishment of the Bank of England in 1694, the final link in the chain binding economic development exclusively to past savings and human labor was broken. It became possible to have economic growth by using technology on a large scale. Development was no longer constrained by limited financing of small-scale technology but by virtually unlimited human imagination—which is to say, practically not limited at all.

There was, however, a problem. The new financing techniques as a rule benefitted only those who already controlled wealth. In this way, the rich came to monopolize ownership of the new capital instruments of the Industrial Revolution. Most people were cut off from enjoying the full benefits of economic participation through lack of access to money and credit, the principal means of acquiring private property in the new capital instruments.

Overall, most people were limited to being suppliers of human labor or recipients of public or private assistance. Labor, however, was decreasing in value as an economic input relative to advancing technology. In addition, increasing demands were being made on public funds and private charity as more and more people became unable to support themselves by labor alone.

Large numbers of people were forced into destitution as a way of life instead of as a temporary condition, while a small number became immensely wealthy. Through their access to money and credit, this meant that the wealthy could not only acquire existing capital but enjoy a virtual monopoly over new future inventions.

The rich became richer at an accelerating rate as technology advanced and became increasingly productive, while the poorest of the poor often lost even bare subsistence as they were displaced from traditional employment and small ownership. As is the case today, the failure of existing political and religious institutions to address the situation adequately, particularly the European monarchies and the Catholic Church, caused not merely discontent but growing anger and resentment.

Revolution and Reaction

Many people who hoped for fundamental social, political, and religious change were disappointed with what they saw as the failure of the French Revolution and its betrayal by Napoléon Buonaparte. To many radicals, *liberté, egalité,* and *fraternité* seemed as distant as they had before the Revolution. Reactionaries added to the growing discontent by attempting to return to the pre-revolutionary *status quo*, or, more accurately, an idealized version of it that was as unrealistic as the vision of the new world order of the radicals.

Eventually, the radical liberal position centered on a collectivist, or what Alexis de Tocqueville called the Franco-European, version of liberal democracy based on the sovereignty of humanity. For their part, moderate liberals (the ancestors of today's conservatives) coalesced around an individualist liberal democracy (which de Tocqueville called English) that assumed only a small elite is effectively sovereign.

At the same time, the personalist version of liberal democracy de Tocqueville saw in the United States of the 1830s, based on the sovereignty of each person, was contradicted by slavery, treatment of native peoples, the political and economic disenfranchisement of women, and (what is often overlooked) hampered by an appallingly inadequate financial system.[21]

De Tocqueville's visit also coincided with the wave of religious socialism known as "the Second Great Awakening." This added chauvinistic patriotism—what came to be called "Americanism" (a label as misleading as "modernism")—to its innovative concepts of God and man.[22]

Accounting in part for the differences between what de Tocqueville saw and the situation just a decade later, the Second Great Awakening hit its peak from the 1820s to the 1840s. It changed many fundamental American assumptions

---

[21] See Congressman George Tucker, *The Theory of Money and Banks Investigated* (Boston, Massachusetts: Charles C. Little and James Brown, 1839).

[22] J. D. Dickey, *American Demagogue: The Great Awakening and the Rise and Fall of Populism* (New York: Pegasus Books, 2019), 274–77.

about politics and religion, spawning new religions and utopian movements.[23]

There was, however, one institution that looked to the
future without forgetting the past: the papacy. Surprising
many people today, before his election, Pope Pius VII had
declared there is no necessary conflict between democracy
and Christianity.[24] Even his imprisonment by Napoléon had
not diminished his zeal for reform, although reactionary elements in the Papal States and among the European Catholic
powers prevented anything other than token reforms from
being carried out in the wake of the social chaos left by the
Man of Destiny.

Faced with the necessity of placating reactionaries and
keeping radicals and moderates in check without surrendering the remnants of papal independence or asserting power
he did not have in the first place, Pope Leo XII ceased reform
efforts and functioned in the civil order as something of a
benevolent despot. Pope Pius VIII showed definite signs of
wanting to restart Pius VII's program but died a year after
his election. It was left to Pope Gregory XVI to deal with the
rising tide of discontent and revolution spreading through
Europe in the late 1820s and early 1830s.[25]

---

[23]   Ibid. Andrew Jackson's economic and fiscal policies accompany-
       ing his quarrel with Nicholas Biddle and the Second Bank of the
       United States contributed greatly to the social and economic cha-
       os of the period.

[24]   J. N. D. Kelly, *The Oxford Dictionary of Popes* (New York: Oxford
       University Press, 1986), 303; E. E. Y. Hales, *Pio Nono: A Study
       in European Politics and Religion in the Nineteenth Century* (New
       York: P.J. Kenedy & Sons, 1954), 35.

[25]   Similar forces in the United States led to a great increase in utopi-

In the Wake of Revolution

Gregory XVI's pontificate did not begin auspiciously, nor has history been particularly kind to him, or appreciative of his accomplishments. His election in 1831 sparked rebellions by radicals who feared he was a tool of the reactionary Prince Metternich[26] of Austria.[27]

Had they known it, the radicals had far more to fear from the new pope's scholarship than from his political acumen or military might (or lack thereof). It was in fact philosophy, not firearms, that Gregory XVI used in his efforts to bring order out of the political, religious, and social confusion that characterized post-Napoleonic Europe.

It was clear something had to be done. Politics and religion, as well as nature, abhor a vacuum. The new ideas and schemes that sprang up seemingly everywhere to fill the void left by the perceived inadequacies of traditional institutions in Church and State rivaled those of today in number, if nothing else.

From Gregory's perspective (as might be expected), of most concern were the philosophical and religious innovations that would become known as socialism and modernism (ultrasupernaturalism). In the early nineteenth century,

---

anism and the quest for the City upon the Hill. See Adam Morris, *American Messiahs: False Prophets of a Damned Nation* (New York: W.W. Norton and Company, 2019); Chris Jennings, *Paradise Now: The Story of American Utopianism* (New York: Random House, 2016); J. D. Dickey, *American Demagogue*.

26   Klemens Wenzel Nepomuk Lothar, Prince von Metternich-Winneburg zu Beilstein.

27   "Pius IX and the Revolutions at Rome," *The North American Review* 74, no. 154 (January 1852): 31.

however, these went together and were generally labeled *démocratie religieuse*, "the Democratic Religion."[28]

Promoting socialism as an alternative religion to Catholicism may have originated with Claude Henri de Rouvroy, comte de Saint-Simon, to whom Monsignor Benson referred in the letter to his mother. According to Saint-Simon, Christianity had been useful in its day, but that day was past. A new religion was needed to replace Christianity, not merely reform it along economic and humanitarian lines.[29]

To anyone conversant with subsequent efforts at economic and social reform, especially the Great Reset and other proposals, Saint-Simon's New Christianity sounds very familiar. In 1803, he began publishing works detailing his religious, social, political, and economic ideas. The plan was to "associate" all of society in a unified whole, integrating production with a moral code based on science.[30] Because the moral code was scientific, objective, and presumably reason-based instead of faith-based or religious, it could be coercively enforced.

The Church of Saint-Simon

About 1817, Saint-Simon replaced Augustin Thierry as his secretary with Auguste Comte, the future founder of positivism.[31] Over the next two years, Saint-Simon and Comte

---

28   Literally "the Religion of Democracy," but in context it is construed and translated as "the Democratic Religion." See Pierre Leroux, "*De l'individualisme et du socialisme*," in Œuvres de Pierre Leroux (1825-1850) (Paris: *Société typographique*, 1850), 376.

29   Julian Strube, "Socialism and Esotericism in July Monarchy France," *History of Religions*, July 2016, 2.

30   Ibid., 2–3.

31   "Saint-Simon and Saint-Simonism," Georges Goyau, *The Catho-*

decided that society needed to be run by a religious authority, but not one based on a traditional concept of God. After Saint-Simon's death, Comte would invent his own "Religion of Humanity," asserting society itself as divine with no need of a transcendent God.

Developing these ideas, Saint-Simon and Comte thought society should be organized like a medieval theocracy. Instead of a transcendent God as the basis of morality, people would share scientifically determined moral values and a common social vision. Anticipating "the Council for Inclusive Capitalism With The Vatican,"[32] there would be an industrial hierarchy in place of civil governors or ecclesiastical authorities.

Saint-Simon's industrial hierarchy would have economic, political, and military power, the last of which would fade away as there was an end to conflict between classes and universal prosperity and harmony ensued in a scientifically and morally directed economy.[33] Democratic only in name, the whole of society, construed as exclusively economic in

lic Encyclopedia, vol. 13 (New York: Robert Appleton Company, 1912).

32   "[A] historic new partnership between some of the world's largest investment and business leaders and the Vatican, . . . led by a core group of global leaders, known as 'Guardians for Inclusive Capitalism,' who meet annually with Pope Francis and Cardinal Turkson." Bank of America Newsroom, "The Council for Inclusive Capitalism With The Vatican, A New Alliance of Global Business Leaders, Launches," December 8, 2020, https://newsroom.banko famerica.com/content/newsroom/press-releases/2020/12/the-co uncil-for-inclusive-capitalism-with-the-vatican--a-new-all.html.

33   "Saint-Simon," *Encyclopedia Britannica*, 19: 14th Edition, 1956, Print.

nature, would be devoted to material improvement, with special emphasis on uplifting the poor.[34]

In his posthumous book, *Le Nouveau Christianisme* (1825), "The New Christianity," Saint-Simon declared himself the prophet of a "true Christianity." This was a universal religion returning to the pure doctrine of Christ. The goal was to establish a rational, scientific, positivist religion. A global social organization would direct economic life and bring an end to poverty. This would be through "the spirit of association" fostered by peace and the brotherhood of man.[35]

Saint-Simon's New Christianity would "resolve Christianity into its essential elements"[36] by focusing on the moral teachings and removing anything purely spiritual. This would combine civil, religious, and domestic society—State, Church, and Family—into one, presumably more efficient unit that would make material well-being its sole priority. As summarized in the precept that became the fundamental dogma of socialism, "The whole of society ought to strive towards the amelioration of the moral and physical existence of the poorest class; society ought to organize itself in the way best adapted for attaining this end."[37]

After his death, Saint-Simon's followers proclaimed themselves the Apostles of their Messiah or "Revelator," Saint-Simon, and formed *Le Église Saint-Simonienne*, "the Church

---

[34]   Ibid.
[35]   Ibid.
[36]   Ibid.
[37]   Ibid.

of Saint-Simonism." Saint-Amand Bazard and Barthélemy Prosper Enfantin were selected as "Supreme Fathers."[38]

Although extremely influential in its day, the Saint-Simonian organization was rent by schism and involvement in the Occult. "Lax notions as to the relation of the sexes" and a series of "extravagant entertainments" (possibly a euphemism for orgies) discredited the movement.[39] It eventually faded away as an identifiable organization. Significantly, the first published work of Blessed Antoine-Frédéric Ozanam—best known today as the founder of the Society of Saint Vincent de Paul—was a pamphlet harshly critiquing the Saint-Simonians.[40]

Pierre Leroux, a Saint-Simonian, coined the term *socialisme* ("socialism") in 1833/1834 as a pejorative to mean the opposite of *individualisme*.[41] By 1847, however, Leroux noted that socialism had come to be used to describe every form of *démocratie religieuse*.[42] To stress the originality of their "scientific socialism," Friedrich Engels and Karl Marx debated

---

[38]   Strube, "Socialism and Esotericism in July Monarchy France," 3.

[39]   "Men and women giving themselves to many without ever ceasing to be to one another, but whose love on the contrary would be as a divine Banquet." "Societary Theories," *The American Review: A Whig Journal* 1, no. 6 (June 1848), 640.

[40]   *Réflexions sur la Doctrine de Saint-Simon* (1831).

[41]   The term "socialist" antedates the term "socialism," being used at least as early as 1827, appearing in the London *Cooperative Magazine* in November of that year. John F. C. Harrison, *Quest for the New Moral World: Robert Owen and the Owenites in Britain and America* (New York: Charles Scribner's Sons, 1969), 45.

[42]   Leroux, "*De l'individualisme et du socialisme*," in Œuvres de Pierre Leroux, 376.

what term to use. They selected communism because they felt others had already coopted the word "socialism."[43]

3.2. The Theory of Certitude

As should be clear, efforts to reset society, whether Church, State, or Family, have been going on much longer than many people today realize. In the previous section, we looked at the Saint Simonian movement which first presented socialism as a new type of religion, a "New Christianity."

While the Saint-Simonian organization (but not its influence) eventually dissolved, there were other prophets and proponents of the Democratic Religion that concerned Pope Gregory XVI. To name only a few, there was the Associationism of François Marie Charles Fourier, the Icarian communism[44] of Étienne Cabet, the Fourierism of Fourier's disciples Victor Prosper Considerant and Albert Brisbane, the Universal Catholicism and magic of Alphonse-Louis Constant (who on becoming a ceremonial magician changed his name to Éliphas Lévi Zahed), and the proposals of the English industrialist Robert Owen, who founded the utopian community of New Harmony, Indiana (near Evansville) in the 1820s.

---

43   Harrison, *Quest for the New Moral World*, 45.

44   Cabet's system is invariably referred to as "Icarian socialism" today, but Cabet insisted he was a communist, not a socialist. Julian Strube, "Contested Christianities: Communism and Religion in July Monarchy France," *Socialist Imaginations: Utopias, Myths, and the Masses* (New York: Routledge, 2018) preprint, 1–2.

The First Modernist

As far as Gregory XVI was concerned, however, the
greatest danger came from the "novelties" promoted by
l'abbé Hugues-Félicité Robert de Lamennais. The "Neo-
Catholicism" of this "tormented, headstrong Breton priest"[45]
was based on changing fundamental Christian doctrines to
justify and conform to socialism.

As a result, Charles Périn, a professor at the University of
Louvain who appears to have been the first to define modernism in today's Catholic sense, regarded de Lamennais as
the first modernist. In *Le Modernisme dans l'Église d'après
les lettres inédites de Lamennais* (Paris, 1881), Périn defined
moderate modernism as "liberalism[46] of every degree and
shade," and extreme modernism as "the ambition to eliminate God from all public life."

Unfortunately, de Lamennais was a true genius. His errors
were of such incredible subtlety that to this day, even in many
otherwise orthodox circles, he is regarded as the unjustly
persecuted founder of liberal or social Catholicism.[47]

---

[45]　Philip Spencer, *Politics of Belief in Nineteenth-Century France*
(London: Faber and Faber Limited, 1954), 39.

[46]　Of the radical collectivist variety and the moderate or conservative
individualist type. Périn evidently did not consider personalist liberalism true liberalism.

[47]　See, e.g., George Weigel, *The Irony of Modern Catholic History:
How the Church Rediscovered Itself and Challenged the Modern
World to Reform* (New York: Basic Books, 2019), 33–37; W. G.
Roe, *Lamennais and England: The Reception of Lamennais's Reli-
gious Ideas in England in the Nineteenth Century* (London: Oxford
University Press, 1966); Peter N. Stearns, *Priest and Revolution-
ary: Lamennais and the Dilemma of French Catholicism* (New York:
Harper and Row, Publishers, 1967).

At one point, impressed with de Lamennais's obvious talents and his extraordinary zeal in opposing religious indifferentism (the belief that differences in religious belief are not important) and Gallicanism (the national church administratively free from papal control), Pope Leo XII considered making him a cardinal. The pope's better judgement, however, stopped him from giving the red hat to the "unhealthy, unkempt little bourgeois."[48] As he characterized de Lamennais, "He is an *esaltato*, a distinguished man of talents, knowledge, and good faith. But he is one of those lovers of perfection who, if one should leave them alone, would overthrow the whole world."[49]

Decades later, Alexis de Tocqueville agreed with this assessment. After a run-in with de Lamennais during the constitutional debates of the Second French Republic over a procedural issue too trivial to mention here but which threatened to disrupt the entire convention, de Tocqueville expressed his disgust. In his *Recollections*, he declared de Lamennais had "a pride great enough to walk over the heads of kings and bid defiance to God."[50]

---

[48]   Spencer, *Politics of Belief in Nineteenth-Century France*, 39.
[49]   Dudon, *Lamennais et le Saint-Siège* (Paris, 1911), 29; quoted in Heinrich A. Rommen, *The State in Catholic Thought: A Treatise in Political Philosophy* (St. Louis, Missouri: B. Herder Book Company, 1947), 436n.
[50]   Alexis de Tocqueville, *The Recollections of Alexis de Tocqueville* (Cleveland, Ohio: The World Publishing Company, 1959), 191.

Abstraction vs. Actuality

De Lamennais's principal error, and the one from which all his other errors derived, was to believe that the ideas he created in his own mind had a higher level of existence independent of the very mind that created them. Thus, he worshipped the People but quarreled incessantly with people, idolized the papacy, but despised every pope.

However, this was nothing more than what other socialists had done and would continue to do. What made de Lamennais more dangerous than the others in Gregory XVI's eyes was the way the Abbé mixed truth, falsehood, and nonsense to form a superficially consistent synthesis of socialism and Catholic doctrine based on his "theory of certitude." This transformed the Neo-Catholic movement from a sect advocating supreme papal authority in matters of faith and discipline—ultramontane—asserting papal claims against the rising secularism of radical liberalism to a Catholicized version of the Democratic Religion: a Catholic socialism supported by ultrasupernaturalist theology.

Most simply stated, de Lamennais's theory of certitude is that God vested humanity, not individual human persons, with the capacity to become more fully human—that is, virtuous. That meant only society or the collective could be saved, and only by establishing and maintaining the Kingdom of God on Earth.[51] This would be a perfect society in

---

[51]　The idea of collective salvation is a recurring theme in millennialist socialism and New Age thought. It was an important aspect of Guido List's *Armanenschaft*, as well as Theosophy, Ariosophy, and Nazi occultist ideology, in which it was thought to be an essential precondition for the establishment of the Thousand Year Reich.

which individuals are constrained by law to be virtuous. Humanity as a whole is condemned or redeemed, depending on whether it rejects or accepts the perfect social order, respectively, while individuals are saved by their faith and acceptance of the social order.

At the same time, de Lamennais accepted the Aristotelian-Thomist primacy of the intellect over the will in matters pertaining to natural law, and thus an understanding of natural law as based on reason—but with a twist. He made the intellect subordinate to the will in natural matters as well as supernatural, thereby subsuming the natural completely into the supernatural, reason to faith, and justice to charity.

De Lamennais failed to realize that the will completes and fulfils the intellect in supernatural matters, and vice versa, just as the supernatural itself fulfills and completes the natural: faith fulfills and completes reason, and charity fulfills and completes justice. The will does not replace the intellect, any more than the supernatural replaces the natural, faith replaces reason, or charity replaces justice.

As de Lamennais argued, however, because only humanity can become virtuous, and natural law is discerned by reason, only the collective, or humanity, can decide what constitutes right and wrong, or good and evil. Although it was probably not his intention, he replaced the moral absolutes of the natural law discerned by objective reason with popular opinion determined by subjective faith.

Nicholas Goodrick-Clarke, *The Occult Roots of Nazism* (London, UK: Tauris Parke, 2004), 84–89, 203.

Exaggerating Infallibility

To fit his theory of certitude into a Catholic framework, de Lamennais greatly exaggerated the concept of infallibility. He applied it to the pope's temporal and administrative power as well as to his spiritual authority. In so doing, de Lamennais confused that which is human with what is divine, inverting the natural and the supernatural orders.

This was a fatal error, as Sheen noted in *God and Intelligence.*[52] To explain, in Catholic belief, the Church as the Mystical Body of Christ is both divine and human. This makes perfect sense in Catholicism, for Jesus, who is considered the Church's Founder, is believed to be both true God and true man.

As a human institution, the Church is organized and run by imperfect people, including the pope. Like all other ordinary human beings, the pope can make mistakes in purely human matters such as science—including philosophy, theology, and economics—but also Church discipline, policy, administration, and governance.

At the same time, the Church is a divine institution constantly guided and animated by the Holy Spirit. Catholics believe that this guidance extends to the pope in his capacity as the Vicar of Christ on Earth. As a result, the pope is held to teach infallibly when, with the intention of doing so, he speaks definitively on matters of faith and morals (which includes the general norms of the natural law) that Catholics have always believed.

---

[52]   Sheen was analyzing the error and did not mention de Lamennais.

Properly understood, then, "papal infallibility"—or, more correctly, "the infallibility of the teaching office of the pope"—is a sort of certification process. By means of his infallible teaching office, the pope can declare that something the Church has always taught as true, but that people may have discussed, interpreted in different ways, or even doubted, is no longer to be questioned.

By claiming that the intellect (reason) resides in humanity instead of in individual human beings, however, de Lamennais inserted the need for an infallible interpreter in matters pertaining to the intellect as well as to faith and morals. Being unable to reason out matters for themselves—so de Lamennais argued—people must be told right from wrong by some infallible authority. This authority, so he claimed, is the pope, the final, indeed only arbiter of everything concerning both faith and reason.[53]

Changing the Nature of Truth

The theory of certitude is the essence of ultrasupernaturalism, and the reason Périn called de Lamennais the first modernist. It is why socialism and modernism are the social and theological aspects of relativism.

---

[53] G. K. Chesterton appears to have been aware of these implications of de Lamennais's theory of certitude. In his book on Saint Thomas Aquinas, he recounted the true relations between faith and reason and the debate between Aquinas and Siger of Brabant in terms that apply equally to the conflict between Gregory XVI and de Lamennais. See Chesterton, *Saint Thomas Aquinas*, 91-96, 126.

In the modernist or relativist framework, the basis of truth changes from what can be proved by reason (logical argument or empirical evidence) to faith. Faith, in turn, changes from the theological virtue applied to what is not manifestly true but consistent with reason to opinion that can and often does contradict reason. By rejecting the validity of reason and basing everything on faith, charity (the premier supernatural virtue) can override justice (the premier natural virtue).

In de Lamennais's thought, therefore, infallibility became the doctrine that something is true because the pope, Church, or Magisterium says so rather than the traditional, orthodox view that the pope (or Church or Magisterium) says so because it is true. Faith (really opinion) became stronger than "man's miserable intellect"[54] and could contradict reason. As Pope Saint Pius X later summed it up, by putting opinion above what can be proved by reason, modernism is "the synthesis of all heresies."[55]

Any opinion could now be justified if one's faith was strong enough. Church teaching could be used to support socialism, capitalism, and even nihilism or Satanism. It was only necessary to find a statement or incident (or anything

---

[54]   Knox, *Enthusiasm*, 3, 578–80, 585–87.

[55]   *Pascendi Dominici Gregis*, § 39. That is also why the first article in the Oath Against Modernism declares the primacy of the intellect in matters pertaining to natural law: "First of all, I profess that God, the origin and end of all things, can be known with certainty by the natural light of reason from the created world, that is, from the visible works of creation, as a cause from its effects, and that, therefore, his existence can also be demonstrated."

else) that could be twisted to justify a strongly held personal opinion and it was *ipso facto* true.

By making faith instead of reason the basis of natural law, anything goes. In that way, as Dr. Heinrich Albert Rommen, a student of Father Heinrich Pesch, SJ, explained, "Morality depends on the will of God. A thing is good not because it corresponds to the nature of God or, analogically, to the nature of man, but because God so wills. Hence the *lex naturalis* could be other than it is even materially or as to content, because it has no intrinsic connection with God's essence, which is self-conscious in His intellect. The laws of the second table of the Decalogue were no longer unalterable. An evolution set in which would lead to pure moral positivism, indeed to nihilism."[56]

The theory of certitude explains de Lamennais's intense and ostensibly orthodox focus on the problems of religious indifferentism and Gallicanism as well as his rejection of the radical liberal version of the separation of Church and State. After all, if only the pope can tell people what is right and wrong, anyone rejecting or ignoring the claims of the Catholic Church (indifferentism) is damned for not being a Catholic, and a virtual criminal in the civil order—an enemy of the people and a traitor to Christ.

As for Gallicanism, the French version of subordinating the Church to the civil authority, as far as de Lamennais was concerned, it inverted the proper order in which the State is subordinate to the Church. Separation of Church and State,

---

[56]   Heinrich A. Rommen, *The Natural Law: A Study in Legal and Social History and Philosophy* (Indianapolis, Indiana: Liberty Fund, Inc., 1998), 51–52 [edited].

which the radical liberals insisted means that religion is to be completely separate from civil and at times even domestic life, was also anathema to de Lamennais. In common with all ultrasupernaturalists, as Msgr. Ronald Knox noted in *Enthusiasm* (1950),[57] the only acceptable arrangement for de Lamennais was a theocracy, with the pope as ultimate civil and religious authority.

"Extreme and Rash Theories"

There is a great deal of truth mixed in with these errors, making discernment difficult at times. As Charles Forbes René de Montalembert, a friend and associate of de Lamennais, noted years later after breaking with him, "To new and fair practical notions, honest in themselves, which have for the last twenty years been the daily bread of Catholic polemics, we had been foolish enough to add extreme and rash theories; and to defend both with absolute logic, which loses, even when it does not dishonour, every cause."[58]

De Lamennais's theories dramatically highlight the difficulties involved in any program of reform. By changing fundamental assumptions, giving old terms new meanings, and mixing truth and falsehood indiscriminately, reform is given a bad name. Confusion spreads to the point where many people are unable to distinguish between good and evil. This is particularly problematic with the Great Reset, as it confuses

---

57   Knox, *Enthusiasm*, 3, 584–87.
58   Montalembert, from his *Life of Lacordaire*, quoted by John Henry Cardinal Newman, "Note on Essay IV., The Fall of La Mennais," *Essays Critical and Historical* (London: Longmans, Green, and Co., 1897), 173–74.

essential short-term emergency measures with long-term solutions, redefines fundamental rights, and makes appeals to emotion. Unfortunately, as we will see in the next section, the problem did not end with mere confusion.

3.3. The Renegade Abbé and Friends

By mixing truth, falsehood, and novelties indiscriminately, *l'abbe* Félicité de Lamennais was able to convince many people down to the present day of his orthodoxy. Like the Great Reset, whether intentional or not, the more convoluted and confusing a program is, the more accepted it may become.

Making matters worse was the fact that, for various reasons, the early-nineteenth-century popes were not popular. As a result, some people supported socialism simply because it was opposed to orthodox Christianity as symbolized by the Catholic Church in the person of the Vicar of Christ.

The Birth of Catholic Social Teaching

Gregory XVI could not let de Lamennais's theories go unchallenged, especially after the Abbé, Montalembert, and Jean-Baptiste Henri Dominique Lacordaire (who later helped restore the Dominican Order in France) made an uninvited trip to Rome to present their case. Calling themselves "the Pilgrims of God and Liberty," they eventually obtained an audience with the pope, although not on their terms.[59]

Prior to the meeting, the pope had already let the Pilgrims know, even though he was not pleased by it, they had permission to continue their political activities if they

---

[59]   Ibid.

toned down the rhetoric.[60] As for de Lamennais's theological and philosophical theories, a decision would be forthcoming. Gregory XVI was, in fact, suspicious of de Lamennais's orthodoxy, remarking later, "That dangerous man deserved to be brought before the Holy Office."[61]

During the meeting, impressed with their efforts to defend the Church (but not the manner of it), Gregory XVI confined the conversation to artistic and religious matters.[62] Afterwards, having received the permission they sought and gained the audience they demanded, Montalembert and Lacordaire tried to persuade de Lamennais to return to France, but he was far from satisfied. He had not come for permission and a chat but an enthusiastic endorsement, and he would not settle for anything less.

Montalembert and Lacordaire eventually made their way back to France. De Lamennais stayed, nursing his grudge against the pope and other churchmen and politicians who refused to see things his way.

In the meantime, Gregory XVI received word of what had happened in Poland during the November Uprising of 1830–31. This began as a riot sparked by an attempt to assassinate the Russian governor, Grand Duke Konstantin Pavlovich. Russians and Polish collaborators were lynched,

---

60   Thomas Bokenkotter, *Church and Revolution: Catholics in the Struggle for Democracy and Social Justice* (New York: Doubleday, 1998), 55–56.

61   E. L. Woodward, *Three Studies in European Conservatism*, 265, quoted by Spencer, *Politics of Belief in Nineteenth-Century France*, 47.

62   Bokenkotter, *Church and Revolution*, 56; Spencer, *Politics of Belief in Nineteenth-Century France*, 46–47.

resulting in reprisals that ended any remaining fiction of Polish autonomy.[63]

The First Social Encyclical

As pope, Gregory XVI would almost certainly have ignored the uprising, at least officially, had it not been for two circumstances. One, because Polish liberals sided with Napoléon against Russia, Prussia, and Austria to regain independence, the uprising became associated with the collectivist type of liberal democracy de Lamennais favored, and thus with socialism, ultrasupernaturalism, and the occult.[64]

This was largely through the efforts of the anti-Catholic "New Christian" Ludwik Królikowski, "an ardent propagandist" for the uprising who was tied in with the Saint-Simonians.[65] The activities of the radical "national apostate"

---

[63]   Adam Zamoyski, *The Polish Way: A Thousand-Year History of the Poles and Their Culture* (New York: Hippocrene Books, 1994), 269–76.

[64]   The three Partitions of 1772, 1792, and 1794 divided the country between Russia, Prussia, and Austria and erased Poland from the map of Europe. Many Polish intellectuals took refuge in France after the Third Partition, the purges of 1823, and the Decembrist Coup of 1825, and associated with the Saint-Simonians and others. Zamoyski, *The Polish Way*, 268–69.

[65]   Piotr Kuligowski (2018) "The Utopian Impulse and Searching for the Kingdom of God: Ludwik Królikowski's (1799-1879) Romantic Utopianism in Transnational Perspective," *Slovêne* 7, no. 2, 199–226. See also Bogdan Janski, Diary, 1830-1839 (Rome, Italy: Resurrection Studies, 2000); Bogdan Janski, *Letters*, 1828-1839 (Rome, Italy: Resurrection Studies, 2011); Ernest A. Varosi, *The Spiritual Legacy of Bogdan Janski* (Rome, Italy: Resurrection Studies, 2007).

Adam Gurowski and his connections with Saint-Simon and Fourier were also significant.[66]

Perhaps the determining factor, however, involved a renegade priest, Father Piotr Wojciech Ściegienny, who had circulated a forged encyclical, *Złota Książeczka* ("The Golden Book"). In Gregory's name, the people were urged to rise and destroy their presumed oppressors, including most priests and prelates of the Church, and redistribute their wealth.

For decades, the forgery continued to be accepted as genuine in rural districts. It was a strong influence on the development of Polish socialism and popular understanding of Catholic social teaching.[67] It was also a source for Mariavitism, a Polish socialist and ultrasupernaturalist heresy in the late nineteenth and early twentieth centuries that sought to establish the Kingdom of God on Earth.[68]

On June 9, 1832, therefore, Gregory XVI issued *Cum Primum*, "On Civil Obedience." This was primarily directed at the uprising, although without mentioning Królikowski, Father Ściegienny, or the false encyclical. Outraged at what he considered the pope's betrayal of democracy, and possibly aware that the pope was about to render the final decision on his theories, de Lamennais left Rome in early August.

---

[66]   Norman Davies, *God's Playground: A History of Poland, Volume II, 1795 to the Present* (New York: Columbia University Press, 1984), 31–32.

[67]   Piotr Kuligowski, "Sword of Christ: Christian Inspirations of Polish Socialism Before the January Uprising," *Journal of Polish Education, Culture and Society*, no. 1 (2012): 120.

[68]   Lukasz Liniewicz, "Mariavitism: Mystical, Social, National, A Polish Religious Answer to the Challenges of Modernity," Master Thesis, School of Theology, Tilburg University, 2012/2013.

A few days later, August 15, 1832, Gregory XVI issued the first social encyclical, *Mirari Vos*, "On Liberalism and Religious Indifferentism." The bulk of the document addressed collectivist liberal doctrines de Lamennais himself condemned, even as he relied on them for his theories, as well as the theory of certitude and other "novelties," although not by name.

Words of a Non-Believer

At first, De Lamennais submitted, but then he wrote letters expressing his true feelings. Some recipients made the contents public, including the archbishop of Toulouse, whom de Lamennais sent a particularly intemperate one.[69] At that point, Gregory XVI demanded de Lamennais submit again in writing, and the French priest complied. Within a matter of hours, however, de Lamennais changed his mind. He repudiated his priesthood, renounced Christianity, and eventually declared himself the prophet of a new Religion of Humanity.

Given de Lamennais's theory that the pope speaks infallibly on virtually everything, his rejection of papal authority may at first seem inexplicable. It makes perfect sense within an ultrasupernaturalist framework, however, which permits contradictions if they agree with one's own opinion. If the infallible pope rejects his own infallibility, then—obviously—he could not have been infallible in the first place. The only truly infallible doctrine is the faith one has in one's own opinion, even if that opinion changes. Thus,

---

[69]   Lancelot C. Sheppard, *Lacordaire: A Biographical Essay* (New York: The Macmillan Company, 1964), 43.

in ultrasupernaturalism, truth changes as opinions change, depending on whatever one believes in. It is not any particular doctrine that matters but one's belief in it. Ultrasupernaturalism does not consist of any specific body of doctrine but of an understanding of truth itself as changeable; the only absolute is that there are no absolutes.

Matters did not stop there. In May 1834, de Lamennais published *Les Paroles d'un Croyant,* "Words of a Believer." Translated into many languages, the little pamphlet condemned a conspiracy of kings and priests against the people in apocalyptic terms. It sold tens of thousands of copies.

In response, Gregory XVI issued the second social encyclical, *Singulari Nos,* "On the Errors of Lamennais." The pope condemned *Les Paroles d'un Croyant* as "small in size, [but] enormous in wickedness."[70] He specifically warned the hierarchy to be on guard against ideas—*rerum novarum,* "new things"[71]—that undermine truth, replace God with man, and destabilize the social order.

The Principle of Social Justice

Continuing his efforts to counter the New Things, which eventually became known as socialism, modernism, and the New Age, Gregory XVI sponsored the Thomist revival. He thereby established sound philosophy and natural law as the principal weapons against socialism and ultrasupernaturalism. He also encouraged the work of Monsignor Luigi

---

70 *Singulari Nos,* § 2.
71 Ibid., § 8.

Aloysius Taparelli d'Azeglio, SJ, who was the first to use the term "social justice" in a Catholic sense.

By the 1830s, the term "social justice" had been used in many ways. The socialists were starting to use it to describe redistribution of existing wealth, as well as the replacement of justice with charity, reason with faith, and so on. This made sense within the context of socialism as the Democratic Religion, and the consequent rejection of the natural virtues, especially justice, and their replacement with the supernatural virtues, notably charity.

In response, in the late 1830s, Taparelli, a leader in the Thomist revival, reoriented the idea of social justice along Catholic, natural law lines. His concept of social justice was a specific, identifiable principle, although not a particular virtue with a definable act of its own.[72] He intended his theory as an alternative to the Democratic Religion and Neo-Platonism of the socialists, particularly de Lamennais.

Taparelli conceived social justice as a guiding principle to reform human institutions. The idea was to conform institutions to the demands of individual human nature and the common good, bringing people together in solidarity. Taparelli's theory was that all human matters, especially social improvement and the general welfare, must be subordinate to the natural law as understood in Aristotelian-Thomism and to the Magisterium of the Church.

There are thus absolutes—natural rights inhering in each human person, such as life, liberty, and private property—that

---

[72]   A. Taparelli, *Saggio Teorico di Diritto Naturale* (1845); cf.. William J. Ferree, *The Act of Social Justice* (Washington, DC: Catholic University of America Press, 1942), 83.

must remain sacred and inviolate, regardless of the needs of individuals or society. Taparelli's principle of social justice went no further than that. He does not appear to have construed it as a virtue in the classical sense. His achievement, critical as it was, was therefore not a fully developed theory of social ethics but of individual ethics with a good intention toward the common good.[73]

Unfortunately, as is the case today with the Great Reset, as social conditions worsened, people wanted results. They became impatient with rarified and highly technical theories that, while diagnosing the problem accurately, did nothing to offer a solution to poverty, social alienation, and injustice.

Unlike the Great Reset, however, lack of specificity in papal condemnations as well as the failure to present a viable alternative to what was condemned virtually ensured that people would ignore essential instruction and guidance. Even Gregory XVI's attempt in 1839 to correct the horror of slavery in the United States, *In Supremo Apostolatus* ("On the Slave Trade"), was dismissed as irrelevant or ineffectual theorizing.[74]

3.4. The Frustrated Reformer

On June 14, 1846, the College of Cardinals elected Giovanni Maria Mastai Ferretti, a moderate personalist liberal and

---

[73]   William J. Ferree, *Introduction to Social Justice* (New York: Paulist Press, 1948), 10.

[74]   The encyclical may have been prompted by the 1838 slave auction by the Jesuits in Maryland to provide funding for Georgetown University. See Joel S. Panzer, *The Popes and Slavery* (New York: Alba House, 1996) for an overview of papal condemnations of slavery over the centuries.

supporter of democracy, as Pope Pius IX. A protégé of Pope Pius VII, he was the first head of the Catholic Church to have visited the Americas, having accompanied a papal mission to Chile from 1823 to 1825.

The Black Legend of Pio No-No

Not surprisingly, the new pope was harshly criticized by both radicals and reactionaries. The former considered him too orthodox and conservative, while the latter believed him to be unorthodox and liberal.

According to the usual accounts, Pius IX started out as a reformer, but when confronted with the harsh reality of true (i.e., individualist and collectivist) liberalism, he became an ultra-reactionary. As legend has it, he became the "Pio No-No" of modernist myth who simply responded "no, no" to every attempt to implement reforms. There is no evidence that he ever did so.

Still, there is just barely enough truth in the *Leyenda Negra* of Pius IX to keep it alive and nullify the accomplishments and goals of the longest pontificate in history. Part of the problem is that few people, especially liberals, seem to realize that "liberalism" has different meanings, depending on how one views the human person.

As noted, there is the collectivist type of radical liberalism in which the collective is sovereign and has rights that actual human beings do not. This often manifests as some form of socialism as well as collectivism and is supported theologically by ultrasupernaturalism. This is what usually falls under the heading of liberalism today.

Then there is the individualist type of moderate or conservative liberalism in which an elite is effectively sovereign. Often, adherents of this type of liberalism will assert that everyone has rights but that they are only effective for the elite who have some special characteristic that other people lack. This is usually tied to some form of capitalism as well as individualism. Perhaps confusingly, this is also supported theologically by ultrasupernaturalism, although today it usually falls under the heading of conservatism.

What confuses matters even more today is the fact that as radical and moderate liberalism draw closer together to form what Hilaire Belloc called "the Servile State" (although not quite as he envisioned it), it becomes increasingly difficult to distinguish between capitalism and socialism. George Bernard Shaw, for example, insisted that "only communism [socialism] remains,"[75] while the stakeholder and inclusive capitalism of the Great Reset appear to be indistinguishable from democratic socialism.[76]

What is almost always omitted from the discussion is the personalist type of liberalism that is consistent with natural law and thus with Catholic social teaching. As applied in the United States and chronicled by Alexis de Tocqueville, personalist liberalism is the type praised by most popes since

---

[75]   "Shaw's Greatness Declared Vapid," *Evening Star*, November 27, 1931, B-11. Chesterton's response to Shaw's insistence that everything is socialism because everything is social seems to have been to point out, then, that if use of capital is capitalism, then everything is capitalism. G. K. Chesterton, *The Outline of Sanity, Collected Works, Vol. V* (San Francisco: Ignatius Press, 1987), 43.

[76]   "Rise of the Democratic Socialists," *The Week*, July 30, 2018, http://theweek.com/articles/786937/rise-democratic-socialists.

Pius VII[77] and is based on the sovereignty of every human being. While today often confused with individualist or "conservative" liberalism, personalist liberalism is fundamentally different from both moderate liberalism and radical liberalism, so much so that the popes have often avoided even calling it liberalism.[78]

Hijacking the Reform

Reactionaries viewed Pope Pius IX's election with alarm and were very nearly able to prevent it. They knew he was a protégé of Pius VII and had firsthand experience of the new republics in South America, having traveled there as a special envoy during that pontificate. Given their distrust of new ideas, they had every reason to be suspicious of his liberalism.

Pius IX did nothing to quell their fears. To forestall threatened insurrections, the new pope immediately announced a program of political reforms intended to remove the causes of legitimate grievances. His first act was to declare an amnesty for all political prisoners. This worried Metternich, who believed the radicals would simply take the first opportunity to seize power.

Metternich was not wrong. Pius IX instituted sweeping political reforms throughout the Papal States, including a democratically elected legislature, a lay civil administration

---

77   Rommen, *The State in Catholic Thought*, 481.
78   See Joseph Ratzinger and Marcello Pera, *Without Roots: The West, Relativism, Christianity, Islam* (New York: Basic Books, 2006), 70-75; Joseph Ratzinger, *Europe: Today and Tomorrow* (San Francisco: Ignatius Press, 2004), 28, 72–74.

and prime minister, and a constitution modeled on that of the United States.[79] The only power Pius IX reserved as civil ruler was the veto over any legislation that in his opinion violated the rights of the Church.[80]

Unfortunately, the only politically experienced people in the Papal States were the radical liberals, who were able to gain many elective and appointed offices largely because others simply did not know how to go about being an empowered citizenry. Two years after Pius IX's election when the revolutions of 1848 swept through Europe, they made their move.

Demanding reforms the pope had already granted, armed radical bands seized strategic points throughout the country, assassinated the prime minister and many others, and imprisoned Pius IX in his own palace. They demanded that he dissolve the Church, resign as pope, and turn the country over to them. Following a daring escape arranged by some foreign ambassadors, the pope took refuge in the city of Gaeta in the Kingdom of the Two Sicilies.

Despite the stream of envoys from the revolutionary government assuring him of his personal safety and inviolability should he return, Pius IX refused to negotiate with those who today would be regarded as terrorists. This is the probable source of the Black Legend of "Pio No-No"—a prudential and certainly common sense response to insurgents who had

---

[79]   British Prime Minister William Ewert Gladstone mistakenly believed Pius IX's "Fundamental Statute" was based on the unwritten English constitution. "Pius IX and the Revolutions at Rome," *The North American Review* 74, no. 154 (January 1852): 52.

[80]   Ibid.; Rommen, *The State in Catholic Thought*, 481, 605.

called for his abdication and the destruction of the Church, and murdered the leader of the legitimate government.

Forestalling Reform

After the French restored Pius IX, radicals in the French legislature—including de Lamennais—demanded that the pope implement many of the changes demanded by the revolutionaries in consideration of their help. Fortunately, however, Alexis de Tocqueville was French Foreign Minister.

The unquestioned champion of democracy pointed out that Pius IX had already implemented many of the changes. To do any more before the political situation could be stabilized would very likely cause another revolution. In de Tocqueville's opinion, the radicals would again seize the opportunity to try and take over the government.[81]

Unfortunately, the political situation went from bad to worse as Austria, France, and Sardinia continued to vie with the various factions of the Italian unification movement to establish spheres of influence and expand territory. Pius IX was still able to implement limited administrative reforms and sponsor educational and economic development. By 1861, however, there was nothing left to reform as Sardinia seized all the Papal States except Rome and its immediate environs, and then Rome in 1871.

Nevertheless, Pius IX accomplished much more than history credits him. His attempt to add political reform to the Church's social program failed, but that did not invalidate the principle of personal sovereignty in either religious or

---

[81]   De Tocqueville, *Recollections*, 314.

civil society. He continued the Thomist revival, strengthened the Church doctrinally and administratively, and carefully explained the errors and dangers of ultrasupernaturalism and socialism in a series of encyclicals and other teachings.

The First Vatican Council

Perhaps Pius IX's greatest achievement in the field of social teaching, however, was calling the First Vatican Council in an effort to settle the question of the New Things definitively and dogmatically. Unfortunately, the work of the council fathers was cut short by the withdrawal of French troops protecting Rome for service against Prussia. This allowed Sardinia to complete the conquest of Italy.

Nevertheless, the council fathers promulgated two key definitions that utterly destroyed any intellectual or religious justification for de Lamennais's theory of certitude. These were the primacy of the intellect in matters pertaining to natural law and the infallibility of the teaching office of the Roman pontiff in matters relating to faith and morals.

We discussed papal infallibility above. It is only necessary to repeat that where de Lamennais insisted that the pope's power to teach authoritatively extended to science and reason, the council limited infallibility to faith and morals, and then only under certain conditions. Some orthodox commentators, notably Saint John Henry Newman, were concerned that the council fathers intended to expand infallibility in a misguided effort to counter the New Things more effectively but soon realized their fears were groundless.[82]

---

[82]   Saint John Henry Newman had explicitly repudiated an exagger-

At the heart of opposition to the New Things, and thus the foundation of Catholic social teaching, was the definition of the primacy of the intellect in matters pertaining to natural law and the temporal order.[83] In supernatural or spiritual matters, as Aquinas explained, the will is preeminent.[84] The problem, however, was replacement of natural law with private interpretations of supernatural law—the essence of ultrasupernaturalism.[85]

It was therefore essential to define the primacy of the intellect in natural matters. This was because de Lamennais and all subsequent theological relativists—Knox's ultrasupernaturalists—made a special point of denigrating or attacking human reason. Contrary to traditional Catholic teaching,[86] they asserted the primacy of faith alone, rejecting reason and justice. That is why Dr. Ralph McInerny of the University

---

ated interpretation of papal infallibility in his *Essay in Aid of a Grammar of Assent* (1870). The *Grammar* had its origin in Newman's efforts during the late 1850s and early 1860s to argue a middle way between those like de Lamennais, who based everything on faith even when it contradicted reason, and others such as his friend William Froude (1810-1879), who rejected faith and believed that theological conclusions reached by human reason were uncertain. Wilfred Ward, *Life of John Henry Cardinal Newman* (London: Longmans, Green, and Co., 1913), II.307; Alejandro Sada Mier y Terán, "The Legitimacy of Certitude in Newman's *Grammar of Assent,*" *Yearbook of the Irish Philosophical Society*, 2014/15, ed. Angelo Bottone (Maynooth, Éire: Irish Philosophical Society, 2015), 49–63.

[83]   I q. 83, a. 2, c.

[84]   Ibid.

[85]   Sheen, *Religion Without God*, 95–97.

[86]   Karol Wojtyła, "The Problem of the Separation of Experience from the Act in Ethics," *Person and Community: Selected Essays* (New York: Peter Lang, 2008), 23.

of Notre Dame declared that fideism is the single greatest danger to the Catholic Church today.[87]

As Sheen pointed out in *God and Intelligence*, Aquinas based his entire philosophy of common sense on the first principle of reason. This is stated negatively as nothing can both "be" and "not be" at the same time under the same conditions. Its positive statement is that which is true is as true and is true in the same way as everything else that is true. Within a Thomist framework, then, it is impossible that a faith-based truth can contradict reason, or that a reason-based truth can contradict faith.

The true sense of the primacy of the intellect is not that either reason or faith is necessarily false if an apparent contradiction appears but that a true understanding of either faith or reason must be achieved by applying the human intellect to the question to discern the truth. If there seems to be a contradiction, it must be resolved, not merely dismissed by asserting the superiority of faith over reason or vice versa.[88]

Within the Aristotelian-Thomist framework, the supernatural ("above nature") virtue of faith is "above" natural reason and applies to that which cannot be proved by reason. At the same time, nothing held by faith can contradict that which has been proved by reason.

Reason ("intellect") therefore has a primacy over faith ("will") in the sense that it comes first in natural matters, and faith, which deals with the supernatural, cannot contradict

---

87   Ralph M. McInerny, *Miracles: A Catholic View* (Huntington, Indiana: Our Sunday Visitor, 1986), 22.

88   Wojtyła, "The Problem of the Separation of Experience from the Act in Ethics," *Person and Community*, 23–44.

reason. The primacy of the intellect in natural matters does not mean that reason is greater than faith, or true when faith is false. Even in matters of faith where the will is preeminent, reason must never be rejected. As the council fathers declared, "If anyone says that the one, true God, our creator and lord, cannot be known with certainty from the things that have been made,[89] by the natural light of human reason[90]: let him be anathema."[91]

This was repeated in the first article of the Oath Against Modernism and again in section 2 of *Humani Generis*, as well as implied in encyclicals and other documents dealing with the problem of ultrasupernaturalism. Pius IX did not, therefore, abandon Gregory XVI's reliance on scholastic philosophy, especially that of Aquinas, in trying to counter the New Things. Instead, he added an attempt to reform political institutions so that the intellectual and spiritual sovereignty of the human person—both rejected by de Lamennais and other socialists—could be fostered in a suitable civil environment.

A Fatal Omission

Papal efforts to counter ultrasupernaturalism and socialism, however, left a fatal omission. They did not present a sound economic program to empower every human being with direct ownership of both labor and capital. This is essential for at least three reasons.

---

[89] That is, by the empirical evidence of the human senses.
[90] That is, by the human intellect.
[91] Vatican I, Canon 2.1.

First, power follows property. If people are to lead virtuous lives, they must have the power to act virtuously and build habits of doing good.

Second, political democracy cannot be sustained without economic democracy. A free people must be free in deed as well as word, and that means free of the very dependency on the government, a private employer, or any other locus of concentrated power on which the wage and welfare system of, for example, the Great Reset rely.

Third, capitalism and socialism both deprive ordinary people of private property in capital. Capitalism does this by asserting that something other than mere humanity is needed to be an owner even if private property is recognized as a natural right, while socialism asserts that real ownership resides in the collective or humanity. Even those forms of socialism that allow private ownership only do so as an expedient that can be revoked or—as in the Great Reset—redefined so that it is effectively meaningless. It is not considered a natural and inalienable right in the Aristotelian-Thomist sense.

3.5. The Struggle for Sanity

Following his election in 1878, Pope Leo XIII continued Blessed Pope Pius IX's efforts to contain and counter socialism and ultrasupernaturalism. The new pope had seen what happened to Pius IX's political reform efforts at the hands of radical liberalism.

While bishop of Perugia, Leo XIII's own economic and political reforms had been completely overturned by Sardinia's conquest of the Papal States. He knew the risks of implementing political reforms, much less trying to counter the New Things of socialism and ultrasupernaturalism, without first instructing people in authentic political principles and sound philosophy.

This Leo XIII proceeded to do. While uniquely his own, however, it cannot be said that Leo XIII's teachings differed materially from those of Pius IX in substance, form, or content prior to 1891. He condemned the evils of modern society, especially socialism and modernism, although the term "modernism" in this context would not appear until 1881. Matters seemed to have reached a stalemate.

The Georgist Wild Cards

Then, beginning in 1886, what comes across to modern readers as an improbable, even surreal series of events took the conflict between the New Things and Catholicism to an entirely new level. In that year, the agrarian socialist Henry George decided to run for mayor of New York City. What he hoped to accomplish remains a mystery to this day, but the campaign and its aftermath were a game changer.[92]

George, who had been strongly influenced as a child by the religious socialism and chauvinistic patriotism of the Second Great Awakening, had made a name for himself as the author of *Progress and Poverty* (1879). This was one of the two most influential nineteenth-century socialist books coming out of the United States. (The other was Edward Bellamy's *Looking Backward: 2000-1887*, 1888.)

---

[92]   Henry W. Farnam, "Progress and Poverty in Politics," *The New Englander and Yale Review* 46, no. 205 (April 1887): 340.

Although George insisted that he was not a socialist on the rather specious grounds that in his opinion socialism can only exist in barbarian or degenerate cultures,[93] his basic theory, known as "Georgism," was essentially the same as all other forms of socialism. His innovation (or so he assumed; Marx had advocated the abolition of private property in land earlier in *The Communist Manifesto*) was that no individual human person can legitimately own land or anything else created by God. In George's view, private ownership is limited to what human beings create with their own labor and nothing else. Only humanity, not human beings, has the right to own land.[94] George did not address the question whether owning livestock is legitimate.

Shortly before running for mayor, and although he was not Catholic, George had joined forces with Father Edward McGlynn of the New York Archdiocese. A perennial thorn in the side of the Church even before his ordination, Father McGlynn had also been influenced in childhood by the Second Great Awakening. He believed strongly that religion must be democratic and subordinate to the will of the People in doctrine and practice—what was coming to be called "Americanism."[95]

McGlynn was an avowed socialist with flexible views regarding doctrine and obedience.[96] He was on good terms

---

[93]   Henry George, *Progress and Poverty* (New York: Robert Schalkenbach Foundation, 1992), 319–21.

[94]   Ibid., 336–40.

[95]   Cf. *Testem Benevolentiae Nostrae.*

[96]   At one point Father McGlynn explored the idea of establishing his own independent parish, but the project came to nothing due to lack of funding. Alfred Isacsson, *The Determined Doctor: The*

with anti-Catholic individuals and Protestant clergy, such as Henry Ward Beecher and Howard Crosby.[97] Even his best friend among his brother clergy, Father Richard Lalor Burtsell, who advocated women's ordination,[98] thought that some of McGlynn's views were too radical.[99]

Father Isaac Hecker, colleague of Orestes Brownson and founder of the Paulists, sympathized with McGlynn's concern for the poor. As a former socialist himself, however, he believed that the New Christianity was not the answer.[100] Hecker also looked askance at McGlynn's attitude toward authority and his obsession with "gossipy Church politics."[101]

During the campaign, George claimed the endorsement of Bishop Thomas Nulty of Meath, Ireland, and Edward Cardinal Manning, primate of England. Nulty, however, had completely repudiated George and his theories years before and had issued a public statement to that effect.[102] The Irish bishop had also personally assured Leo XIII of his complete fidelity to the teachings of the Catholic Church, not those of George.[103]

Story of Edward McGlynn (Tarrytown, New York: Vestigium Press, 1990), 14–17.

97 Stephen Bell, *Rebel, Priest and Prophet: A Biography of Dr. Edward McGlynn* (New York: The Devin-Adair Company, 1937), 17.

98 Ibid., 55.

99 Ibid.

100 Walter Elliott, *The Life of Father Hecker* (New York: The Columbus Press, 1891), 47–48, 53.

101 David J. O'Brien, *Isaac Hecker: An American Catholic* (New York: Paulist Press, 1992), 332–34.

102 "The Most Rev. Dr. Nulty," *New Zealand Tablet*, March 17, 1882, 13.

103 "Bishop Nulty is Dead, An Irish Catholic Prelate Who Was Prom-

Manning had met with George on George's trip to the United Kingdom in 1883–1884, during which George claimed the cardinal had endorsed his views. Learning of this immediately following the campaign, Manning wrote two open letters to the New York newspapers.

His Eminence's first letter diplomatically repudiated George's claim of an endorsement.[104] The second, written after George declared that Manning had in the first letter again endorsed him,[105] implied in much less diplomatic terms that George had deceived him.[106] As he wrote, "The Catholic church is not opposed to the present labor movement or Mr. Henry George, unless they fall into socialism. There must be a very wide distinction made between the socialist and the workingman. I saw in a telegram some time ago that Mr. George had said the Catholic church had never confirmed the principle of property in land. This is not true. Exactly the reverse is the fact. The church has, from the beginning, taught the right of property in land."[107]

inent in the Fight Against 'Landlordism'," *The New York Times*, December 25, 1898.

[104] "Cardinal Manning on the Attitude of the Catholic Church," *The Milwaukee Journal*, December 14, 1886, 1.

[105] Washington, DC *Evening Star*, December 18, 1886, 4.

[106] "A Conference of Prelates," *The New York Sun*, December 15, 1886, 1; "Henry George's Theories. Cardinal Manning Tells of His Talk with George About Them." *The New York Times*, December 18, 1886.

[107] "Cardinal Manning on the Attitude of the Catholic Church."

The Road to Excommunication

During the campaign, in response to a request from Tammany Hall, Father Thomas Scott Preston, protonotary apostolic of the New York Archdiocese, had issued an opinion as to the orthodoxy of George's theories. As Preston explained in an article published a few years later, George's theories are "contrary to the law of God, [and] destructive of the best interests of society."[108]

George blamed his loss to the Democratic reforming candidate, Abram Stevens Hewitt, on voter fraud and collusion between corrupt politicians and venal Catholic prelates. This was simple resentment. Horace Greeley, a socialist, praised the election for its fairness and cleanness,[109] while objective historians claim that Preston's letter had no effect on the election.[110]

Realistically, George would have lost the election in any event. Republican bosses, worried by George's popularity, ran a reform candidate of their own: Theodore Roosevelt Jr. Roosevelt agreed to run when the Republican bosses promised not to tell people to vote for Hewitt to ensure George's defeat.

Although Roosevelt pulled votes from both Hewitt and George and had a good chance of winning, Republican leaders told their people to vote for Hewitt anyway. Roosevelt never forgave them for their betrayal.[111]

---

108   Thomas S. Preston, "Socialism and the Church," *The Forum* V, no. 2 (April 1888).

109   "How City Votes Were Cast. The Day of Election Fine and Quiet." *The New York Tribune*, November 3, 1886, 1.

110   Edmund Morris, *The Rise of Theodore Roosevelt* (New York: Random House, 2010), 350–51.

111   Ibid.

Commenting on the election, McGlynn, too, hinted that the Catholic Church was responsible for George's defeat. In the December 1886 issue of the *North American Review*, he reiterated his belief that George was the prophet of the new gospel of Georgism come to replace the corrupt Catholic Church.[112]

Prefiguring the Great Reset, McGlynn believed George was destined by heaven to reform Christianity and create a perfect society on earth by applying the principles of Georgism.[113] Summoned to the Vatican by Leo XIII personally to explain his actions, McGlynn at first agreed, but then refused, making a series of increasingly specious excuses.[114]

Soon after the election, George founded a newspaper, *The Standard*,[115] in which he relentlessly attacked the Church for opposing socialism. As Michael Davitt, president of the Irish National Land League, declared during a lecture on Home Rule he gave in Glasgow, Scotland, on Saturday, January 15, 1887, the week following the first issue of George's new

---

[112] Edward McGlynn, "Lessons of the New York City Election," *The North American Review* 143, no. 361 (December 1886): 571–76.

[113] Ibid.

[114] "McGlynn Refuses," *Desert News*, February 2, 1887, 37; "Corrigan Sustained: A Letter from the Pope Regarding the Dr. McGlynn Affair," The Daily Argus News, May 24, 1887, 1; "The Crisis at Hand: Will Dr. McGlynn Obey the Summons of the Pope?" *The Meriden Daily Republican*, May 24, 1887, 1; Henry George, Jr., *The Life of Henry George* (New York: Doubleday and McClure Company, 1900), 488–95.

[115] Three other newspapers had been started during the campaign to support George. Henry W. Farnam, "Progress and Poverty in Politics," *The New Englander and Yale Review* 46, no. 205 (April 1887): 341.

journal, "Mr George's newspaper is the organ of the new labour movement, yet it chiefly attacks the Church, which cannot be the object of the labour party. Mr George gives Father M'Glynn bad advice in telling him not to visit Rome to defend himself."[116]

Finally, after repeated warnings,[117] McGlynn was excommunicated for disobedience on Monday July 4, 1887. The excommunication was effective July 5 due to the holiday as the registered letter could not be delivered until the following day.[118]

---

[116]   "Mr Davitt and Mr Henry George," *The Glasgow Herald*, January 18, 1887, 5.

[117]   Corrigan Sustained: A Letter from the Pope Regarding the Dr. McGlynn Affair," *The Daily Argus News*, May 24, 1887, 1; "The Crisis at Hand: Will Dr. McGlynn Obey the Summons of the Pope?" *The Meriden Daily Republican*, May 24, 1887, 1.

[118]   "Defiant Dr. McGlynn," *The True Witness and Catholic Chronicle*, July 13, 1887, 1.

CHAPTER 4

The Servile State

4.1. A New Kind of Social Encyclical

At the height of the frenzy caused by the antics of Henry George and Father Edward McGlynn during and after the 1886 New York City mayoral campaign, Bishop Bernard John McQuaid of Rochester, New York, wrote a series of letters to Archbishop Michael Augustine Corrigan of New York City. In one of them, McQuaid noted that "many of [George's and McGlynn's] poor people have been led astray by the use of the names of Cardinal Manning and Bishop Nulty" to give the impression that the Catholic Church endorsed socialism. McQuaid then commented that "the Holy Father will probably issue a dogmatic decision on the question."[1]

A Change in Tactics

McQuaid's letter appears to be the first hint of what would eventually be issued in 1891 as *Rerum Novarum*, "On the Condition of Labor." Considered by many authorities to be

---

[1] Letter of January 22, 1887 from McQuaid to Corrigan (University of Notre Dame Archives).

the first social encyclical, that is clearly not the case. This is obvious from the fact that the formal title is an allusion to Gregory XVI's 1834 encyclical *Singulari Nos*, "On the Errors of Lamennais," which referred to socialism and ultrasupernaturalism as *rerum novarum*—"new things."

This does not detract from the genuinely revolutionary nature of the document. While not the first social encyclical, *Rerum Novarum* was a new kind of social encyclical. Starting with *Mirari Vos* in 1832, previous social encyclicals had condemned errors and presented authentic doctrine. In *Rerum Novarum*, Leo XIII did that too but added a specific suggested program as an alternative to socialist proposals.

Not that the road had been particularly smooth. Following his excommunication for disobedience, McGlynn published a vitriolic article in the *North American Review* condemning the Catholic Church for requiring clergy to wear the Roman collar and not accepting socialism. Most of his ire, however, was directed at the alleged mandate for parishes to establish parochial schools regardless of cost and indoctrinate children in anti-American beliefs under pain of excommunication.[2]

For his part, George alienated many supporters by insulting—or allowing to be insulted—William O'Brien, editor

---

[2]   Edward McGlynn, "The New Know-Nothingism and the Old," *The North American Review* 145, no. 369 (August 1887): 192–205. Archbishop John Ireland's 1890 address to the National Educational Association of the United States, "State Schools and Parish Schools," may have been in part a response to McGlynn's article. Archbishop John Ireland, *The Church and Modern Society, Vol. I & II* (St. Paul, Minnesota: The Pioneer Press, 1905), I.215-232.

of *The United Irishman*, journal of the Irish National Land
League.[3] Without O'Brien's knowledge, George announced
the Irish leader as the featured speaker at the largest pro-
George rally ever assembled. O'Brien declined, saying he
was in New York to promote Irish nationalism, not Henry
George. Georgists' subsequent display of petulant bad tem-
per disgusted many people.[4]

Repeated attempts to persuade McGlynn to comply
with the two conditions for lifting his excommunication—
apologize to those whom he had insulted and go to Rome
as originally ordered—were rejected as often as they were
made. Instead, McGlynn invariably chose to grandstand
and air his grievances, real and (mostly) imagined.[5]

On one occasion, McGlynn outraged Catholics and Prot-
estants alike by delivering a "vulgar tirade" in which he called

---

[3]   The Irish National Land League, *Conradh na Talún*, founded
       1879, suppressed in 1881, and revived in 1882 as the Irish Na-
       tional League. The organization in the United States retained the
       name National Land League.

[4]   "Angry with O'Brien," *Washington Evening Star*, June 6, 1887, 1;
       "The Big Labor Parade," *Bridgeport Morning News*, June 6, 1887,
       1; "Mr. O'Brien Commended: All But the George People Say He
       Did Well," *The New York Times*, June 7, 1887.

[5]   "Another Foolish Priest," *Meriden Daily Republican*, August 4,
       1887, 1; "Rebellious Priests," *The Toronto Daily Mail*, August
       15, 1887; J. U. Heinzle, "Galileo Galilei and Dr. McGlynn,"
       The Catholic World 46, no. 271 (October 1887); "Will Be Taken
       Back," *The Boston Evening Transcript*, October 27, 1887, 1; "Dr.
       McGlynn Talks Back," *The New York Sun*, November 6, 1887, 11;
       "Dr. McGlynn Must Recant to Regain Favour," *The Toronto Daily
       Mail*, July 17, 1890, 1; "Dr. M'Glynn Restored," *The Irish Cana-
       dian*, August 28, 1890, 4.

Leo XIII an imbecile.[6] Anxious to keep his name before the public, especially after he announced his candidacy for president in opposition to George,[7] McGlynn claimed there were attempts made to bribe him into compliance that he "scornfully rejected,"[8] although no evidence of any such offers exists.

What broke the stalemate was *Rerum Novarum*, issued May 15, 1891. Socialists were taken completely by surprise. They had expected the usual condemnations which were, of course, included.[9] What caught them off guard was Leo XIII's alternative to socialism, which can be summed up in two key points:

- Redistribution that the socialists present as mandatory and a permanent solution, is a voluntary and temporary charitable expedient except in "extreme cases" when duly constituted authority can enforce limited redistribution by law.[10]
- In contrast to the socialist abolition of private property, there is to be a restructuring of the social order to shift economic life from the wage system to an ownership system that will encourage "as many as possible of the people to become owners."[11]

---

[6] "Look On This Picture And On This," *Waterbury Evening Democrat*, January 13, 1888, 2.

[7] "Dr. McGlynn and Mr. George: Former Master and Pupil are Very Much at Odds," *The New York Evening World*, February 11, 1888, 1.

[8] "Defiant McGlynn. Henry George's Ex-Partner Says He Is Still On the Warpath," *Sacramento Daily Record-Union*, December 3, 1888, 1.

[9] *Rerum Novarum*, §§ 4-5, 14-17.

[10] Ibid., § 22.

[11] Ibid., § 46.

Repeated Omissions

There was, however, a serious omission from the papal program, and it was again fatal. Not being conversant with modern financing techniques, the only suggestion Leo XIII had about how ordinary people can become capital owners is to pay workers more so they can accumulate savings.[12]

There are two problems with the pope's recommendation. One, increasing pay without a corresponding increase in productivity typically raises the price level, often more than the wage increase. This usually nullifies any wage increase, making it virtually impossible to save.[13]

Two, relying on past savings to finance new capital not only restricts ownership to those with savings but also decreases disposable income and reduces consumer purchasing power. Having fewer customers with money to buy goods and services makes any new capital less likely to be profitable and thus less able to pay for itself out of the future profits it generates.[14]

As Louis Kelso and Mortimer Adler advocated in their second book, *The New Capitalists* (1961), financing with *future increases in production* instead of past decreases in consumption, solves these problems. Both capitalists and socialists, however, were quick to seize on the presumed impossibility of financing new capital while creating new owners to justify their own

---

[12]   Ibid.

[13]   Walter Reuther, Testimony before the Joint Economic Committee of Congress, February 20, 1967.

[14]   Harold G. Moulton, *The Formation of Capital* (Washington, DC: The Brookings Institution, 1935), 28–29.

positions. Capitalists asserted that what the pope proposed supported them, at least if they treated workers better.

The Socialist Counterattack

Socialists, at first taken aback, quickly regrouped and developed two responses. First was to go on the attack and claim that the pope did not understand true socialism and the tenets of the Democratic Religion.

That was the approach of Henry George. Taking *Rerum Novarum* as a condemnation of himself and his theories and thus as a personal affront, he responded in kind. He published an open letter twice the length of the encyclical itself, taking the position that Leo XIII did not understand Catholic social teaching.[15]

Second was to claim that *Rerum Novarum* was the manifesto of the New Christianity. This was the approach taken by Marie-Eugène-Melchior, vicomte de Vogüé, de facto leader of the New Christian movement. He declared the encyclical validated everything the socialists and ultrasupernaturalists had demanded from the beginning.[16]

De Vogüé's and other socialists' and ultrasupernaturalists' reinterpretation of natural law is the source of the idea

---

[15]   Henry George, *The Condition of Labor: An Open Letter to Pope Leo XIII* (New York: Doubleday & McClure Co., 1891).

[16]   Vicomte Eugène Melchior de Vogüé, "The Neo-Christian Movement in France," *Harper's New Monthly Magazine*, January 1892. See also Aline Gorren, "The Moral Revival in France," *The Atlantic Monthly*, September 1893, Lillian Parker Wallace, *Leo XIII and the Rise of Socialism* (Durham, North Carolina: Duke University Press, 1966), and similar works justifying socialism as consistent with Catholic doctrine.

that moderate socialism (or capitalism) and Catholic social teaching are merely different names for the same thing. Combined with other aspects of ultrasupernaturalism, it popularized what G. K. Chesterton would call "the Double Mind of Man."[17]

In this way, Catholic social teaching became separated from reality. The Church was torn by her members' many competing views. Some saw her mission as purely spiritual, others interpreted it as exclusively temporal, while yet others ignored these contradictions. Some even claimed to see no contradictions, trying to believe and disbelieve at the same time, putting their faith and reason into conflict.

The wage system common to both capitalism and socialism cemented contradiction and separation from reality into social thought. By reinterpreting *Rerum Novarum* as "the living wage encyclical," capitalists and socialists of all types and degrees effectively cut the great mass of people off from the opportunity and means to participate fully in economic life as both workers and owners.

Inevitably, the wage and welfare system as the primary means by which people met their material needs also influenced most people's degree of participation in civil, domestic, and even religious life. This separated the means of existence from the reason for existence. Reflecting the total focus of the Democratic Religion on material betterment, work became solely a way to meet consumption needs, not an essential part of human personal development.[18]

---

[17]   Chesterton, *Saint Thomas Aquinas*, 92–93.
[18]   Cf. *Laborem Exercens*, § 7.

Family life—including education—became outwardly directed and centered on employment and income, weakening family bonds. Religious faith also deteriorated as people realized (often unconsciously) that there were profound conflicts between what they heard from modernist clergy and intellectuals, both capitalist and socialist, and the realities of everyday life.

The idea spread that being a "good Catholic" means rejecting orthodoxy based on reason and accepting ultrasupernaturalism based on faith alone. Those who were confused by this inversion of the natural and the supernatural, or who objected, were labeled heretics and dissenters, even "traitors to Christ."

McGlynn's Responses

Most people have always relied on faith instead of reason in religion. Still, at least in the Abrahamic faiths, there has always been a solid foundation of reason to back them up. This was why the popes have used reason, especially the philosophy of Aquinas, as the first line of defense against ultrasupernaturalism and socialism. It was why people like Newman, Benson, Chesterton, and Sheen kept insisting that faith and reason—common sense—must never contradict one another.

McGlynn's response was thus more typical than it might appear at first glance, perhaps explaining why he is still regarded in certain circles as something of an ultrasupernaturalist prophet or saint, and certainly a martyr.[19] He

---

[19]   John A. Ryan, *Social Doctrine in Action: A Personal History* (New

shifted his position constantly from one extreme to another, sometimes claiming to agree completely with the encyclical and other times condemning it.[20] He eventually took de Vogüé's stance that *Rerum Novarum* advocates non-Marxist, Neo-Catholic socialism.[21]

To the two conditions for lifting McGlynn's excommunication—apologize and travel to Rome to explain his actions to the pope—a third was added: accept *Rerum Novarum* in its true sense without reservation. This increased the pressure to reconcile him to the Church as soon as possible.[22]

Eventually, amid great bombast and misdirection, McGlynn met the conditions and was reconciled to the Church.[23] Explicitly adjuring socialism was not one of the

---

York: Harper & Brothers, Publishers, 1941), 20.

[20]   "Mr. M'Glynn Refuses to Comply," *The Hartford Weekly Times*, November 29, 1891, 3; "Still a Single Tax Man: Dr. McGlynn Reiterates the Views that Unfrocked Him," *The Day*, January 2, 1893, 1; "Dr. McGlynn and His Hostility to Tammany Hall Reported to Have Been the Secret of Archbishop Corrigan's Hostility to the Doctor," *The Lewiston Evening Journal*, January 19, 1893, 1, 7.

[21]   E. Cahill, *The Framework of a Christian State* (Dublin, Éire: M.H. Gill and Son, Ltd., 1932), 301–6, 534–35; Wallace, *Leo XIII and the Rise of Socialism*, 183–84.

[22]   Michael A. Corrigan, *Private Record of the Case of Rev. Edward McGlynn*, ms. cir. 1895, 417–18; "McGlynn Assails Parochial Schools at New York," *Meriden Daily Republican*, December 19, 1892, 3.

[23]   "M'Glynn Makes His Peace: The Noted Recalcitrant Priest Has His Authority Restored," *Aurora Daily Express*, December 24, 1892; "United States Nuncio: Monsignor Satolli Made Permanent Delegate," *Baltimore Sunday Herald*, January 15, 1893, 1; "Dr. McGlynn Sails Out on the Stormy Atlantic and is Given a Rousing Reception in Which Archbishop Corrigan is Hissed,"

requirements, however,[24] and Archbishop Corrigan refused to give him an assignment.[25]

Finally, however, McGlynn publicly repudiated George's doctrines and immediately received a parish.[26] He then issued statements to the effect that he both had and had not recanted.[27] On his deathbed, McGlynn dictated a letter in which he implied he had attempted to deceive the pope and Corrigan.[28]

Both Pope Saint Pius X and Pope Benedict XV continued papal efforts to counter socialism and ultrasupernaturalism. Pius X, for example, instituted the Oath Against Modernism, the first article of which affirms the primacy of the

---

Lewiston Evening Journal, February 9, 1893, 6.

[24]   Except by implication in accepting *Rerum Novarum*, which ultrasupernaturalists and socialists like McGlynn did with mental reservations. This was revealed in McGlynn's own account of his interview with Leo XIII in which he equivocated by giving evasive answers to the pope's direct questions. Bell, *Rebel, Priest and Prophet*, 249–51.

[25]   "Archdiocese to be Divided," *Argus Daily News*, July 3, 1893, 1; Bell, *Rebel, Priest and Prophet*, 251–54.

[26]   "Parish for M'Glynn: He Recants and Will Soon Be Completely Forgiven," *Meriden Daily Republican*, December 19, 1894, 3; "Surprise to Catholics: Dr. Edward M'Glynn Has Made a Complete Recantation," *New Haven Journal-Courier*, December 19, 1894, 4.

[27]   "M'Glynn's Restoration: Rev. Dr. Burtsell Makes a Statement Regarding the Matter," *Indianapolis Journal*, December 21, 1894, 1; cf. *Alexandria Gazette and Advertiser*, December 20, 1894, 2; *Boston Evening Transcript*, December 24, 1894, 4; "Dr. M'Glynn in His New Parish," *The New York Sun*, January 7, 1895, 7; "Dr. McGlynn Indorses George," *The New York Times*, October 28, 1897.

[28]   Sylvester L. Malone, *Dr. Edward McGlynn* (New York: Dr. McGlynn Monument Association, 1918), 53.

intellect in the natural order,[29] and issued *Lamentabili Sane* (1907) and *Pascendi Dominici Gregis* (1907). Benedict XV believed that the New Things caused the First World War[30] but reminded people that change is not evil *per se*; we must be prepared to do "old things, but in a new way."[31]

4.2. Wolves in Sheep's Clothing

Effective opposition to proposals such as the Great Reset, Georgism, or any other form of socialism requires not only sound principles but a viable alternative and a feasible means to implement it. *Rerum Novarum* presented sound principles and a viable alternative to socialism but fell short when it came to the question of financing.

George's Continuing Influence

Leo XIII's belief that raising wages would enable workers to save to purchase capital was unrealistic and virtually guaranteed rejection of the program. It also implicitly restricted ownership to workers, which suggested to some readers agreement with the socialist principle that only labor creates wealth.

Consequently, Henry George and Father McGlynn were neutralized, but not Georgism or the reinterpretation of Catholic social teaching as moderate socialism. Ironically,

---

[29]   *Sacrorum Antistitum*, motu proprio of September 1, 1910.

[30]   *Ad Beatissimi Apostolorum*, § 12.

[31]   Ibid., § 25. Although expressed in religious terms, Benedict XV's analysis of the causes of the war agrees with that of many historians, e.g., J. W. Burrow, *The Crisis of Reason: European Thought, 1848-1914* (New Haven, Connecticut: Yale University Press, 2000).

McGlynn's and George's falls had less to do with *Rerum Novarum* than with their own arrogance. Had McGlynn simply obeyed the original summons to Rome as his friends advised before George talked him out of it, and had George not insulted William O'Brien, they would probably have remained in good standing with the public. Instead, they degenerated into cult figures, largely forgotten today except by academics and economic historians.

Not so their influence, which continued long after their deaths. Many people today are astounded when they discover that much of what they believe to be incontrovertible truth in politics and religion is often nothing more than warmed-over and expanded Georgism. Nowhere is this more evident than in the Fabian Society, an offshoot of the Fellowship of the New Life founded in 1883 to establish the Kingdom of God on Earth—that is, "the cultivation of a perfect character in each and all" in this life through pacifism, vegetarianism, and simple living.[32] Soon, members of the group wanted to use the power of the State to transform Christianity and bring society around to their views; "Christianity and Socialism are said to be convertible terms."[33]

Inspired by its founders' enthusiasm for the theories of Henry George,[34] members of the fellowship founded the

---

[32]   Colin Spencer, *The Heretic's Feast: A History of Vegetarianism* (London: Fourth Estate Classic Publisher, 1996), 283.

[33]   Edward R. Pease, *A History of the Fabian Society* (Lincoln, U.K.: Frank Cass & Co., Ltd., 1963), 25; M. Kaufmann, *Christian Socialism* (London: Kegan Paul, Trench & Co, 1888), xii, 14n, 22n, 33, 190n.

[34]   Ibid., 28.

Fabian Society as their political arm on January 4, 1884.[35] As one of the organizers acknowledged, "To George belongs the extraordinary merit of recognising the right way of social salvation. . . . From Henry George I think it may be taken that the early Fabians learned to associate the new gospel with the old political method."[36]

George shared with the Fabians "a desire to explore the possibilities, within existing economic theory, of using legislation to regulate the economy for the general good,"[37] As George Holland Sabine commented, "Fabian economics was for the most part not Marxian but an extension of the theory of economic rent to the accumulation of capital, on lines already suggested by Henry George. Fabian policy was based on the justice and the desirability of recapturing unearned [i.e., non-labor] increment for social purposes."[38]

Consistent with their emblem of the wolf in sheep's clothing, the Fabian Society worked secretly until success was within their grasp. According to George Bernard Shaw, their goal was to infiltrate organizations and turn them socialist without (if possible) using the term "socialism" or letting people realize that what they had been led to accept, and even champion, was socialist.[39]

---

[35]   Ibid., 28–33.
[36]   Ibid., 20–21.
[37]   George H. Sabine, *A History of Political Theory, Third Edition* (New York: Holt, Rinehart and Winston, 1961), 693; Harold G. Moulton, *The New Philosophy of Public Debt* (Washington, DC: The Brookings Institution, 1943), 71–89.
[38]   Sabine, *A History of Political Theory*, 740.
[39]   "The Fading Fabians," *The Boston Evening Transcript*, November 27, 1908, 10.

Fabian Influence on Catholicism

Many of the Fabians had a misplaced devotion to Saint Francis of Assisi, who is often venerated today for reasons that would probably astound him. The Fabians, for example, regarded *Il Poverello* as a proto socialist oppressed by a tyrannical Church.[40]

Fabians also venerated the Spirituals or Fraticelli, offshoots of the Franciscans,[41] as the only real Christians of the Middle Ages. This was due to the Fraticelli doctrine that the Church established by Christ had become corrupt and worldly through ownership.[42]

According to the Fraticelli, Christ's Church had been revived by Saint Francis of Assisi, the Paraclete foretold by Jesus. "The Little Poor Man" had ushered in the New Age of the Holy Spirit characterized by direct rule by God and the abolition of private property, marriage and family, organized religion, and political authority.

As presumably commanded by Saint Francis, the natural order was to be abolished on earth and replaced with the supernatural order. This, to Chesterton, was the invention

---

[40]   See G. B. Shaw, ed., *Fabian Essays in Socialism* (London: The Fabian Society, 1889), sexologist Havelock Ellis's essay "St. Francis and Others," collected in *Affirmations* (Boston: Houghton Mifflin Co., 1926), and Shaw's preface to *Back to Methuselah*.

[41]   Technically, the Fraticelli were an offshoot of the Spirituals, although the terms are often used interchangeably.

[42]   Ronald Knox, *Enthusiasm: A Chapter in the History of Religion* (New York: Oxford University Press, 1961), 110–11.

of a new religion under the name of Christianity[43]—a prefiguring of socialism as the New Christianity.[44]

Fabian influence has been enormous. Some authorities believe that John Maynard Keynes, the economic architect of the modern world, was a member of the society. There is a great deal of circumstantial evidence to support this claim, but no proof.

Keynes's protégé, Ernst Friedrich "Fritz" Schumacher, was certainly a Fabian.[45] Despite that, many Catholics have accepted Schumacher's "New Age Guide to Economics," *Small Is Beautiful* (1973)[46] that advocates the abolition of

---

[43]   G. K. Chesterton, *Saint Francis of Assisi* (London: Hodder and Stoughton, Ltd., 1923), 174–75.

[44]   Cf. J. D. Dickey, *American Demagogue: The Great Awakening and the Rise and Fall of Populism* (New York: Pegasus Books, 2019), 164.

[45]   Schumacher was the author of *Export Policy and Full Employment, Fabian Research Series No. 77* (London: Fabian Publications, 1943), a publication of the New Fabian Research Bureau, a privilege permitted only to members of the Fabian "inner circle." Pease, *A History of the Fabian Society*, 182–84. He was also a member of the post-World War II British government, controlled by the Fabians.

[46]   E. F. Schumacher, *Small Is Beautiful* (New York: HarperCollins, 1973). Those forms of socialism influenced by Theosophy and Ariosophy, such as Fabian socialism and its offshoots and National Socialism (Nazism), respectively, stressed the "small is beautiful" ethos and the importance of the peasantry and "rooting in the soil" (*Bodenstandigkeit*) for national health and racial purity. Nicholas Goodrick-Clarke, *The Occult Roots of Nazism* (London, UK: Tauris Parke, 2004), 78–89, 123–24; Burrow, *The Crisis of Reason*, 222. This concept also found its way into Nazi law. "Wunderlich, the National Socialist Conception of Landed Property," 12 Social Research 60 at 61, 66, 72 (1945), quoted in Howard R. Williams, *Cases and Materials on the Law of Property* (Brooklyn: The

private property, and *A Guide for the Perplexed* (1979)[47] that posits truth changes at different levels of consciousness, as compatible with Catholic social doctrine. *Small Is Beautiful* was even cited in the 1986 US bishop's pastoral letter on the economy, *Economic Justice for All.*[48]

Later Influence in the United States

From the late nineteenth century on, the impact of Georgism and the New Things on the Catholic Church in the United States has also been significant. In large part this was due to the influence of Monsignor John Augustine Ryan. At the height of George's popularity in the 1880s, Ryan, then in his early teens, read *Progress and Poverty.*[49] He also became "much interested in the proposals for economic reform advocated by Donnelly, the Farmers' Alliance,[50] and the Knights of Labor."[51]

"Donnelly" was Ignatius Loyola Donnelly, whom Ryan idolized[52] and credited with "exercis[ing] more influence upon [his] political and economic thinking than any other

---

Foundation Press, Inc., 1954), 46–48. Belloc and Chesterton's distributism was, in part, an effort to correct these errors, but was subsumed into Fabian socialism and its offshoots (guild socialism, social credit) by later distributists.

47   E. F. Schumacher, *A Guide for the Perplexed* (New York: Harper Collins, 1977).

48   Chapter III, note 116.

49   Ryan, *Social Doctrine in Action*, 9.

50   An agrarian reform movement founded by Donnelly that eventually merged into the Populist Party.

51   Ryan, *Social Doctrine in Action*, 12.

52   Francis L. Broderick, *Right Reverend New Dealer: John A. Ryan* (New York: The Macmillan Company, 1963), 9.

factor."[53] An attorney, politician, and writer, Donnelly was born a Catholic but became a spiritualist.[54] A populist who hated William Jennings Bryan,[55] he advocated socialism and corresponded with and supported George.[56] He has been described as "America's 'Prince of Cranks.'"[57]

A primary source for the Theosophy of Madame Helena Petrovna Blavatsky,[58] Donnelly wrote histories of the Antediluvian world dictated by his spirit guide.[59] According to Ryan, Donnelly's science fiction and fantasy novels[60] contain innovative concepts that were integrated into his political thought.[61]

---

[53] Ryan, *Social Doctrine in Action*, 12.

[54] Walter Monfried, "The Astonishingly Inconsistent Ignatius Donnelly," *The Milwaukee Journal*, August 19, 1974, 10.

[55] "Anti-Trust Leaders At Variance Over Watered Stock," *Boston Evening Transcript*, February 14, 1900, 4. Bryan was opposed to George's proposals, as he made clear on more than one occasion, although George never ceased trying to gain his endorsement.

[56] Helen McCann White, *Guide to a Microfilm Edition of the Ignatius Donnelly Papers* (St. Paul, Minnesota: The Minnesota Historical Society, 1968), 24.

[57] Walter Monfried, "America's 'Prince of Cranks'," *The Milwaukee Journal*, May 15, 1953, 8.

[58] Helena Petrovna Blavatsky, *The Secret Doctrine, The Synthesis of Science, Religion, and Philosophy* (New York: The Theosophical Society, 1888), II.221n, II.266n, II.276n, II.333, II.334, II.741n, II.745, II.746n, II.761n, II.782, II.782n, II.786n, II.791, II.792–93.

[59] Ignatius Donnelly, *Atlantis: The Antediluvian World* (1882); *Ragnarok: The Age of Fire and Gravel* (1883).

[60] Ignatius Donnelly (as Edmund Boisgilbert), *Caesar's Column* (1890); *Doctor Huguet: A Novel* (1891); (as Ignatius Donnelly) *The Golden Bottle, or, The Story of Ephraim Benezet of Kansas* (1892).

[61] Ryan, *Social Doctrine in Action*, 15–16.

Chesterton alluded to Donnelly as "some American crank" for his Shakespearean cryptogram theory.[62] His obituary characterized him as ruled "by his imagination more than logic,"[63] and stated that "though he was a man of great mental powers he was dominated by the erratic and unfounded."[64]

Ryan's political and economic theories reflect Donnelly's theosophical influence and George's socialist thought. They are detailed in *A Living Wage* (1906),[65] *Distributive Justice* (1916),[66] and other works. Principally, Ryan's contribution was to expand George's agrarian socialism from land to all forms of capital.

In constructing his paradigm and to fit it within an ultra-supernaturalist framework, Ryan subsumed the natural into the supernatural. In *A Living Wage*, like de Lamennais, he redefined natural law—especially private property—to base it on subjective faith instead of objective reason.[67] He derived the basic idea in *Distributive Justice* from the American

62	G. K. Chesterton, *The Everlasting Man* (New York: Image Books, 1955), 206. The belief that mystical sages and magicians in the past left encoded messages to their future disciples is common in occult and spiritualist mythology. Guido "von" List claimed that the medieval masons who built Saint Stephen's Cathedral in Vienna carved allegorical references into the stonework conveying ancient Aryan doctrines to future generations. Goodrick-Clarke, *The Occult Roots of Nazism*, 74.

63	"Ignatius Donnelly," *The Toledo Weekly Blade*, January 10, 1901, 4.

64	Ibid.

65	John A. Ryan, *A Living Wage* (New York: Grosset and Dunlap, Publishers, 1906).

66	John A. Ryan, *Distributive Justice* (New York: The Macmillan Company, 1916).

67	Ryan, *A Living Wage*, 48.

disciples of the French socialist Charles Fourier.[68] Fourier advocated a new form of distributive justice to replace the classical version of Aristotle and Aquinas.[69] There would be a distribution of worldly goods sufficient for everyone's needs without regard to productive input.

Fourier's theories and his plan for a perfect world, sanitized for Americans by Albert Brisbane,[70] were presented in *Théorie des Quatre Mouvements*, "The Theory of the Four Movements" (1808), and later works. To establish his credentials as a prophet of Divine Humanity, Fourier declared himself the successor of Jesus and Sir Isaac Newton and founded a new scientific religion. His followers claimed to be the only true Christians.[71]

Orestes Brownson rejected Fourierism as intentional perversions of Catholic doctrine and liturgy,[72] declaring it false and anti-Christian.[73] In Fourier's system, the evolution of collective man toward the perfect society is the evolution

---

[68] Adam Morris, *American Messiahs: False Prophets of a Damned Nation* (New York: W.W. Norton and Company, 2019), 82–83.

[69] *Compendium of the Social Doctrine of the Church*, § 201.

[70] Chris Jennings, *Paradise Now: The Story of American Utopianism* (New York: Random House, 2016), 166, 172–77, 179; "The Fate of Reformers," *The National Era*, Washington, D.C., September 2, 1855; "The Free Love System," *Littell's Living Age 46*, no. 592 (September 29, 1855): 815–821.

[71] Gareth Stedman Jones, "Introduction," Charles Fourier, *The Theory of the Four Movements* (Cambridge, UK: Cambridge University Press, 2006), xxv–xxvi.

[72] Orestes A. Brownson, *Essays and Reviews, Chiefly on Theology, Politics, and Socialism* (New York: D. & J. Sadlier & Co., 1852), 499–500.

[73] *Brownson's Quarterly Review*, July 1844; cf. Chesterton, *Saint Francis of Assisi*.

of God Himself. As Fulton Sheen noted in other modernist thought, Fourier believed that collective man evolves into the immanent God, while the transcendent God gradually dies.[74] Fourier also declared that released sexual power would transform the Aurora Borealis ("the Northern Crown") into a source of heat,[75] oceans would turn to lemonade, the Sahara would be turned into fertile farmland, and the North Pole become a sunny paradise.[76]

Reinterpreting Rerum Novarum

In addition to changing the basis of natural law, Ryan reinterpreted *Rerum Novarum* to justify a vast expansion of State power explicitly repudiated in the document itself.[77] As historian Eric Frederick Goldman related:

> Ryan proceeded to apply the *Rerum Novarum* in a way scarcely distinguishable from the Reform Darwinists[78] of Protestants and Jews. . . . After Ryan had

---

[74]   Gregory S. Butler, *In Search of the American Spirit: The Political Thought of Orestes Brownson* (Carbondale, Illinois: Southern Illinois University Press, 1992), 130–31.

[75]   Fourier, *The Theory of the Four Movements*, 47–56.

[76]   Ibid., 50; Jennings, *Paradise Now*, 168.

[77]   *Rerum Novarum*, § 7.

[78]   Cf. *Pascendi Dominici Gregis*, § 13. Reform or Social Darwinism was influenced by the utopian and religious socialists and their emphasis on the need for social regeneration by improving or changing human nature by spiritual enlightenment, selective breeding, or some combination thereof. Whether Reform or Social Darwinism—the difference is largely semantic—it has little or nothing to do with the evolutionary theory developed by Charles Darwin. Morris, *American Messiahs*, 83, 121, 152, 163–65, 186, 203; William G. McLoughlin, *Revivals, Awakenings, and Reform: An Essay*

been hurling the *Rerum Novarum* at his enemies for years, a reform-minded rabbi achieved a masterpiece of superfluity by saying to the priest: "You have a very great advantage over men in my position. . . . You can hang your 'radical' utterances on a papal encyclical."

"Yes," I suppose there is something to that," said Father Ryan, smiling.[79]

Ryan's social program was similar to that of the populist Jacob Sechler Coxey Jr., a theosophist. In 1894, when Ryan was in his mid-twenties, Coxey's widely publicized army had marched across the country to demand inflation-financed government assistance during the Great Depression of 1893–1898.[80]

As analyzed by the solidarist economist Dr. Franz Herman Mueller, a student of Father Heinrich Pesch, SJ, Ryan assumed the whole message of *Rerum Novarum* was summed up in section 36: "Whenever the general interest or any particular class suffers, or is threatened with harm, which can in no other way be met or prevented, the public authority must step in to deal with it." As Mueller commented, "Ryan

---

on Religion and Social Change in America, 1607-1977 (Chicago, Illinois: University of Chicago Press, 1978), 4, 144, 145, 150–62, 163–64, 187, 189. Reform or Social Darwinism was also a significant influence on Nazi ideology, along with theosophy and the rejection of orthodox Christianity. Goodrick-Clarke, *Occult Roots of Nazism*, 2.

[79]   Eric F. Goldman, *Rendezvous with Destiny: A History of Modern American Reform* (New York: Vintage Books, 1956), 86.

[80]   Carlos A. Schwantes, *Coxey's Army: An American Odyssey* (Lincoln, Nebraska: University of Nebraska Press, 1985).

relates that the first time he read *Rerum Novarum* he was most impressed by the passage in Section 28.[81] Actually this passage is a clear statement of the principle of subsidiarity, but at that time Ryan seems to have been fascinated by the pope's acceptance of State intervention and overlooked the important qualifications made by Leo. . . . Ryan all through his life felt that what governments normally do, and what appears to be practically necessary, may be regarded as belonging to the proper functions of government—a rather pragmatic point of view."[82]

Ryan's program included minimum wage and maximum hours laws,[83] compulsory arbitration,[84] State employment bureaus,[85] and unemployment insurance.[86] Ryan also advocated "State labor colonies" for recalcitrants and hardcore unemployables that "could be of great benefit to certain classes of the unemployed."[87] Regimentation of the workforce would be accompanied "by gradual nationalization of railroads, power companies, water works, municipal

---

[81]   Mueller used another edition of the encyclical with different numbering than the current official Vatican translation.

[82]   Franz H. Mueller, *The Church and the Social Question* (Washington, DC: American Enterprise Institute for Policy Research, 1984), 96.

[83]   John A. Ryan, "A Program of Social Reform by Legislation," New York: Catholic World Press, 1909, quoted in Mueller, *The Church and the Social Question*, 105 (Republished in 1919, but poorly edited).

[84]   Mueller, *The Church and the Social Question*, 104–5.

[85]   Ibid.

[86]   Ibid.

[87]   Ryan, "A Program of Social Reform by Legislation."

transportation, and telephones."[88] Wealth above a predetermined level would be confiscated and redistributed.[89]

The American Bishops' Program of 1919 contained many elements of Ryan's proposal. In particular, "The industry in which a man is employed should provide him with all that is necessary to meet all the needs of his entire life."[90] As Mueller commented, "It is hard to understand why neither Ryan nor the Catholic War Council realized, or so it seems, the 'corporatist' [i.e., Fascist] implications of this statement."[91]

Ryan's chief accomplishment was to make *Rerum Novarum* mean the opposite of what Leo XIII had intended. Further, just as the post-World War II era brought the Fabians to power in England, Ryan's preeminence in the United States ensured that his interpretation of Catholic social teaching would be regarded as authentic and authoritative. As Mueller observed, "Perhaps the only nation in which the Catholic social movement—and a 'movement' it now was—could continue to operate with almost undiminished vigor was the United States. Under the leadership of John A. Ryan social Catholicism in this country enjoyed during the depression

---

[88] Mueller, *The Church and the Social Question*, 105. Ryan's proposal for industrial armies may have been suggested by Marx, Fourier (Jennings, *Paradise Now*, 240), or Edward Bellamy's utopian socialist novel, *Looking Backward* (Morris, American Messiahs, 166).

[89] Cahill, *The Framework of a Christian State*, 568–69.

[90] Mueller, *The Church and the Social Question*, 107. Cf. "I would rather see a man employed in private industry. But if he can't find that kind of a job, the government should give him one." "Restaurant Union Hears Judge Smith," *The Pittsburgh Press*, June 20, 1939, 6.

[91] Mueller, *The Church and the Social Question*, 107.

something approaching official recognition. . . . Ryan rose, in a manner, to be the architect of social legislation in this country, enjoying the special confidence of President Franklin D. Roosevelt."[92]

Socialism and Solidarism

Although he does not appear to have been influenced directly by Henry George, the French sociologist David Émile Durkheim profoundly influenced ultrasupernaturalism and today's popular understanding of religion. A disciple of Saint-Simon,[93] Durkheim is credited with the first scientific treatment of solidarism, a term he applied to a socialist—"entirely positivist"[94]—form of corporatism (fascism).

Durkheim presented his religious theories in *Les Forms Élémentaires de la Vie Religieuse* (1912), "The Elementary Forms of Religious Life."[95] Fulton Sheen characterized Durkheim's view of God as "a divinized society."[96] As Joseph Alois Schumpeter put it, for Durkheim, "religion is the group's worship of itself."[97]

This is a logical conclusion drawn from Durkheim's belief that religion is a social, rather than a spiritual, phenomenon.

---

[92]   Ibid., 117–18.
[93]   Julian Strube, "Socialist Religion and the Emergence of Occultism," *Religion* 46, no. 3 (2016): 264.
[94]   Joseph A. Schumpeter, *History of Economic Analysis* (New York: Oxford University Press, 1954), 413.
[95]   Allen & Unwin in London and Macmillan and Co. in New York published the first English edition simultaneously in 1915.
[96]   Fulton J. Sheen, *Religion Without God* (New York: Garden City Books, 1954), 54.
[97]   Schumpeter, *History of Economic Analysis*, 794.

Durkheim's thought is similar to (if not the same as) the secular mindset guiding the Great Reset and related proposals.

4.3. Defenders of the Faith

As is the case today with the growing opposition to the Great Reset and similar proposals, Monsignor Ryan, the Fabians, and other heirs of Henry George did not go unchallenged. In England, G. K. Chesterton and Hilaire Belloc locked horns with the Fabian Society, while in the United States, Fulton Sheen, "the American Chesterton," came into conflict with Ryan. On the continent, Fr. Heinrich Pesch, SJ, worked to reorient Durkheim's solidarism to conform to natural law and Catholic teaching.

Chesterton vs. the Fabians

Chesterton was at one time a member of the Fabian Society but resigned during the Boer War, evidently as the result of his conversion to Christianity and profound differences with the Fabian philosophy. George Bernard Shaw, who believed Belloc exercised some mysterious influence over Chesterton, insisted that he (Chesterton) did not understand that he was really a socialist, and spent the next thirty years fruitlessly trying to convince him of it.

Sometime before 1910, Chesterton and others began publishing articles advocating a policy of widespread capital ownership in the *New Age* and *New Witness* magazines. This eventually came to be called distributism.[98] The articles

---

[98]   G. K. Chesterton, *The Outline of Sanity*, in *Collected Works*, vol. 5 (San Francisco: Ignatius Press, 1987), 45.

were based in part on "idle arguments" Chesterton had with Charles Frederick Gurney Masterman, a Christian socialist politician who was a friend of Herbert George Wells and on good terms with the Fabians.[99]

In 1909, Masterman published *The Condition of England* (1909).[100] His goal was to present specifics that would justify imposition of the ideal socialist world and establish the Kingdom of God on Earth. He rejected theories as "generalizations about realities."[101]

In response, Chesterton reworked his articles as "a thundering gallop of theory" titled *What's Wrong With the World* (1910). He countered each of Masterman's pragmatic collectivist proposals with a theoretical personalist principle.

A few years later, Hilaire Belloc published *The Servile State* (1912), a harsh critique of the Fabian program. Belloc refuted the Fabian goal of socialized capitalism (or capitalized socialism), especially the demand that people gain income only through wage labor, a requirement to be enforced by greatly increasing the powers of the State.[102]

Silence not being a Fabian virtue, responses soon appeared. Shaw, who rarely left anything unsaid, and Chesterton engaged in debates that never resolved anything. At the same time, however, modern literature was enriched by

---

[99]   G. K. Chesterton, *What's Wrong With the World, in Collected Works*, vol. 5 (San Francisco: Ignatius Press, 1987), 35.

[100]   C. F. G. Masterman, *The Condition of England* (London: Methuen and Co., 1909). Alzina Stone Dale, *The Outline of Sanity: A Life of G.K. Chesterton* (Grand Rapids, Michigan: William B. Eerdman's Publishing Company, 1982), 140–41.

[101]   Masterman, *The Condition of England*, vii.

[102]   Pease, *History of the Fabian Society*, 229–30.

a "battle of the books" in which Fabians skirmished with Chesterton and Belloc.

Richard Henry Tawney, "the most influential theorist and exponent of socialism in Britain in the 20th century,"[103] opened the game with *The Acquisitive Society* in 1920. As co-head of the Fabian Society from 1920 to 1933, Tawney presented a much-distorted view of history, with special emphasis on the corrupt Church that had oppressed the Fraticelli and deviated from the true socialist teachings of Jesus.

Chesterton countered with the real story, *Saint Francis of Assisi*, in 1923. He argued that far from being a socialist or a rebel, Saint Francis—and the Catholic Church—supported private property, not the abolition of it. He then responded to former Fabian H. G. Wells's *Outline of History* (1920) in 1925 with *The Everlasting Man*.[104]

Tawney came back in 1926 with *Religion and the Rise of Capitalism*, presenting ultrasupernaturalism as authentic Christian doctrine and socialism as applied Christianity. Again making the Catholic Church the villain, Tawney added insult to injury by claiming that distributism—promoted by Chesterton and Belloc as a progressive (in the Theodore Roosevelt sense) application of Catholic social teaching—was really reactionary and Protestant.[105]

---

[103]   Back cover of Lawrence Goldman, *The Life of R.H. Tawney: Socialism and History* (London: Bloomsbury, 2014).

[104]   Belloc also responded to Wells's *Outline* in a more ad hominem manner, which resulted in an acrimonious exchange that did not resolve anything.

[105]   R. H. Tawney, *Religion and the Rise of Capitalism: A Historical Study* (New York: Harcourt, Brace and Company, 1952), 92.

Chesterton had the last word with *Saint Thomas Aquinas: The "Dumb Ox"* (1933). In what Étienne Gilson called "the best book ever written on St. Thomas,"[106] the "Apostle of Common Sense" refuted the ultrasupernaturalist principles behind Fabianism and defended the primacy of the intellect against irrational faith in matters pertaining to natural law.

Despite the best efforts of Chesterton, Belloc, and a few others, however, distributism never caught on the way Fabianism did. In large part this was because relatively few people seemed to grasp the subtle but extremely important differences between the two systems. As Shaw berated Chesterton on more than one occasion, "Distributism is plumb-centre Socialism." Shaw insisted Chesterton was wasting his time "trying to establish a false anti-thesis" between them.[107]

Shaw's assertion was based on Chesterton's refusal to give him anything specific he could ridicule[108] and Belloc's insistence on recommending specifics that even he knew could not work.[109] As a result of this confusion, the distributist movement lacked clear principles and goals. It became a de facto personality cult centered on Chesterton himself rather than on the ideas.

"Fanatical types" were involved from the beginning,[110] with "many ideologies hiding under the cloak of

106   Maisie Ward, *Gilbert Keith Chesterton* (New York: Sheed & Ward, 1943), 620.
107   Dale, *The Outline of Sanity*, 265.
108   Louis Biancolli, ed., *The Book of Great Conversations* (New York: Simon and Schuster, 1948), 498–506.
109   See Hilaire Belloc, *An Essay on the Restoration of Property* (New York: Sheed and Ward, Inc., 1936).
110   Dale, *The Outline of Sanity*, 245.

Distributism."[111] Chesterton being incapable of excluding anyone, the movement became a magnet for "cranks." As he noted, "We have had some very fantastic human forms lingering about our office."[112] Meetings of the Distributist League became so unpleasant that Chesterton eventually stopped attending, except for the annual celebration.[113]

Chesterton died June 14, 1936, whereupon distributism came to an end as anything coherent or even distinct from Fabianism or any other kind of socialism. "Gilbert's death signified the end of the philosophy, if that is what it was, as a serious proposition. He had kept it alive; squabbles and lack of direction tore the movement apart."[114]

Fulton Sheen vs. the Modernist Monsignor

Fulton Sheen did not fare any better with Monsignor Ryan at the Catholic University of America. Bishop Thomas Joseph Shahan, rector of the CUA, had been one of the examiners in the McGlynn case[115] and appears to have been suspicious of Henry George's influence on Ryan.

Shahan evidently brought Sheen into the university as a sort of protégé to deal with the problems caused by Ryan, as Sheen's doctoral thesis[116] demonstrated the unsoundness

---

[111]   Michael Coren, *Gilbert: The Man Who Was G.K. Chesterton* (New York: Paragon House, 1990), 264.

[112]   *G.K.'s Weekly*, April 24, 1926.

[113]   Michael Ffinch, *G. K. Chesterton* (San Francisco: Harper and Row, Publishers, 1986), 315–16.

[114]   Coren, *Gilbert*, 243.

[115]   The others were Rev. Dr. Thomas Bouquillon, Rev. Dr. Thomas O'Gorman, and Rev. Dr. Charles P. Grannan.

[116]   *God and Intelligence in Modern Philosophy* (1925).

of certain modernist theories on which Ryan relied in his social thought.[117] Not surprisingly, considering the threat that Sheen's work represented to Ryan's theories, Sheen was made unwelcome from the first in the School of Sacred Sciences. The school was under the control of Ryan,[118] although Ryan could do nothing overt while Shahan was rector.

At the end of 1927, however, Shahan retired and was replaced with Monsignor James Hugh Ryan, no relation to Monsignor John Augustine Ryan. Shahan's departure marked the beginning of what Sheen later described as a period of great suffering, tantamount to a crucifixion. As he noted in the preface to *Life of Christ* (1958), "This book was written to find solace in the Cross of Christ, as for about ten years of my life I endured a great trial."[119]

Once Sheen's patron, Bishop Shahan, was out of the picture, John A. Ryan immediately began forcing confrontations. Incidents were manufactured. "Theologians were . . . charging Sheen with heresy in order to get him removed from the faculty."[120] A graduate student Sheen was advising was harassed to get at Sheen.[121]

Ryan denied any involvement and claimed Sheen was delusional. He asserted the charges "'all emanated from Dr.

---

[117]   E.g., the modernist ideas of distributive justice and collective man evolving into an immanent God found in the thought of Charles Fourier and David Émile Durkheim.

[118]   Kathleen L. Riley, *Fulton J. Sheen: An American Catholic Response to the Twentieth Century* (New York: Society of St. Paul, 2004), 12.

[119]   Fulton J. Sheen, *Life of Christ* (New York: Image Books, 1977), 9.

[120]   Thomas C. Reeves, *America's Bishop: The Life and Times of Fulton J. Sheen* (San Francisco: Encounter Books, 2001), 71.

[121]   Riley, *Fulton J. Sheen*, 14; Reeves, *America's Bishop*, 71.

Sheen's very vivid imagination' and 'he made them quite generally known around the university and off campus.'"[122]

Matters came to a head when Rector James H. Ryan refused to approve the appointment of Msgr. John A. Ryan's handpicked successor at the School of Sacred Sciences, Dr. Francis Joseph Haas, until Haas obtained a Doctor of Divinity. John A. Ryan circulated a petition to remove the rector and demanded that every professor in the school sign it. Sheen refused.[123] As he related, "The next day there appeared on the bulletin board of the School of Theology a notice to the effect that all of the classes of Dr. Fulton J. Sheen had been suspended in the School of Theology. James H. Ryan, the rector, knew the reason—namely, because I had defended him. He then transferred me to the School of Philosophy."[124]

On May 13, 1931, Ryan testified before one of the committees investigating the problems in the School of Sacred Sciences. He glossed over his role in the incidents and put the blame wholly on Sheen. As related by Kathleen L. Riley, "Later, during the course of the investigations launched by the two special committees, other references to Sheen's status and personality conflicts emerged. In 1931, Fr. John A. Ryan told the committee that Dr. Sheen was transferred because he was unhappy; he seemed to feel that he was not fitted for

---

[122]   Reeves, *America's Bishop*, 71.
[123]   Fulton J. Sheen, *Treasure in Clay: The Autobiography of Fulton J. Sheen* (Garden City, New York: Doubleday & Company, Inc., 1979), 45.
[124]   Ibid., 45–46.

the work in theology and was academically unprepared to teach the classes he was asked to teach."[125]

John A. Ryan's efforts to neutralize Sheen did not end there. He was probably the source of the rumor—completely false—that Sheen had delivered a secret report about James H. Ryan to Vatican secretary of state Eugenio Maria Giuseppe Giovanni Cardinal Pacelli. This was allegedly the eventual cause of Rector Ryan's removal from office in 1935.[126] Later, when John A. Ryan was allied with Father Charles Edward Coughlin, the "radio priest,"[127] there was an effort made to persuade Sheen to stop his own increasingly popular radio broadcasts that competed with those of Coughlin.[128]

A few years after that, some of Ryan's students formed the Catholic Radical Alliance of Pittsburgh, and attacked Sheen in print for allegedly being an enemy of organized labor.[129] On that occasion, Sheen was able to prove what he had really said, a matter of public record that completely refuted the accusation.[130] Around this time, Father Charles Owen

---

[125]   "Ryan to the Visiting Committee, May 13, 1931—McNicholas Papers, ACHA," cited by Riley, *Fulton J. Sheen*, 15.

[126]   Sheen, *Treasure in Clay*, 46–47. More likely, it was James H. Ryan's failure to deal effectively with John A. Ryan that resulted in his removal.

[127]   Dr. Harry Elmer Barnes, "Father Coughlin," *The Pittsburgh Press*, December 24, 1933, 4; Donald Pond, "The Crusader of the Air: Boos for Al [Smith] Mark Father Coughlin's Attack on 'Happy Warrior'," *The Pittsburgh Press*, January 9, 1934, 21.

[128]   Sheen, *Treasure in Clay*, 78.

[129]   "Rev. Rice Hits Msgr. Sheen's Labor Views: Catholic Radical Alliance Spokesman Replies to Orator's Charges" *The Pittsburgh Press*, March 2, 1938, 5.

[130]   A radio address by Sheen delivered February 6, 1938.

Rice, chief spokesman of the Alliance, hinted that Sheen was a "traitor to Christ" for opposing socialism.[131]

Fortunately, Sheen's media ministry allowed him to survive Ryan's sabotage of his academic career. He went on to become "America's bishop" and one of the most popular figures in the golden age of television.

Like his English counterpart, Chesterton, Sheen is not remembered for his efforts to deal with ultrasupernaturalism and socialism but for his cleverness, wit, and spiritual guidance. These are notable, but they are not what either Sheen or Chesterton considered the most important aspects of their work.

Sheen's books reflect this development, which can be divided into three broad categories. His purely academic works, *God and Intelligence* and *Religion Without God* (1928), are directed against the New Things. They focus on the lack of sound reasoning to support ultrasupernaturalism and socialism without identifying the source of the problem in the early nineteenth century. Instead, they give a brilliant analysis of the later phase of the intellectual development

---

[131]   Rice "branded Catholic 'friends of the present system,' as 'traitors to Christ'." (Pamphlet, Catholic University of America Archives, CIO central office papers, 1937-1941, quoted in Neil Betten, "Charles Owen Rice," *Pennsylvania Magazine of History and Biography* 94, 524.) As he declared, "I am a radical, a Catholic radical. I believe that the present social and economic system is a mess and should be changed from top to bottom." (Oral history interview with Rice, February 6, 1958, 1, Rice Papers, Pennsylvania State University Archives, quoted in Betten, "Charles Owen Rice," ibid.).

of the ultrasupernaturalist and socialist movement from the election of Leo XIII in 1878.

The second group of Sheen's books presents his critique of applied ultrasupernaturalism and socialism, particularly as seen in Nazism and communism. In works such as *Freedom Under God* (1940), *Philosophies at War* (1943), and *Communism and the Conscience of the West* (1948), he detailed the conflict between what we can call a personalist culture as promoted by Catholic social teaching and an ultrasupernaturalist culture promoted by the world. His final group of books concentrated on that personal spirituality for which he is best remembered.

Solidarism's Redeemer

Our third Defender of the Faith often gets overlooked only because he was never as well-known as either Chesterton or Sheen, although he was their intellectual equal, and his social thought rivals theirs. Unfortunately, Fr. Heinrich Pesch's writings were not published in English while he was alive, and his thoughts were surpassed by doctrinal developments shortly after being published in the original German.

Many authorities believe Pesch made the most original contribution to Central European Catholic thought before 1918. Often credited with being the founder of solidarism, he should more accurately be viewed as its redeemer, at least from a Catholic perspective.

Pesch began with the ultrasupernaturalist-socialist version of solidarism developed by Durkheim, based in part on the positivism of Comte and the New Christianity of

Saint-Simon. Bringing Durkheim's concepts into conformity with the principles of Aristotelian-Thomism—particularly private property as a natural right[132]—Pesch transformed solidarism from a statist/totalitarian philosophy, into a natural law, "person centered" system, but without making it a form of individualism.[133]

In Pesch's solidarism, the human person is at the center of the social system, and thus also at the center of economic activity. For Pesch, society is neither a mere voluntary aggregate of individuals nor an amorphous collective, a "substance" or abstraction independent of the individuals who compose it.[134]

Pesch explained that society is a union of individuals working toward common goals, but without prejudice to individual goals; the human person is not to be subsumed into the collective, any more than the natural order is to be absorbed by the supernatural order.[135] Keeping in mind that Pesch was an Aristotelian-Thomist, and thus recognized that God's intellect and will are in perfect union and do not have separate acts, Pesch defined solidarism as "the reciprocity

---

[132]   Gustav Gundlach, "Solidarist Economics, Philosophy and Socio-economic Theory in Pesch" *Social Order*, April 1951, 185.

[133]   Richard E. Mulcahy, *The Economics of Heinrich Pesch* (New York: Henry Holt and Company, 1952), 6.

[134]   Alfred Diamant, *Austrian Catholics and the First Republic: Democracy, Capitalism, and the Social Order 1918-1934* (Princeton, New Jersey: Princeton University Press, 1960), 161.

[135]   Cf. Karol Wojtyła, "Thomistic Personalism," *Person and Community: Selected Essays* (New York: Peter Lang, 2008), 174.

and mutuality of human interests . . . based on the rational nature of the human personality."[136]

Although Pesch did not consider social justice a particular virtue—a development at the center of Pope Pius XI's social doctrine[137]—the Holy Father did incorporate some of Pesch's concepts into *Quadragesimo Anno* and *Divini Redemptoris*. This was through the *Königswinterkreis* discussion group composed largely of Pesch's students, two members of which, Father Oswald von Nell-Breuning, SJ, and Father Gustav Gundlach, SJ, were called to the Vatican in 1931 for consultation.

Despite the profundity of his thought, Pesch has suffered egregiously from latter day disciples who fail to see the distinction between his Christian solidarism and Durkheim's fascist-socialist version. Like what happened to both Chesterton and Sheen's works, the tendency has been to impose a socialist and ultrasupernaturalist interpretation on Pesch's solidarism, turning it into the very thing it was intended to counter.

In effect, Chesterton, Sheen, and Pesch had two serious omissions from their writings that made them less effective foils to the New Things, even in many cases having their thought reinterpreted as socialism and ultrasupernaturalism. These lacunae caused the real importance of their work to be ignored. The first omission was the failure to recognize a particular act of social justice. This meant that no one had direct access to the common good and full participation for anyone was out of the question.

---

[136]   Diamant, *Austrian Catholics and the First Republic*, 161.
[137]   William J. Ferree, *The Act of Social Justice* (Washington, DC: Catholic University of America Press, 1942), 84–85.

The second omission was that they had no feasible way to finance expanded capital ownership as a means of opening full participation in the common good to all. As we will see in the next section, these two omissions allowed ultrasupernaturalists and socialists to control the development of popular understanding of economic and social justice and turn it in ways they wanted it to go—that is, in the direction of the Great Reset.

4.4. The Democratic Religion in Action

The Great Reset and similar proposals have been compared to the New Deal and often promoted as an expansion of the program. Are the New Deal and the global economy based on its principles, however, consistent with the demands of human dignity—that is, with the natural law and the requirement that every person have access to the opportunity and means to participate fully in the common good?

The Not-So-New Deal and the Catholic Vote

Some authorities trace the origins of the New Deal[138] not to Theodore Roosevelt's Square Deal[139]—although President Franklin Delano Roosevelt clearly wanted people to draw that conclusion—but to the proposals of Jacob Sechler Coxey, mentioned earlier. Maintaining that the New Deal

---

[138] Elliot A. Rosen, "Roosevelt and the Brains Trust: An Historiographical Overview," *Political Science Quarterly* 87, no. 4 (1972): 531–57.

[139] See Theodore Roosevelt, *Social Justice and Popular Rule: Essays, Addresses, and Public Statements Relating to the Progressive Movement (1910-1916)* (New York: Charles Scribner's Sons, 1926).

was influenced or inspired by Catholic social teaching is even more problematical, although that impression, too, was deliberately given.[140]

Franklin Roosevelt's prejudice against and suspicion of Jews and orthodox Catholics as fundamentally un-American were well-known.[141] This was a potential political liability, because to secure his election in 1932, he needed "the Catholic vote" that four years earlier had so worried Herbert Clark Hoover by throwing its support to "the Happy Warrior," Alfred Emanuel "Al" Smith.[142]

At the same time, Roosevelt could not afford to alienate the anti-Catholic and New Christian Democrats that had voted Republican in 1928. He managed to accomplish both goals by building alliances with Catholic and Jewish leaders whom he misled or who were willing to swallow his insults for what they believed to be the greater good.[143]

The key to Roosevelt's success in this respect was the effort of his campaign manager, James Aloysius Farley, a staunch Catholic and a Knight of Malta. As campaign manager for Al Smith in the 1928 election, Farley had failed to persuade Americans to accept an anti-racist and progressive (in the Theodore Roosevelt sense) Catholic as a national candidate.

---

[140]   See Broderick, *Right Reverend New Dealer*, 241–42; also, Kenneth J. Heineman, *A Catholic New Deal: Religion and Reform in Depression Pittsburgh* (University Park, Pennsylvania: The Pennsylvania State University Press, 1999).

[141]   George J. Marlin, *The American Catholic Voter: 200 Years of Political Impact* (South Bend, Indiana: St. Augustine's Press, 2006), 192–94.

[142]   Ibid., 183–91.

[143]   Ibid., 193–94, 206.

Farley was, however, overwhelmingly successful in selling a progressive, liberal, political, and economic agenda to Catholics, women, and African Americans, paving the way for Franklin Roosevelt's election. This support among key voting blocs was essential for popular acceptance of the New Deal. An intelligent and astute politician who had influence with the "Brain(s) Trust" (inspired by and modeled on the New Fabian Research Bureau), but not a philosopher or theologian, Farley appears to have been honestly unaware of the significant differences between what the popes were saying and the president's program.

Contrary to legend, Ryan, *Quadragesimo Anno*, and Catholic social teaching did not shape the New Deal. This false idea comes from the fact that during the campaign, Roosevelt gave a speech in Detroit, a "Catholic city," probably guided or contributed to by Farley, and that he actively courted the support of Fr. Charles Coughlin, about whom Farley expressed serious reservations. This earned Farley Coughlin's enmity and the vituperation of Huey Pierce Long Jr.[144] Farley regarded FDR's failure to defend him against Long's attacks as a betrayal. He felt that the president used people when convenient and ignored or discarded them when they were no longer useful.[145]

This feeling became a certainty when it became obvious by 1938 that the New Deal was dead in the water. Roosevelt attempted what Farley described as a failed purge to rid his administration of the ideologically unfit, and Farley found

---

[144]   James A. Farley, *Jim Farley's Story: The Roosevelt Years* (New York: McGraw-Hill Book Company, Inc., 1948), 5052, 128.
[145]   Ibid., 178.

himself excluded from Roosevelt's inner circle. Nevertheless, he stuck with the president because he believed it to be his duty to the Democratic Party and to the country.[146]

Ryan's academic credentials took a distant back seat to Coughlin's working-class appeal and Farley's political expertise. Farley made no mention of Ryan in either of his books, although Ryan had at one time repeatedly approached Farley to give a government job to Maurice Ryan, his younger brother.[147]

One of Ryan's biographers inadvertently portrayed him as a wannabe power broker who was constantly slighted by FDR except when the president needed someone to wave the Catholic flag, especially after Coughlin turned against him.[148] Although—contrary to canon law—he publicly endorsed Roosevelt,[149] Ryan's only official reward was a ten-month appointment to the three-person Industrial Appeals Board of the National Recovery Administration in 1934.[150]

Possibly inspired by his idol Donnelly, Ryan had hungered for political power since at least the days of the Wilson administration. He had slavishly followed that president's lead in everything. He even condemned the Easter Rising in Dublin in 1916, although many of the revolutionaries espoused socialist views indistinguishable from Ryan's own.[151]

---

[146]   Ibid., 120–50.

[147]   Broderick, *Right Reverend New Dealer*, 212.

[148]   Ibid., 241.

[149]   Ibid., 222.

[150]   Ibid., 217; Heineman, *A Catholic New Deal*, 102.

[151]   Charles Callan Tansill, *America and the Fight for Irish Freedom, 1866-1922* (New York: Devin-Adair Co., 1957), 204n.

Catholic Opposition to the New Deal

All was not rosy, however. Some members of the US Catholic hierarchy spoke of "increasing agitation of 'cunning propagandists'."[152] A few organizations, such as the Central Bureau of the Catholic Central Verein of America in Saint Louis,[153] expressed grave reservations about Roosevelt's plans and their lack of consistency with Catholic doctrine.

In this regard, mention should be made of recent efforts to transform Dorothy Day back into a socialist[154] and promote her as a supporter of the New Deal.[155] On the contrary, she was strongly opposed to what she saw as the anti-personalist agenda and the overtly statist approach of Roosevelt's program.[156] As Day declared in her autobiography, she and Peter Maurin "wanted none of the state relief" of the New Deal,[157] which they believed to be misguided.[158]

Significantly, in contrast to the Keynesian (and New Deal) emphasis on full employment through the wage system and "the euthanasia of the rentier" (small owner)

---

[152]   Mueller, *The Church and the Social Question*, 119.

[153]   Ibid., 118–120.

[154]   See, e.g., Dean Dettloff, "The Catholic Case for Communism," *America* magazine, July 23, 2019, https://www.americamagazine .org/faith/2019/07/23/catholic-case-communism.

[155]   Harry Murray, "Dorothy Day, Welfare Reform, and Personal Responsibility," *St. John's Law Review* 73, no. 3, (Summer 1999).

[156]   Kurt Buhring, "Day and Niebuhr on the Great Depression," Lance Richey and Adam Deville, ed., *Dorothy Day and the Church: Past, Present, and Future* (Solidarity Hall, 2016), 393–406.

[157]   Dorothy Day, *The Long Loneliness: The Autobiography of the Legendary Catholic Social Activist* (San Francisco, California: HarperOne, 2009), 180.

[158]   Buhring, "Day and Niebuhr," 401.

Keynes advocated, Maurin criticized organized labor. This was because, in his opinion, it rejected responsibility and contributed to the Servile State "instead of aiming for the ownership of the means of production."[159] Day rejected the New Deal in part because it sought "security for the worker, not ownership."[160]

Still, despite the scattered opposition, and although they could not be said to have influenced it, between them, Farley, Ryan, and Coughlin secured the support of the bulk of the hierarchy and of many Catholics for the New Deal at a critical time.[161]

Liberal Catholicism's Uncivil War

It was an uneasy alliance, however. When Coughlin decided that he could not accept the second phase of the New Deal, he split from Roosevelt and shifted his allegiance to Huey Long, "the Kingfish." It was then that Coughlin engaged in a running battle with Ryan,[162] while Long attacked Farley. Ironi-

---

159   Day, *The Long Loneliness*, 222; cf. Walter Reuther, Testimony before the Joint Economic Committee of Congress, February 20, 1967.

160   David L. Gregory, "Dorothy Day and the Transformation of Work: Lessons for Labor," *Dorothy Day and the Catholic Worker Movement: Centenary Essays* (Milwaukee, Wisconsin: Marquette University Press, 2001), 284.

161   Broderick, *Right Reverend New Dealer*, 241–42; Arnold Sparr, "Chesterton and Catholic Moments: Some Reflections on Catholic Revivals, Past and Present," *Records of the American Catholic Historical Society of Philadelphia* 103, no. 2 (Fall 1992): 20.

162   "Monsignor Raps Father Coughlin: The Right Rev. John A. Ryan Speaks Under Democratic Auspices," *The Spokesman-Review*, October 9, 1936, 2; "Father Coughlin Will Answer Monsignor

cally, many elements of Long's "Share Our Wealth" program appear to have been lifted from Monsignor Ryan's proposals.

At one point, the rhetoric and barrage of accusation and counter-accusation between Ryan and Coughlin became so heated that Archbishop Michael Joseph Curley of Baltimore called on both men to "do a great favor to the church and to the country at large" by "retir[ing] for some time to the Carthusian order, where perpetual silence is observed."[163] When Eugenio Cardinal Pacelli, Pius XI's secretary of state and the future Pope Pius XII, visited the United States in part to investigate the situation (denied initially[164]), he refused to comment on, or have anything to do directly with either Coughlin or Ryan.[165]

Coughlin was now a serious embarrassment for FDR, and much more of a challenge for the president's ingenuity than Farley. In addition, the radio priest's economic and monetary theories were too obviously heavily influenced by

---

Ryan," *Lewiston Daily Sun*, October 2, 1936, 1.

[163] "Church Organ Raps Priests: Paper Says Coughlin And Ryan Should 'Rest A While'," *Reading Eagle*, October 16, 1936, 2; "Coughlin and Ryan Asked to 'Shut Up'," *The Florence Times*, October 16, 1936, 1.

[164] "Papal Aide to Sail on Trip to America: Vacation Trip to Be Incognito, With Coughlin's Activities Not a Factor," *The Washington Star*, October 1, 1936, A-12.

[165] "Pacelli Sails for America: Papal Secretary's Visit Linked With Coughlin," *The Times-News*, Hendersonville, North Carolina, October 1, 1936, 1; "Cardinal Pacelli Arrives in New York for Visit," *Lewiston Daily Sun*, October 2, 1936, 1; Joseph Alsop and Robert Kintner, "The Capital Parade: Passage in Pope's Encyclical Declared Rebuke for Coughlin," *The Washington Star*, November 15, 1939, A-11.

socialism and anti-Semitism,[166] while his arguments relied on ad hominem attacks and "straw man" logical fallacies.[167]

With the Catholic vote secured, the ethical Farley became expendable. Encouraged by Roosevelt to run for president in 1940 after being personally assured several times by FDR that the president had absolutely no intention of running again,[168] and to demonstrate his opposition to a third term, Farley sought the Democratic nomination.

Almost immediately, Roosevelt allowed himself to be drafted in a carefully orchestrated spontaneous demonstration, making Farley appear a fool.[169] Although the president's mother, Sara, and Eleanor pleaded with him to stay on and manage FDR's campaign,[170] Farley retired from public life and accepted a position with Coca Cola.[171]

With the rabblerousing Coughlin out of the way and the politically astute Farley neutralized, the only Catholic FDR had to deal with was the easily controlled Ryan. This he did by keeping Ryan hanging with half-promises and allowing him to give the Inauguration Benediction in 1937 and 1945.

---

166   Coughlin's economic advisor was Gertrude Margaret Coogan (1898-1986), whose writings, especially *Money Creators* (1935), are a mainstay and primary source for conspiracy theorists, holocaust deniers, historical revisionists, and Neo-Nazis.

167   See, e.g., Chas. E. Coughlin, *A Series of Lectures on Social Justice* (Royal Oak, Michigan: The Radio League of the Little Flower), 1935.

168   Farley, *Jim Farley's Story*, 151–91, 217–82.

169   Ibid., 284–91.

170   Ibid., 307–17.

171   Ibid., 323.

"An Enormous Fabian School"

The New Deal was not an isolated case of the implementation of the New Things in a leading world economy. The postwar government in Great Britain, satirized by Evelyn Waugh in his novella *Love Among the Ruins* (1953), was a much-touted triumph of the Fabian Society, which years before had joined forces with the British Labour Party.

More than two hundred society members were elected to Parliament in 1945, a landslide victory for Labour. Many of them became ministers in the administration of Prime Minister Clement Richard Attlee, while other Fabians, such as E. F. Schumacher, received political appointments. Seeing the assembled members all together in conclave, Zena Parker (the wife of prominent Fabian John Parker) exclaimed, "It looks just like an enormous Fabian School."

What makes the Fabian postwar British government significant is that there was no nonsense about pretending to be democratic in either the European or American sense. It was the logical fulfilment of what Belloc had seen developing half a century before and chronicled in *The Servile State*: a superficial blending of capitalism and socialism in which an elite presumably takes care of the great mass of people.

This was also the underlying premise of John Maynard Keynes, whose political and economic theories derived from those of Walter Bagehot and were applied in the New Deal.[172] Bagehot, who despised the United States[173] and greatly

---

[172]   John Maynard Keynes, "The Works of Bagehot," *The Economic Journal* 25 (1915):369–75.

[173]   Walter Bagehot, *The English Constitution* (Portland, Oregon: Sussex Academic Press, 1997), 120–25.

admired Thomas Hobbes,[174] believed that ordinary people are not fit to rule themselves. As proposed by inclusive capitalism and the stakeholder capitalism of the Great Reset, they require "a *chosen* people" composed of an aristocracy of wealth to take care of them.[175] Annie Besant, Fabian Society member and heir to Madame Blavatsky, declared, "But the general idea is that each man should have power according to his knowledge and capacity. . . . And the keynote is that of my fairy State: From every man according to his capacity; to every man according to his needs. A democratic Socialism, controlled by majority votes, guided by numbers, can never succeed; a truly aristocratic Socialism, controlled by duty, guided by wisdom, is the next step upwards in civilisation."

Disillusion with Fabianism was not restricted to Great Britain and the United States. As he admitted in his memoirs, Lee Kuan Yew, the first prime minister of Singapore after it gained independence in 1959, had been strongly influenced by Fabian theory. By 1993, however, he had completely reversed himself, considering the implementation of the Fabian program an unmitigated disaster. As he said, "[The Fabians] were going to create a just society for the British workers—the beginning of a welfare state, cheap council housing, free medicine and dental treatment, free spectacles, generous unemployment benefits. Of course, for students from the colonies, like Singapore and Malaya, it was a great attraction as the alternative to communism. We did not see until the 1970s that that was the beginning of

---

[174]   Ibid., 120–21.
[175]   Ibid., 17. Emphasis in original.

big problems contributing to the inevitable decline of the British economy."[176]

Solidarism's Slide

The thought of Fr. Heinrich Pesch was at least spared the ignominy of having the gross distortions and misunderstandings that second and third generation disciples forced on it applied in the unforgiving "real world." As Monsignor Taparelli noted more than a century before the near-total application of the New Things throughout the world, mistakes by scientists in the physical sciences can have no effect on how nature operates. Mistakes in philosophy, politics, and theology such as those embodied in the Great Reset, however, have far-reaching consequences in human society.

4.5. Human Rights and the Hijacked Council

From the standpoint of experience and common sense, it is difficult to understand the popularity of the Great Reset and similar proposals. Socialism by any name has a long history of failure, while the degree of government control required to implement the system is a clear offense against the dignity of the human person. We can only assume that the situation has become so desperate that many people willingly embrace a failed experiment.

You cannot make a badly designed system work better by trying harder and spending more of other people's money. Further, and contrary to popular legend, the New Deal did not

---

[176]   Michael Barr, "Lee Kuan Yew's Fabian Phase," *Australian Journal of Politics & History* 46, no. 1 (March 2000): 110–26.

end the Great Depression. According to Dr. Harold Glenn
Moulton, president of the Brookings Institution, and other
authorities, Keynes's economic—and political—prescriptions
prolonged the Great Depression and caused "the Depression
within the Depression" of 1937–1938.[177]

In reality, it was the buildup to World War II that restored
prosperity and brought the somewhat ephemeral goal of
"full employment" to realization during the war. Ironically,
the politicians insisted on financing the war effort using fiscally unsound debt instead of the politically risky method of
raising taxes.

This is directly contrary to Keynesian theory, which spec-
ifies that once full employment is reached, no new money
should be created. Keynes himself urged that the war effort
be financed with taxes alone.[178] Keeping an eye on their
chances for reelection, however, politicians were more concerned with the short-term effect of taxes than in the long-
term effect of debt.

The Rights of Man

Better than most, Pope Pius XII knew what was behind the
war. He did not need to recall Benedict XV's reminder that
the New Things caused World War I. He was fully aware that
stripping people of their natural rights, especially ownership

---

[177]   Harold G. Moulton, *Financial Organization and the Economic
System* (New York: McGraw-Hill Book Company, Inc., 1938),
411–17.

[178]   John Maynard Keynes, *How to Pay for the War: A Radical Plan
for the Chancellor of the Exchequer* (London: Macmillan and Co.,
Ltd., 1940), 9.

of capital, caused the growing alienation of ordinary people from the ability to participate in the common good. This in turn led directly to the rise of capitalism, socialism, and ultra-supernaturalism, to the growing power of the State, and thus to economic and political dictatorships hungry for power.

It comes as no surprise, then, that as early as 1939, the pope began calling for protection of basic human rights, principally life, liberty, and private property. Pronouncements were made regularly throughout the war and were the special focus of Pius XII's 1942, 1943, and 1944 Christmas messages.

Of the Christmas messages, that of 1942, "The Rights of Man," was possibly the most important in Pius XII's eyes. This is almost certainly the case, as he quoted a key section of that Christmas message in his 1950 encyclical *Evangelii Praecones*, "On Promotion of Catholic Missions"—

> The dignity of the human person then, speaking gen-
> erally, requires as a natural foundation of life the right
> to the use of the goods of the earth. To this right cor-
> responds the fundamental obligation to grant private
> ownership of property, if possible, to all. Positive leg-
> islation, regulating private ownership may change and
> more or less restrict its use. But if legislation is to play
> its part in the pacification of the community, it must
> see to it that the worker, who is or will be the father
> of a family, is not condemned to an economic depen-
> dence and servitude which is irreconcilable with his
> rights as a person.[179]

---

[179]   *Evangelii Praecones*, § 52.

Pius XII did not stop there. Frequently during the war, and with increasing emphasis after it, the pope insistently called not merely for peace but a restoration of basic human rights as the only secure foundation for peace. In particular, he repeatedly cited socialism and communism, philosophies built on the abolition of private property in capital, as the chief dangers to civilization, the family, and world peace.

To restore and secure fundamental rights, Pius XII advocated the establishment of some sort of "Society of Peoples" as a means of preserving peace.[180] After the war, President Harry S. Truman and the pope exchanged letters pledging mutual support for securing human rights and initiatives for peace.[181]

Determining Pius XII's role in the United Nations adopting the Universal Declaration of Human Rights is beyond the scope of this book, but it certainly had his full backing. Many conservatives, however, viewed the declaration as communist.

Appealing to Catholics and probably mentioning Pius XII's well-known advocacy for such a statement, Eleanor Roosevelt was able to overcome objections.[182] Key to the declaration, as might be expected from papal insistence on the importance of private property, is Article 17: "(1) Everyone has the right to own property alone as well as in association with others. (2) No one shall be arbitrarily deprived of his property."

---

[180]   "Pope Calls On World For Society of Peoples To Ban Future Wars," *Washington Evening Star*, December 24, 1942, A-2.

[181]   "Text of Truman-Pope Letters," *Washington Evening Star*, August 28, 1947, A-2.

[182]   "How Eleanor Roosevelt Pushed for a Universal Declaration of Human Rights," A&E History, accessed May 10, 2021, https://www.history.com/news/eleanor-roosevelt-universal-declaration-human-rights.

Why Was Vatican II Called?

This makes what happened at the Second Vatican Council even more puzzling. For Catholics and non-Catholics alike, the council was a watershed, a revolutionary event that has been completely misunderstood.

Although, by 1950, the Catholic Church, especially in the United States, appeared to have achieved a very agreeable and quite comfortable accommodation to the modern world, this was deceptive. The Welfare State to which the New Deal gave birth was an indication of serious problems.

Thanks to Ryan, many people considered the New Deal the quintessence of Catholic social teaching. Nevertheless, this new form of the Servile State was based on a "concept of society . . . utterly foreign to Christian truth."[183] Similar to the Great Reset, the New Deal was a complete and total rejection of respect for the dignity of the human person under God and a shift from the sovereignty of individual human beings to that of some form of the collective.

When analyzing the council, virtually everyone begins with the presumably halcyon days of the 1950s, ignoring that a superficial compliance to traditional forms concealed the massive damage caused by ultrasupernaturalism and socialism. This becomes clear when we expand the timeframe of analysis to find out "What Happened to Vatican II."

An Alternative View of the Council

Vatican II was not intended as the precursor to the Great Reset and similar proposals but as a counter to the Kingdom

---

[183]   *Quadragesimo Anno*, § 117.

of God on Earth that had been the goal of the ultrasupernaturalists and socialists from the very beginning. That, at least, was the opinion of Evelyn Waugh, who believed John XXIII worked to reverse the gains made by adherents of the New Things in the century and a half before the council.

Waugh saw great significance in John XXIII's choice of name on his election, as John XXII—excoriated by the Fabians—was the pope who dealt with the Fraticelli, whom the Fabians venerated as the only real Christians for their rejection of private property as a natural right.[184] John XXIII had to deal with a global society formed in large measure by Fabian socialism and the New Deal, sold to American Church by Coughlin and Ryan, and from there to the rest of the Catholic world.

Although it was confined to the little-understood field of the Church's social doctrine, the triumph of Ryan and his carefully selected associates and students at the Catholic University of America in Washington, DC, along with the tactics of the Fabian Society, had taught dissenters an important lesson. Dissent was feasible, even profitable, if proper precautions were taken and a network organized before taking open action.

Lip service had to be paid to orthodoxy, outward forms of obedience maintained, and the attack presented as the true orthodoxy in conformity with what Jesus (or whatever authority was cited) "really meant." Innovative theories (such as the abolition of private property, the sovereignty of the collective, and the rejection of the natural order in favor of the

---

184   Evelyn Waugh, *The Essays, Articles and Reviews of Evelyn Waugh* (London: Penguin Books, 1983), 616–17.

supernatural) could then be rebranded as true Christian doctrine. This would enable someone not only to dissent from fundamental Catholic doctrines and remain in the Church but be revered as a virtual prophet of the New Christianity.

As Ryan's attacks on Sheen demonstrated, this fostered a unique climate of dissent in Catholic academia, especially at the Catholic University of America. During the New Deal, many American Catholics had been convinced by the repeated assurances from credible authorities that de facto socialism is compatible with Catholic teaching. As a result, many people now viewed adherence to traditional concepts of faith and morals on which the Church's social teachings are based as somehow un- or anti-Christian or at the very least heretical.

In the minds of dissenting theologians of the mid-twentieth century, what Saint-Simon, de Lamennais, and others had proclaimed at the dawn of the nineteenth century was nothing less than a religious declaration of independence. This was what Sheen, who saw the implications beyond the Church's social teachings, had protested in radio broadcasts, newspaper columns, and books.

As far as the dissenters from the Church's social doctrine were concerned, however, the day of traditional Christianity was over. Principles of democratic socialism embodied in the New Deal were the first signs of the New Church and heralded the dawn of a New Age for humanity.

In the New Age, the supernatural order would replace the natural order, charity would replace justice, and so on. God's law (as interpreted by the dissenters) would replace man's law and establish the Kingdom of God on Earth.

A Climate of Dissent

People in key positions took advantage of circumstances to move in the same general direction by implementing personal agendas developed within a climate of dissent, even if open rebellion had not been evident until then. These "false prophets," as Robert Cardinal Sarah called them, continue their work to the present day.[185]

As His Eminence noted during his talk at a conference in Paris on May 25, 2019, these ultrasupernaturalists "loudly proclaim change and rupture. . . . They are not seeking the good of the flock. They are mercenaries let in by deceit into the sheepfold." The only remedy, as he said, is to reject innovations that change fundamental principles and always do old things in new ways:

> The Catholic doctrine we have received from the apostles is the only solid foundation we can find. If everyone defends his own opinion, theological hypotheses, novelties, or a pastoral approach that contradicts the demands of the Gospel and the perennial Magisterium of the Church, then division will spread everywhere.
>
> I am wounded when I see so many pastors selling off Catholic doctrine and sowing division among the faithful. We owe the Christian people a clear teaching, firm and stable. How can we allow bishops and

---

[185] Conference given by Robert Cardinal Sarah at Église Saint François-Xavier in Paris, May 25, 2019, *Catholic World Report*, accessed June 29, 2021, https://www.catholicworldreport.com/2019/12/29/cardinal-sarah-we-must-rebuild-the-cathedral-we-do-not-need-to-invent-a-new-church/.

episcopal conferences to contradict one another? Where confusion reigns, God cannot dwell! For God is Light and Truth.

Unity of faith assumes the unity of the magisterium across space and time. When we are confronted with a new teaching, it must always be interpreted in continuity with the teaching that preceded. If we introduce ruptures and revolutions, we destroy the unity that governs the holy Church across the ages. This does not mean that we are condemned to a theological fixism. But all evolution must lead to a better understanding and deepening of the past.[186]

Such "false prophets" imposed reinterpretations of the Church's social teachings on the council documents to conform them to ultrasupernaturalism and the Democratic Religion of socialism. This was almost as if by chance and applied wholesale to other areas to create a superficial consistency.

Even though this involved altering the interpretation of the council documents and often the facts, it is evident that specific doctrines were not the real issue. It was the idea of absolutes that had to go, whether in Church (immutable doctrine), State (inherent natural rights), or family (traditional marriage, even sexual identity). The belief that something was not subject to change even under pressure of the greatest need or desire had to be eliminated.

Change for the sake of change—pure ultrasupernaturalism leading ultimately to the rejection of all religious and

---

[186]   Ibid.

moral principles and the belief that life is meaningless, i.e., nihilism[187]—was the motive of the dissenters, and sometimes the only point on which they agreed. The resulting confusion accelerated acceptance of the New Things and shifted power to the dissenters and away from the institutional Church and the hierarchy, especially the pope.

The Fatal Omission Strikes Again

How was this possible? In our opinion, it began with socialism itself, which rejects the single most powerful weapon in the arsenal of Catholic social teaching: widespread capital ownership. Both Leo XIII and Pius XI put great emphasis on this.[188]

A meaningful private property stake in capital is important not simply for individual income but also for society at large. Ownership conveys power, and thus the ability to resist the New Things.[189] As political philosophers from Aristotle down to Mortimer Adler have reminded us, private property in capital is the chief means by which people connect to society and participate in the institutions of the common good.

The problem was that while the popes are infallible in matters of faith and morals under the usual conditions, infallibility does not extend to science, including the science of

[187]   Heinrich A. Rommen, *The Natural Law: A Study in Legal and Social History and Philosophy* (Indianapolis, Indiana: Liberty Fund, Inc., 1998), 52.

[188]   *Rerum Novarum*, §§ 4–6, 8, 11–16, 22, 38, 46–47, 57; *Quadragesimo Anno*, §§ 32, 44–49, 57–61, 63.

[189]   *Centesimus Annus*, §§ 3, 5, 12–21, 43, 61.

finance. Consequently, several popes suggested that the only means of gaining ownership is to increase wages, thereby presumably allowing workers to save and purchase capital.

Unfortunately, this method of capital finance is not generally feasible, especially on a large scale. The required decrease in consumption demand and the rise in production costs render it self-defeating at best. Expanded ownership was simply not discussed during the council, although it is the single best practical means by which ordinary people can participate in the struggle to counter the New Things.

Ironically, it was shortly before the council that Louis Kelso and Mortimer Adler published two books that explained the principles and techniques by means of which the great mass of people not only would prefer to become owners but have the opportunity and means to do so. These were *The Capitalist Manifesto* (1958) and *The New Capitalists* (1961), containing the core theory which, when combined with Catholic social doctrine, is the best response and alternative to the Great Reset and similar proposals.

CHAPTER 5

"A New Pastoral Theology"

5.1. Surrender, the City Upon the Hill, or Social Justice?

Many people have compared the Great Reset and similar proposals to the New Deal. At the same time, a significant number of Catholics believe the New Deal was an application of the Church's social doctrine. Finally, there is a fixed belief, especially in Catholic academia and among the hierarchy, that Msgr. John A. Ryan's interpretation of Catholic social doctrine is authoritative.

Ryan Improvises History

As noted previously, Ryan's interpretation of Catholic doctrine and the natural law was badly flawed. This undermined fundamental concepts of natural law not only for Catholics but for people of all faiths and philosophies. It is therefore important to understand how Ryan's defective understanding of important concepts attained its present unquestioned status.

As Ryan related, Bishop Thomas Shahan, past Rector of the Catholic University of America, exclaimed after the release of *Quadragesimo Anno*, "Well, this is a great vindication for John Ryan."[1] This was similar to other endorsements, favorable comments on his work, and encouragement from leading churchmen that Ryan claimed he had received, such as from Cardinal Gibbons[2] and Archbishop Ireland.[3]

We can only take Ryan's word about such claims which appear in his autobiography *Social Doctrine in Action* (1941), as none of them can be verified. All the individuals cited were dead by the time Ryan made the information public and there are no other sources to support his statements.

Frankly, not only is the timing suspicious, what Ryan reported in many cases contradicted facts as well as the known positions of Gibbons and Ireland. As for Shahan's alleged comment, circumstances reveal it is even more dubious than those attributed to Gibbons and Ireland.

On May 13, 1931, Ryan had testified before a special Visiting Committee at Catholic University.[4] This was one of two committees appointed to investigate certain irregularities in the school of theology for which Ryan was believed to be responsible. *Quadragesimo Anno* was released May 15, 1931. "[A] few days later"[5]—on or about May 17—Ryan claimed Shahan made his comment.

---

1   John A. Ryan, *Social Doctrine in Action: A Personal History* (New York: Harper & Brothers, Publishers, 1941), 242.
2   Ibid., 18–21, 128, 129.
3   Ibid., 21–28, 42, 43, 62, 69, 70, 128–31.
4   Kathleen L. Riley, *Fulton J. Sheen: An American Catholic Response to the Twentieth Century* (New York: Society of St. Paul, 2004), 15.
5   Ryan, *Social Doctrine in Action*, 242.

In his May 13 testimony, Ryan had made damaging—and demonstrably false—statements about Fulton Sheen, who was (in a sense) Shahan's protégé. Further, Ryan had been the cause of Sheen's ouster from the School of Sacred Sciences.[6]

The Visiting Committee was, in part, charged with looking into John A. Ryan's efforts to remove James H. Ryan as rector. It would have been therefore not only imprudent and irregular but also grossly improper for Shahan as past rector to comment on anything connected with John A. Ryan while the Visiting Committee was in session, unless called to testify. It is inconceivable that Shahan would have made any statement in support of John A. Ryan, thereby undercutting the current rector's position and authority as well as implying that Ryan's accusations against Sheen were valid.

The plain fact is that *Quadragesimo Anno*, Pius XI's encyclical "On the Restructuring of the Social Order," did not inspire or justify the New Deal, nor did it "vindicate" Ryan. Instead, a strong case could be made that the encyclical was (at least in part) a response of sorts to the errors being spread by Ryan through his distortions of *Rerum Novarum*.[7] There is, therefore, no basis for claiming that the Great Reset or other proposals characterized as expansions of or improvements on the New Deal are compatible with a natural law approach to economics or are consistent with Catholic social teaching—or Jewish, Islamic, or pagan, for that matter.

---

[6]   Fulton J. Sheen, *Treasure in Clay: The Autobiography of Fulton J. Sheen* (Garden City, New York: Doubleday & Company, Inc., 1979), 45–46.

[7]   See *Quadragesimo Anno*, §§ 14, 40, 44.

Responding to Relativism

This is not to say that many people are not sincerely searching for alternatives to today's seemingly overwhelming and
endless crises. The problem is when people of any faith or
philosophy distance themselves from the natural law based
on reason and accept some version of manufactured reality—such as the New Things—that dismisses or deviates
from a reason-based approach derived from human nature.
What results may by chance be consistent with the demands
of human dignity, but more often than not ends up being
anti- or un-human.

Take, for example, the two most common responses in
Catholic circles to modern society, and to the Great Reset
and similar proposals. This is not to say that people of other
faiths and philosophies are not going down the same path,
possibly to an even greater degree. Here, however, we are
presenting a natural law response to the current situation,
framed within the context of Thomistic personalism as articulated in the work of Pope Saint John Paul II,[8] and thus
within the larger framework of Catholic social teaching and
the theories of economic justice presented by Louis Kelso
and Mortimer Adler.

The first response to today's situation is to surrender to it.
This generally means promoting some version of capitalism,
socialism, or the Servile State. In effect, this gives in partially
or completely to the socialist and ultrasupernaturalist idea

---

[8]   Karol Wojtyła, "Thomistic Personalism," *Person and Community:
        Selected Essays* (New York: Peter Lang, 2008), 165–75.

that existence relates only to this world, and the only issue of importance is meeting people's material needs.

This, as already noted, is the goal of the New Things that Catholic social doctrine was developed to counter. As Cardinal Sarah noted,[9] it is blatantly materialistic and fosters war, love of money, poverty, racism, consumerism, and pretty much every other ism that one can imagine.

Unfortunately, many people today interpret Catholic social teaching as directed exclusively to meeting material needs and not to the full development of the human person. This reinterpretation provides a solid foundation and receptive audience for such programs and proposals as the New Deal, the Great Reset, stakeholder capitalism, universal basic income, inclusive capitalism, and so on. Surrendering to a materialist understanding of life validates and justifies everything intended to improve the quality of life as defined by those with property, and thus power. The end justifies the means and might makes right.

Retreat to the Catacombs

As historian Christopher Dawson noted more than once in chronicling the spiritual and cultural decline of the West, the second response is to reject modern culture and, in a sense, "retreat to the catacombs" to get away from the world of sin. This response, while still grossly inadequate, at least acknowledges that there must be objective and even absolute

---

9   Cardinal Sarah, Conference, *Catholic World Report*, accessed June 29, 2021, https://www.catholicworldreport.com/2019/12/29/car dinal-sarah-we-must-rebuild-the-cathedral-we-do-not-need-to-in vent-a-new-church/.

standards of human conduct—that is, the natural law. It is not, however, the Aristotelian-Thomist understanding of natural law in its strictest sense—that is, based on reason guided and illuminated by faith.

Instead, while lip service may be paid to reason, and the necessity of faith and reason going together, there is a subtle shift in the basis of natural law from reason to faith, and from justice to charity. This was the error of Hugo Grotius, the so-called "Father of Natural Law," who was chiefly responsible for the change, or at least the most consistent in developing his theories.[10]

In Grotius's theory, the basis of the natural law changes from God's nature reflected in that of human beings to God's commands as interpreted by some accepted authority. Something ceases to be right because God—and thus human nature—*is* so and becomes right because God (or whatever one puts in the place of God) *says* so. Law changes from being reasonable and natural (*lex ratio*, "law is reason") to being arbitrary and supernatural (*lex voluntas*, "law is will")—the "Triumph of the Will."

If "law is will," the Lawgiver or any other absolute standard becomes unnecessary once you have the law. As Grotius explained, "What we have been saying would have a degree of validity even if we should concede that which cannot be conceded without the utmost wickedness, that there is no God, or that the affairs of men are of no concern to Him."[11]

---

10   Heinrich A. Rommen, *The Natural Law: A Study in Legal and So-cial History and Philosophy* (Indianapolis, Indiana: Liberty Fund, Inc., 1998), 62–66.

11   Hugo Grotius, *De Jure Belli ac Pacis Libri Tres*, Proloegomena, II,

While Grotius's analysis was not as crudely stated as Kallikles the Sophist's "might makes right," the result is the same. Instead of a worldview based on empirical evidence and logical consistency, an individual puts his faith in that which controls him or is most compatible with his own opinion.

People become divided into the godly (those with whom you agree) and the ungodly (those with whom you disagree), into persons (who have rights) and non-persons (who have no rights), or even in extreme instances into humans ("us") and non-humans ("them"). This often ends in theological relativism—modernism, what Msgr. Ronald Knox called enthusiasm or ultrasupernaturalism.

Ultrasupernaturalism

According to Knox, the ultrasupernaturalist believes himself to be a member of a group especially chosen by God, either to save the world or survive as a remnant once Satan or who- or whatever has taken to himself the ungodly, the worldly, or the unawakened. Inevitably, the ultrasupernaturalist believes he must separate himself from the ungodly, especially if he does not have the power to force them to become virtuous on his terms. As Knox explained:

> God's elect people, although they must perforce live cheek by jowl with the sons of perdition, claim another citizenship and own another allegiance. For the sake of peace and charity, they will submit themselves to every ordinance of man, but always under protest; worldly

Oxford-London, 1925. Cited in Rommen, *The Natural Law*, 62.

> governments, being of purely human institution, have
> no real mandate to exercise authority, and sinful folk
> have no real rights, although, out of courtesy, their
> fancied rights must be respected. Always the enthu-
> siast hankers after a theocracy, in which the anoma-
> lies of the present situation will be done away, and the
> righteous bear rule openly. Disappointed of this hope,
> a group of sectaries will sometimes go out into the wil-
> derness, and set up a little theocracy of their own.[12]

Ultrasupernaturalists are suffused with the idea that the surrounding culture is too sinful to tolerate or even to survive.
The only recourse is to retreat to the wilderness (or some
equivalent) and build a city upon the hill where life can be
lived in a godly manner.

Generally, those who view themselves as godly pay some
attention to meeting the surrounding culture's needs. This
is usually in terms of inspiring or coercing a conversion to
Catholicism, or whatever faith or philosophy motivates the
individual or group. Forced conversions, however, are rarely
if ever real conversions. Coercing people to believe something contrary to their consciences violates fundamental
principles of natural law and personality itself.

Then there is the growing tendency not merely to regard the
ungodly as having no rights[13] but to act on it. This makes anyone outside the elect or the number of the chosen fair game.
After all, did not Saint Paul himself say that all things are lawful

---

[12]   Ibid., 3.
[13]   Ronald Knox, *Enthusiasm: A Chapter in the History of Religion*
        (New York: Oxford University Press, 1961), 3, 584.

to the elect?[14] This gave ultrasupernaturalists a useful text for reinterpretation and justification through the centuries.[15]

In this way, it becomes allowable to do what you will to the ungodly. More, the conviction grows that God commands you to lie, cheat, and steal, even torture and kill anyone stubborn enough not to accept your views, or—horror of horrors!—perversely accepts them the wrong way. Knox chronicled incidents carried out at God's alleged command ranging from human sacrifice[16] and an attorney who embezzled an inheritance[17] to pacifist Quakers in Cromwell's army who slaughtered unarmed children, women, and men as well as their opponents in battle as readily as did their fellow Ironsides.[18] As Knox explained, "Their doctrine was, not that nobody has a right to take the sword, but that no worldly person has a right to take the sword. Dominion is founded on grace; if you are not in a state of grace, you have, strictly speaking, no rights, and therefore no authority either to government or to make war—least of all on the saints."[19]

Today's demonization of political opponents, civil or religious ostracism of those who think or believe differently, and riots are simply a replay of what has been going on for millennia. Once the self-appointed godly gain power, or try to, it is usually only a matter of time before they begin forcing others to act virtuously or simply eliminate them

---

[14]   1 Cor. 6:12, 10:23; Rom. 14:14.

[15]   Knox, *Enthusiasm*, 15, 19.

[16]   Ibid., 582.

[17]   Ibid., 584–85.

[18]   William Cobbett noted a series of similar incidents in his *History of the Protestant Reformation in England and Ireland* (1827).

[19]   Knox, Enthusiasm, 148.

with the guillotine or the gas chamber. As Knox concluded, "But what if the saints contrive to set up the theocratic kingdom which is, always, the subject of their dreams? Is it so clear that they have no right to enforce their own superior enlightenment on the world? The Peasants' Revolt and the defence of Munster give the answer to your question."[20]

Merely separating from the sinful world and undertaking a Great Trek is mild by comparison, although still not consistent with Catholic social teaching or a personalist approach to social and economic reform.

The City upon the Hill

Retreating into the wilderness is not an option for most people these days. Some, however, still attempt to follow the examples that characterized the Second Great Awakening. They seek to found new communities or establish a counterculture within the existing culture so that real Christians—or any other group—can live the way they believe God intended.[21]

As conditions have deteriorated over the past few decades, many authors have advocated variations of the "City upon the Hill" alternative, encouraging a siege mentality, while some individuals and groups have worked to establish separate towns or transform existing communities. Literary examples include *The Benedict Option* (2017),[22] *Strangers*

---

20   Ibid.

21   J. D. Dickey, *American Demagogue: The Great Awakening and the Rise and Fall of Populism* (New York: Pegasus Books, 2019), 274–77.

22   Rod Dreher, *The Benedict Option: A Strategy for Christians in a*

in a Strange Land (2017)[23] and *Out of the Ashes* (2017).[24] Calling to mind the seemingly countless utopian experiments of the nineteenth century (Brook Farm, New Harmony, Icaria, etc.[25]) are Hyattsville, Maryland,[26] the Daniel Berrigan Center/Benincasa Community, New York,[27] Front Royal, Virginia, and Ave Maria, Florida, among others.

Some may protest that the named books do not, in fact, advocate actual separation from the rest of society. There is some merit in that position, but only up to a point. The three cited works—and many others in a similar vein—all take for granted that American (and global) society has not merely stumbled but has fallen and cannot get up by purely human means.

Once you read these admittedly well-intentioned books, you realize that recommendations to resolve the current crisis are all variations on the assumption that if we cheerfully persevere, pray hard enough, and do what is right regardless of the consequences, all will be well. Why? Because the godly will triumph with God's help. The ungodly will ultimately not be able to stand against them and will surrender

---

Post-Christian Nation (New York: Sentinel, 2017).

23   Charles J. Chaput, *Strangers in a Strange Land: Living the Catholic Faith in a Post-Christian World* (New York: Henry Holt and Company, 2017).

24   Anthony Esolen, *Out of the Ashes: Rebuilding American Culture* (Washington, DC: Regnery Publishing, 2017).

25   Dickey, *American Demagogue*, 276.

26   "All Things Considered," National Public Radio, April 10, 2017, https://www.npr.org/2017/04/10/522714982/catholics-build-intentional-community-of-like-minded-believers.

27   "Young Intentional Community is 'Promise of Vatican II' Realized," *National Catholic Reporter*, August 16, 2019.

or perish, more often than not with a little nudge from the godly to help them on their way.

There is one slight issue with this program. God gave us free will and cannot contradict His nature by forcing us to act against our own will, even if we are doing immense harm thereby. He does not encourage, or tolerate, those little assists to virtue in the form of torture or any other coercion, physical, social, or mental which ultrasupernaturalists seem to find so useful, even necessary, to establish their Kingdom of God on Earth.

We do not need to go into a long philosophical discussion here as to why this is so. It can be boiled down to the fact that God did not make human society, people did. If society is in bad shape, it is not God's fault, but ours. We broke it, and it is up to us to fix it—but not with a Great Reset.

The question then becomes how to do it.

5.2. A Breakthrough in Moral Philosophy

Can you force people to be virtuous?

The quick and easy answer to that question is no, you cannot. As Martin Luther King Jr. said, "Morality cannot be legislated, but behavior can be regulated. Judicial decrees may not change the heart, but they can restrain the heartless."[28]

Coerced Virtue

You can force people to obey the law and refrain from acts that harm other people or the common good, and even to act in ways that benefit others. What you cannot do, either

---

28   Address, Western Michigan University, December 18, 1963.

individually or through the State or community, is make them do something because you want them to do it or because it is the right thing to do.

That, however, is precisely the idea behind the Great Reset and similar proposals. All you need do is change human nature, abolish the natural law, turn human-made society into a Hobbesian "Mortall God," and all will be well.

On the contrary!

Strictly speaking, it is no one else's business why someone does something if it does not harm others. Civil society is concerned with acts, not thoughts. Civilly, motives only matter if they lead to acts. If someone does nothing wrong, he should be safe. "Thought crimes" really matter only to God.

You cannot force people to be virtuous; you can only force people to refrain from non-virtuous acts that harm others directly. Neither can you punish people for what they might do, or for acts that might have caused harm indirectly, such as taking advantage of a flawed system. You cannot punish people for what you think they did but for which you have no proof, either; people are innocent until proven guilty. Finally, as a private person or group, you are not duly constituted authority; you cannot take the law into your own hands.

True, people are frustrated by the condition of society today, but whether we are talking about economic, political, or religious conversion, coercion is always a bad idea. From a non-personalist perspective, however—particularly one trapped within what Kelso and Adler called the slavery of (past) savings—there does not seem to be any alternative if matters remain the same. Society, human nature, or both are corrupt and will have to change, and the only way to do it is to force people to do what is right, even if it violates their rights or offends against their dignity—the major problem with the Great Reset.

At least in Catholic circles, this depressing conclusion appears due to the misinterpretations of *Rerum Novarum* by socialists, capitalists, and ultrasupernaturalists of all degrees. This in turn is likely because two key omissions from the encyclical enabled supporters of the New Things to reject it, ignore it, or turn it to their own purposes.

The first of these was covered in section 4.1: omitting a just and financially feasible means by which ordinary people could become owners of capital. The second omission will be addressed now: some means by which ordinary people can gain direct access to the common good. This is critical, because the common good consists of the vast network of institutions within which people as moral beings become more fully human—that is, virtuous.

Individual Virtue Is Not Sufficient

Strictly speaking, the institutions of the common good do not force anyone to be virtuous or vicious. We have free will and can always resist, even if at a high cost to ourselves and others. Institutions do, however, provide the environment within which people can become virtuous or vicious, and thus encourage virtue or vice, depending on how they are structured.

Unfortunately, while human beings are what Aristotle called "political animals,"[29] there is a strong tendency to act in non-political ways, especially—ironically—in matters

---

29   "Man is by nature a political animal." Aristotle, *The Politics*, 1253a.

relating to politics and political economy. Part of this is due to a lack of understanding of our political nature by individualists (capitalists), collectivists (socialists), and those who try to blend individualism and collectivism into the Servile State or the Great Reset.

Eventually, it dawns on people that no matter what they do, being individually virtuous is not going to solve social problems. It can make matters temporarily better and improve conditions for some of the less fortunate briefly, staving off the inevitable end for a while, but it will not solve the problem. As mentioned above, God is not going to do it for them, no matter how much they insist they are acting in His name.

What usually happens is that people give up on individual efforts and yield to the temptation of collectivism and State action. Surrendering to the State at least has the apparent advantage of being able to use coercion to force people to be virtuous, assuming you believe that human nature can be changed and that those in charge accept your personal vision of the Kingdom of God on Earth.

This is one of the problems with the individualist outlook. It may be that Dorothy Day's "long loneliness" was caused in part by her individualism, which she characterized as anarchism. This was manifest in her belief that, ultimately, all you need is love,[30] which many people seem to have misunderstood, a fact of which Day seemed fully aware. With her emphasis on private property and her utter refusal to allow

---

[30]   Dorothy Day, *The Long Loneliness: The Autobiography of the Legendary Catholic Social Activist* (San Francisco: HarperOne, 2009), 285.

collectivism any validity, especially in the form of action by "Holy Mother the State,"[31] Day made it clear that charity does not replace justice but fulfills and completes it.

Day's suspicion of government action seems to have made her reject the essential role the State must play in restructuring the social order, and thus inhibited a full understanding of social justice on her part. This may be why today's Catholic Worker movement seems in some cases to have embraced with wholehearted fervor the intrusive State action that Day and Peter Maurin with more than a little justification firmly rejected.

Had Day's perspective on *Quadragesimo Anno* differed from Monsignor Ryan's disciples in the Catholic Radical Alliance (CRA) of Pittsburgh, with whom she associated for a time, perhaps matters might have turned out differently. Day eventually broke with the CRA ostensibly over the issue of armed resistance to Hitler, although the suspicion intrudes that the near-worship Ryan and his followers had for the State, redefinition of private property, and utter reliance on the wage system might have had more to do with it.[32]

Forty Years After

What, however, led to *Quadragesimo Anno*? If we take the standard interpretation of the encyclical as a mere reiteration

---

[31]   Kurt Buhring, "Day and Niebuhr on the Great Depression," Lance Richey and Adam Deville, ed., *Dorothy Day and the Church: Past, Present, and Future* (Solidarity Hall, 2016), 400.

[32]   Biographers have speculated why Fulton Sheen seemed to avoid Day; her association with the group that attacked him might explain it.

of *Rerum Novarum*—as did Ryan and countless others—there was no real need for it. Pius XI himself admitted in sections 12 to 39 that the situation had greatly improved since 1891.

As might be expected, there were still serious problems. Conditions had changed as technology and institutions advanced, necessitating a more refined application of Leo XIII's vision. Further, damaging misinterpretations of *Rerum Novarum* circulated, causing dissension:

> Yet since in the course of these same years, certain doubts have arisen concerning either the correct meaning of some parts of Leo's Encyclical or conclusions to be deduced therefrom, which doubts in turn have even among Catholics given rise to controversies that are not always peaceful; and since, furthermore, new needs and changed conditions of our age have made necessary a more precise application of Leo's teaching or even certain additions thereto, We most gladly seize this fitting occasion, in accord with Our Apostolic Office through which We are debtors to all,[33] to answer, so far as in Us lies, these doubts and these demands of the present day.[34]

Despite Pius XI's reiteration and expansion of Leo XIII's work, many people continued to accept without question the claim that *Rerum Novarum* instituted the just wage doctrine, the right of labor to organize, and coercive government

---

[33]   Cf. Rom. 1:14. [Note in text.]
[34]   *Quadragesimo Anno*, § 40; cf. §§ 14, 44.

control of the economy as infallible teaching. Justifying this—as Ryan declared—acceptance of a state-controlled economy was gaining ground every day.[35] Just because the pope has no power to declare applications of doctrine as either doctrines themselves or infallible did not seem to bother too many people, except the pope.

On the other hand, if we assume that Pius XI did something as remarkable with *Quadragesimo Anno* as Leo XIII did with *Rerum Novarum*, the pope's approach starts making sense. This becomes evident from the first moment of his election and his selection of "The Peace of Christ in the Kingdom of Christ" as his motto, the significance of which is lost on many people.

For over a century, the socialists and ultrasupernaturalists had worked obsessively to establish the Kingdom of God on Earth to replace traditional concepts of family, State, and Church, particularly Catholicism. To counter this, and echoing Alexis de Tocqueville's call for "a new science of politics . . . for a new world,"[36] Pius XI said that "the pastoral theology of another day will now no longer suffice."[37] In light of this, his call for "the Reign of Christ the King"—which

---

[35]   Franz H. Mueller, *The Church and the Social Question* (Washington, DC: American Enterprise Institute for Policy Research, 1984), 105.

[36]   De Tocqueville, *Democracy in America*, Author's introduction to Volume I.

[37]   Pius XI, *Discourse to the Ecclesiastical Assistants of the U.C.F.I.*, July 19, 1928. Quoted in Luigi Civardi, *Manual of Catholic Action* (New York: Sheed and Ward, 1936), 178.

is *not* of this world[38]—strikes like a thunderbolt itself, and not merely an echo of Leo XIII's "voice of thunder."[39]

The Reign of Christ the King

Or at least it should—once we understand what Pius XI meant by the Reign of Christ the King, and it is not socialism or anything like it, or the abolition of natural law in favor of supernatural law. Neither is it a temporal sovereignty, nor is the purpose of life material betterment as an end in and of itself, as the socialists insisted.

The Reign of Christ the King does not *and cannot* invert the natural and the supernatural orders and mean that a nation *as a nation* must explicitly or implicitly acknowledge the divinity of Christ. That would be impossible in any event, for "nation" is an abstraction, a human construct, not something made by God.

So, what is it that Pius XI made the centerpiece of his first encyclical in 1922, *Ubi Arcano Dei Consilio*, "On the Peace of Christ in the Kingdom of Christ"? Why did he feel the need in 1925 to institute a new "Feast of Christ the King" so that everyone would grasp the importance of the concept? What is the Reign of Christ the King?

Shocking, or at least upsetting to many people, the Reign of Christ the King is not the theocracy so dear to the hearts of many. Neither is it merely a religious conversion so that Jesus reigns individually in the heart of every person. Instead—and this was Leo XIII's goal—the Reign of

---

38   See John 18:36.
39   *Quadragesimo Anno*, § 9.

Christ the King involves restructuring the entire social order to establish and maintain an institutional environment providing the opportunity and means by which every person can become more fully human—that is, to grow in virtue. As Pius XI explained, the goal of his social doctrine was "the restoration of [the social order] according to the principles of sound philosophy and to its perfection according to the sublime precepts of the law of the Gospel, Our Predecessor, Leo XIII, devoted all his thought and care."[40]

Admittedly, Pius XI's language may not have been the best way to convince people, especially non-Christians, of the universality of Catholic social teaching. It seems to smack of triumphalism and, worse, to exclude anyone who is not Catholic.

A moment's reflection, however, helps us realize that Pius XI really had no choice. From his perspective, it was the only language he could use. To counter the socialist Kingdom of God on Earth that was intended to invert the natural and the supernatural orders and establish a material earthly paradise, he had to present an alternative.

That alternative had to not only guide the establishment and maintenance of an environment within which material needs can be met but also encourage and even assist the full development of every human person, regardless of faith or philosophy, and prepare them for their final ends. To Pius XI, then, the answer to the New Christianity was a proper understanding of the old Christianity.

---

[40]   Ibid., § 76.

Truth Is Universal

This may be difficult to grasp at first, but it is essential to understand the goal of Catholic *social* teaching. The Church's *religious* doctrine is supernatural and is for the salvation of souls and is intended for those who accept Catholicism.

Catholic *social* doctrine is natural and is for the restructuring of the social order. It is for every human being, regardless of faith or philosophy. In *Quadragesimo Anno*, Pius XI stated many times explicitly and by implication that natural law-based Catholic social teaching is for everyone.[41]

This brings us to what Leo XIII omitted from his social doctrine—or, possibly, what he seemed to think was so obvious that it did not need any explanation. That was a specific body of theory and practice that would enable the required reform of institutions to be carried out. He simply hinted that organized action based on sound principles of natural law would do what is necessary.

Unfortunately, most people did not realize the implications of *Rerum Novarum*. They assumed that the pope was taking the usual course of urging them to a greater degree of individual virtue. In accordance with traditional philosophical thought, acting in an individually virtuous manner would indirectly improve the institutions of society.

As had been evident for some time, however, being individually virtuous is not sufficient. This gave the socialists their greatest weapon against traditional politics and religion. As they reasoned, since individual virtue clearly no longer functions properly, or at all in some cases, society

---

[41]   Ibid., §§ 15, 21, 27, 147.

itself needs to be torn down and replaced with something that in their opinion would work: the Democratic Religion. This was why *Rerum Novarum* had either been ignored or reinterpreted as a manifesto for the New Christianity.

Pius XI, however, grasped the underlying problem: that it is impossible to solve a social problem by individual means any more than individual problems can be solved by coercive government control. Individually, you cannot fight city hall any more than socially the community can force people to be virtuous through legislation.[42]

In traditional philosophy, people become virtuous by exercising rights that directly affect their individual good and that of others. This has an indirect beneficial effect on the common good. These are the natural rights of life, liberty, and private property exercised in ways that develop the "particular" natural virtues of prudence, temperance, fortitude, and justice, and the particular supernatural virtues of faith, hope, and charity.

Practicing these particular virtues has an indirect beneficial effect on the common good—that is, the institutions of society. Aristotle called this indirect effect "legal justice," a "general virtue," because the common good benefits most often when the State passes good laws and citizens obey them. Thus, individual virtue affects individual good directly, and the common good indirectly.

---

[42]   The English constitutional scholar Albert Venn Dicey explained in *Lectures on the Relation Between Law and Public Opinion in England During the Nineteenth Century* (1905), that unless "public opinion" supports a law, it will either be disobeyed, or be obeyed in ways contrary to the intent of the legislators.

Logically, Pius XI seems to have assumed that if individual virtue affects individual good directly and the common good indirectly, there must be a social virtue that affects the common good directly, and individual good indirectly. Any task requires the right tools. To restructure the social order, then, the answer is not a more intensive application of *individual* virtue but the judicious and appropriate application of *social* virtue.

That is why human persons have the capacity for both individual virtue and social virtue. We must always keep firmly in mind, however, that individual virtue and social virtue are two very different things and must not be confused. Getting them mixed up is one of those seemingly small errors in the beginning that leads to great errors in the end,[43] and is one of the most serious problems with the Great Reset and similar proposals.

5.3. Social Justice and Personalism

In common with many others, Klaus Schwab of the Great Reset defines "social justice" as providing directly for people's material wellbeing, generally on a large scale or "socially."[44] The term is not, however, a way of describing the social

---

[43] Aquinas, "Introduction," *De Ente et Essentia*; cf. Aristotle, *De Caelo*, 1, 5: "The least initial deviation from the truth is multiplied later a thousandfold."

[44] Mark Doumba, "The Great Reset Must Place Social Justice at Its Centre," World Economic Forum, accessed July 7, 2021, https://www.weforum.org/agenda/2020/07/great-reset-must-place-social-justice-centre/. Conservatives agree on this definition while rejecting its legitimacy; e.g., Jon Miltimore, "Hayek: Social Justice Demands the Unequal Treatment of Individuals," Foundation for

exercise of individual justice or charity, redistribution, or welfare, regardless how great or widespread the need.

A New Idea: Social Virtue

Within the framework of the philosophy of Saint Thomas Aquinas, social justice as developed by Pope Pius XI has a precise meaning. It is the particular virtue directed to the common good. Its purpose is the reform of the institutions of the common good to enable people to practice the individual virtues more effectively. Not unexpectedly, that requires explanation. This is especially so since most people today do not have the background or training to understand the terms with the necessary precision or in the sense they were originally meant.

In his doctoral thesis[45] and, later, in a short pamphlet on the subject, Father William Ferree, SM, PhD, framed his analysis of Pius XI's social doctrine as a kind of "detective story." As Ferree saw it, Pius XI was faced with a very complicated situation. Not only had socialists managed to reinterpret *Rerum Novarum* to mean the opposite of what Leo XIII intended, they also distorted Monsignor Taparelli's notion of social justice by using it to mean redistribution and a substitute for the individual virtues of justice and charity.

Added to that was the general lack of understanding of "social justice" in intellectual circles. As a result, "social

Economic Education, November 13, 2018, https://fee.org/articl es/hayek-social-justice-demands-the-unequal-treatment-of-indivi duals/.

[45]   William J. Ferree, *The Act of Social Justice* (Washington, DC: Catholic University of America Press, 1942).

justice" seemed to be a type of "legal justice," but with a general intention added that the common good be benefitted within the framework of Christianity. That is, Aristotle's legal justice described the indirect effect that the individual practice of the natural virtues of prudence, fortitude, temperance, and justice has on the common good. In addition to the natural virtues, Monsignor Taparelli added the supernatural virtues of faith, hope, and charity on the common good when carried out in conformity with the Magisterium of the Church.

Frankly, that was not much help. It implied that if people are individually virtuous and good Catholics, then society will somehow run efficiently. Pius XI, however, knew that was not the case. It was obvious that being individually virtuous often had little or no effect on the rest of society; "It happens all too frequently" that even people in authority "are helpless to ensure justice."[46]

Rejecting the idea that individual virtue understood in the traditional way is sufficient is what had led to the rise of socialism as the Democratic Religion in the first place. The system was *not* working as the priests and politicians said. Something new and different was obviously needed so that people could once again thrive economically, and the socialists had stepped in to fill the need.

The Virtue of Social Justice

We may never know what led Pius XI to discern social justice as a particular virtue with a direct effect on the common

---

[46]   *Divini Redemptoris*, § 53.

good instead of a general virtue limited to affecting the common good indirectly. He had studied Taparelli's works in depth and, very early in his pontificate, even recommended them to Fulton Sheen.[47] This is an intimation that Sheen was being groomed for some important task, such as fixing the damage Monsignor Ryan had created at the Catholic University of America.[48]

Pius XI realized Aquinas's notion of legal justice in the *Summa Theologica* was radically different from the usual understanding. For eight hundred years, people had assumed Aquinas was simply repeating Aristotle, and legal justice was a general virtue that did not look directly to anything.

Aquinas, however, contradicted this in the question on the cardinal (particular) virtues, among which he included legal justice. As he said, "Legal justice alone directly looks to the common good."[49]

That was not the usual interpretation! Correlating this with the question on justice, Pius XI would have seen the traditional understanding of legal justice: "Legal justice, which is general, directs every [other] virtue to the common good."[50] That is, legal justice is a general virtue with no act of its own but functions through the acts of other virtues.

Here was Aquinas talking out of both sides of his mouth and saying that legal justice both is and is not a particular justice! Investigating further, however, Pius XI would have

---

[47]   Thomas C. Reeves, *America's Bishop: The Life and Times of Fulton J. Sheen* (San Francisco: Encounter Books, 2001), 50.

[48]   Sheen, *Treasure in Clay*, 23.

[49]   Ia IIae, q. 61, a. 5, 4 mm.

[50]   IIa IIae, q. 58, a. 6, 2 mm.

seen the statement, "Legal justice directs man to the common good directly, but to the good of the individual indirectly."[51] Another contradiction!

At some point, Pius XI realized that Aquinas was using the same term for two different things. There was traditional legal justice as a *general* virtue, just as Aristotle said, but also legal justice as a *particular* virtue. The latter seems to have been Aquinas's own contribution, although he made it sound as if he was merely commenting on Aristotle.

Pius XI decided to clarify matters. He would restrict the term "legal justice" to the Aristotelian general virtue ("[give] it to the lawyers"[52]) and apply the new term "social justice" (that the socialists and ultrasupernaturalists had coopted) to Aquinas's particular legal justice. He "announced" (after a fashion) the change in *Studiorum Ducem*, his 1923 encyclical on Aquinas.[53]

Appropriately, this was in the same paragraph that the pope closed by commenting, "It is therefore clear why Modernists are so amply justified in fearing no Doctor of the Church so much as Thomas Aquinas." Of course they feared Aquinas. According to Pius XI, "the Angelic Doctor" had explained why their whole theory of "social justice" was inaccurate centuries before they thought of it![54]

---

51   IIa IIae, q. 58, a. 7, 1 mm.
52   William J. Ferree, *Social Charity* (Arlington, Virginia: Center for Economic and Social Justice, 2003), 16.
53   *Studiorum Ducem*, § 27.
54   Cf. Chesterton's account of the debate between Aquinas and Siger of Brabant in *Saint Thomas Aquinas: "The Dumb Ox"* (New York: Image Books, 1956), 91–96.

Simply put, Aquinas's particular legal justice—henceforth to be known as social justice—is not directed to the good of individuals at all but to the common good: that vast network of institutions within which individuals realize their particular good. As Pius XI explained in *Quadragesimo Anno* and *Divini Redemptoris*, the purpose of social justice is not to substitute for the individual virtues—that is, to make direct provision for individual good. Instead, the purpose of social justice is to make the practice of individual virtue and the realization of individual good possible.

A Missing Piece of the Puzzle

What was missing from Leo XIII's social doctrine was a specific theory that when applied to social problems, makes it possible to effect institutional reforms directly and achieve precise results rather than be limited to the practice of individual virtue while hoping for the best. No longer could the socialists claim that their proposals offered a true solution, however much they might be needed as short-term expedients.

Neither could socialism any longer be considered in any way compatible with Christianity. While socialists presented their beliefs as the only true Christianity, the Democratic Religion was not Christian at all, or Jewish, Muslim, or pagan, for that matter. It was not even democratic in any meaningful fashion. Pius XI stressed this point particularly in *Quadragesimo Anno* when he declared:

> We make this pronouncement: Whether considered
> as a doctrine, or an historical fact, or a movement,

> Socialism, if it remains truly Socialism, cannot be reconciled with the teachings of the Catholic Church because its concept of society itself is utterly foreign to Christian truth. . . . If Socialism, like all errors, contains some truth (which, moreover, the Supreme Pontiffs have never denied), it is based nevertheless on a theory of human society peculiar to itself and irreconcilable with true Christianity. Religious socialism, Christian socialism, are contradictory terms; no one can be at the same time a good Catholic and a true socialist.[55]

Although the pontiff's statement was powerful and direct, one point was not entirely clear: where and how every person fit into the theory. Read from the socialist perspective, this social encyclical and others appeared to limit participation in the common good only to workers. It was as if workers are the only economic and social factor to consider and that only the ability to work makes someone socially acceptable or even a person.[56]

Despite such a narrow view, however, Pius XI's encyclicals clearly state that everyone is equally a person with the same right to participate in economic life through ownership of both labor and of capital. At the same time, however, they can easily be reinterpreted or downplayed by those who, similar to the orientation of the Great Reset, see life entirely from an economic perspective, directed exclusively

---

55   *Quadragesimo Anno*, §§ 117, 120.
56   Cf. the Nazi conept of "useless eaters" for those unable to work and who were considered a drag on society.

to material betterment, or who consider human labor the only real factor of production.

The Personalist Approach

Personalism as developed by Karol Józef Wojtyła—John Paul II—clarified Catholic social doctrine by unequivocally stating that it applies to everyone, not just to workers. Working from the framework provided by the natural law[57] and its application in the social encyclicals (notably *Rerum Novarum*, *Quadragesimo Anno*, and *Divini Redemptoris*), Wojtyła formed his thought within the unique situation of Poland.

Divided between Prussia (and later a united Germany), Russia, and Austria-Hungary in the eighteenth century, Polish national identity had been suppressed for much of the nineteenth, with even the name of the country prohibited at times. Popular Catholicism was a major factor in preserving the culture but had been largely shaped by the Democratic Religion through the series of socialist influenced or inspired uprisings to restore independence, and the forged encyclical *Złota Książeczka* ("the Golden Book").

Successive Nazi and then Russian occupation dimmed some of the enthusiasm for socialism. Still, the belief lingers to this day in many quarters—and not just in Poland—that the real problem was that National Socialism and Marxist Communism are not "real socialism."

---

[57]   Wojtyła, "The Human Person and Natural Law," *Person and Community*, 181–85.

Church, State, and even national identity in Poland were imbued with socialist principles.[58] Wojtyła therefore had the task of reconciling Polish popular Catholicism with traditional orthodox thought without offending Poles' legitimate national aspirations.

Understanding Wojtyła's Thomistic personalism begins with identifying the chief errors of socialism and ultrasupernaturalism through his eyes. The first error is the shift of sovereignty away from the human person and to the abstraction of the collective. The second error is the substitution of changeable human opinions based purely on faith for the absolute reality of God and the natural law discerned as far as possible by human reason.

Solidarism Is Key

Solidarity is a key element in Wojtyła's personalist thought.[59] This is not Émile Durkheim's fascist-socialist solidarity, although that is how many people still interpret it. Wojtyła's solidarism is in the same Aristotelian-Thomist family of thought as that of Fr. Heinrich Pesch.

In Wojtyła's thought, solidarity is a characteristic of groups per se, a principle that fulfills and completes that general justice which permeates all virtue, a sort of "general social charity." As such, it relates to social charity as legal justice relates to social justice—namely, a general virtue as it relates to a particular virtue: "Solidarity is undoubtedly a Christian

---

[58] Norman Davies, *Heart of Europe: A Short History of Poland* (Oxford, UK: Oxford University Press, 1984), 341.

[59] *Solicitudo Rei Socialis*, §§ 38–40.

virtue. In what has been said so far it has been possible to identify many points of contact between solidarity and charity, which is the distinguishing mark of Christ's disciples."[60]

That is, solidarity is an awareness of rights and duties within a particular group that define how sovereign individuals relate as persons to one another and to the group. All people as members of a group have solidarity when they have that awareness and can participate fully as members of that group.

Solidarity is an essential prerequisite for social justice, for only members of groups can carry out acts of social justice. Cooperation is achieved not by absorbing people into the group or collective but by mutual interaction and give-and-take in exercising rights and attaining the common goals and aspirations of the group.

In sharp contrast to the Great Reset, which ignores the human person's inherent rights in favor of collectivist programs, in Wojtyła's personalism, each and every human being, even, or especially, as a member of society, retains his uniqueness and individuality. As Wojtyła explained, "Only the human being as a person is the true center of morality, whereas every society and social group bases its morality on the human being as a person and derives its morality from this source.[61] The concept of social morality is, of course, something very real and continually evolving, but it in no way represents an attempt to substitute society for the

---

[60]   Ibid., § 40.
[61]   Cf. *Divini Redemptoris*, § 29.

human person as the substantial subject of moral values and the proper center of morality."[62]

Personalism is not, strictly speaking, a philosophy in the academic sense—that is, a system of philosophical concepts, such as Thomism or Platonism. Emmanuel Mounier claimed that personalism is not a philosophy in any sense and insisted on calling it a movement.

Not going to Mounier's extreme—which may have contributed to his split from Jacques Maritain—personalism is often described as an intellectual stance or worldview with schools of thought co-existing in many faiths and philosophies.[63] That is why Wojtyła formed his thought within the larger context of Aquinas's philosophy.

Solidarity and personalism are related but are not the same thing. A group can have a high degree of solidarity but not be personalist—for eaxmple, street gangs and Nazis. Construing solidarity as a virtue in the classic sense as ultra-supernaturalists often do—that is, good in and of itself, and the capacity for which is inherent by nature in all human beings—obscures this important distinction. Requiring acceptance of a group's principles as a precondition for recognizing personality violates free will and turns solidarity as conceived in Pesch's and Wojtyła's thought into just another form of socialism and fascism *à la* Durkheim.

62   Wojtyła, "The Problem of the Theory of Morality," *Person and Community*, 155.
63   Thomas D. Williams and Jan Olaf Bengtsson, "Personalism," *Stanford Encyclopedia of Philosophy*, accessed June 29, 2021, https://plato.stanford.edu/.

Personalism enables us to evaluate a philosophy to see how well, or if, it conforms to the particular, even unique needs of every human being as a human person and special creation of God. Wojtyła's personalism brings together the concrete, objective reality of each human person and the abstract, theoretical-moral plane of metaphysics (that is, the natural law) to reconcile the actual to the ideal and bring them together to mutual advantage.[64]

Combining Pius XI's social doctrine with Wojtyła's personalism gives us a complete way of understanding how each human person consistently fits into the social order—and precisely why the Great Reset and similar proposals are not compatible with the natural law and Catholic social doctrine. Specifically, if an interpretation of a doctrine or principle of a faith or philosophy that claims to be personalist or consistent with Catholic social teaching does not respect the dignity of every human person, that interpretation is *by definition* incorrect or faulty. As Wojtyła and others have realized, personalism and the respect for human dignity are inseparable concepts that lie at the heart of Catholic social teaching; one is incomplete without the other. Not even a Great Reset can change that.

5.4. The Laws of Social Justice

The previous section revealed that the Great Reset and similar proposals are inconsistent with the natural law principles applied in the Catholic Church's social doctrine and that of

---

[64]   Gian Franco Svidercoschi, *Stories of Karol: The Unknown Life of John Paul II* (Liguori, Missouri: Liguori/Triumph, 2003), 139–40.

many other faiths and philosophes. This section will begin to look at some of the specific ways in which social justice differs fundamentally from the principles and applications embodied in the Great Reset.

As a particular virtue aimed at perfecting the common good, social justice has certain "laws" within which it must operate. Father Ferree discerned seven laws of social justice in his analysis of Pius XI's social doctrine but noted there are probably many more.

1. That the Common Good Be Kept Inviolate

It does not matter how great our need may be, we may not usurp the institutions of the common good to serve our private ends, no matter how important we think the anticipated results may be for us or for others. The institutions of the common good exist for the benefit of everyone, even (or especially) those whom we particularly dislike, not just favored individuals or groups.[65] A good example is the difficulty many people have gaining access to the means to become capital owners—that is, money and credit. In theory, there is no reason why anyone with a financially feasible project should not be able to obtain sufficient credit to purchase capital, but in practice, that is reserved for the already wealthy.

Violating the rights of a single human being, even to obtain immense benefits for the whole of humanity, is an attack on the entire common good. Ultimately, the common

---

65   William J. Ferree, *Introduction to Social Justice* (New York: Paulist Press, 1948), 34.

good can only exist if natural rights such as private property are held "sacred and inviolable."[66]

Abolishing private property, however, is at the heart of the Great Reset. This is done by expanding the definition of "corporate stakeholder" to include non-owners and non-producers.

In this way, what belongs by natural right to owners and producers is diverted as a matter of course, instead of as an expedient in an emergency or as voluntary charity, to those who neither own nor produce.[67] This is de facto slavery, as slavery is defined as a human being who is totally at the behest of another—that is, has no rights.[68] As Abraham Lincoln said, "It is the same principle in whatever shape it develops itself. It is the same spirit that says, 'You work and toil and earn bread, and I'll eat it.' No matter in what shape it comes, whether from the mouth of a king who seeks to bestride the people of his own nation and live by the fruit of their labor, or from one race of men as an apology for enslaving another race, it is the same tyrannical principle."[69]

Similarly, we cannot legitimately redefine a natural right or ordinarily violate even an unjust law on our own initiative without reference to a higher moral principle, or unless the law forces us personally to do wrong. Deciding for ourselves what laws to obey based solely on a whim or private opinion is pure individualism, virtually anarchy.

---

66   *Rerum Novarum*, § 46.
67   Ibid., § 22.
68   "Slave," *Black's Law Dictionary*.
69   Abraham Lincoln, October 15, 1858, Seventh Debate with Stephen Douglas.

For example, the Fugitive Slave Act of 1850[70] in the United States required that escaped slaves had to be returned to their former owners and that law enforcement officials and citizens had to cooperate. Since the law forced people to act contrary to their consciences and strongly held convictions opposing slavery, it was widely disobeyed. It was the most hated and openly violated federal legislation in US history until the National Prohibition Act of 1919.[71]

On the other hand, regarding slavery as an intolerable evil did not justify killing slave owners, although the laws that enabled people to own slaves were manifestly unjust. Even though many people regarded Nat Turner and John Brown as heroes and martyrs, they were executed for murder and treason.[72]

This is because the common good provides the environment within which individual persons become virtuous by exercising rights. Individual crimes and civil disturbances endanger the common good, thereby inhibiting or preventing people's efforts to become virtuous. Thus, you must obey even a bad law if it is possible to do so unless it forces you personally to harm yourself or others. As Heinrich Rommen explained, "An unjust law . . . is not on that account solely devoid of obligation. An unjust law is not forthwith an immoral law in the strict sense, that is, a law which prescribes a sinful action. In cases of this kind the maintenance of even an imperfect *ordo* takes precedence over resistance to a particular unjust law."[73]

---

[70]   9 Stat. 462.

[71]   41 Stat. 305-323, ch. 85.

[72]   Frederick Douglass supported Brown's goals but not his tactics, believing them to be suicidal.

[73]   Rommen, *The Natural Law*, 227.

That is, the social order is so great a good that even if it is imperfect and not in conformity with nature, ordinarily we must not disobey even an unjust law if it does not force us personally to do wrong. On the other hand, when bad laws, customs, or traditions distort the common good, every person is under a strict obligation in social justice to organize with others to restructure the social order by peaceful (and effective) means. The goal is to make the exercise of individual rights—and thus the development of virtue—once again possible and the social order just overall.

We cannot simply override others' rights or ignore or eliminate inconvenient people to get what we want, even if we have taken the precaution of defining them as unworthy of life. Fine sentiments or impressive rhetoric changes nothing.

In sum, it is not that we *may* not exercise private rights until the common good is corrected. When the common good is flawed or under attack it is often *impossible* to exercise individual rights.

2. Cooperation, Not Conflict

Although becoming more fully human is what defines each of us as persons, the way in which each individual becomes more fully human is unique. Turning an individual or particular good into an ultimate principle exercised without any limits whatsoever necessarily puts that good into conflict with every other particular good.[74]

---

[74] Ferree, *Introduction to Social Justice*, 34–35.

Confiscating wealth from the rich and giving it to the poor only means a change in social classes. Putting the life of a mother above that of her child—or vice versa—justifies getting rid of someone whose life is inconvenient. Asserting that people who cannot sustain themselves by their own labor are "useless eaters" and a drag on the economy denigrates the meaning and purpose for everyone's life. You cannot restore justice by making the system more unjust; two or more wrongs do not make a right.

In a truly free society, there are necessary limits to the exercise of rights, such as life, liberty (freedom of association), and private property. To be just, an effective juridical order bounds a free society[75] in a way that clearly defines the exercise of individual rights, provides a level playing field, and enforces contracts when necessary. A just system encourages virtue and discourages vice; no one is free to use his rights to harm or limit the rights of others.

Only through cooperation—people organizing for the common good—can society be structured and restructured for the good of every member. This does not mean overriding or ignoring some individual goods to gain others or putting individual goods above the common good or vice versa. It means that no goods, individual or social, should be in conflict.

---

[75]   *Centesimus Annus*, § 42.

3. One's First Particular Good Is One's Own Place in the Common Good

The first particular good of every individual or group is how individuals or groups can gain access to the institutions of the common good to fulfill one's human needs, acquire greater virtue, or fulfill a social purpose. This necessarily implies that each person and organization directly relates to, and is responsible for the care and perfecting of a particular aspect or level of the common good.[76] As Ferree explained:

> It must be admitted that this is not the way most of us think at the present time, but that is because we have been badly educated. It must be admitted also that to carry out such a principle in practice looks like too big a job for human nature as we know it; but that is because we are individualists and have missed the point. Of course it is too big a job if each one of us and each of our groups is individually and separately responsible for the welfare of the human race as a whole. But the point is that the human race as a whole is *social*.[77]

All persons and institutions relate to the common good in many ways and at many levels, both as individuals and as members of groups. Each of us as a human person is therefore entitled to equal access to, and full participation in the entirety of the common good, that vast network of laws and institutions within which we realize our individual goods

---

[76] Ferree, *Introduction to Social Justice*, 35–36.

[77] More accurately, *political*. Ferree, *Introduction to Social Justice*, 36.

and become virtuous. In practical terms, we derive our particular or individual goods most directly when we actively participate as persons in the institutions of the social order.[78]

For example, in an ideal economy, every person would own capital, enabling him to "labor in his own vineyard," not merely providing for his and his dependents' material needs, but growing in virtue by exercising his rights and participating in social life. In a less ideal economy, owners of capital and owners of labor would cooperate with each other, each contributing what he has to the economic process, but still exercising rights and growing more fully human. Under the Great Reset, however, people would presumably get what they need without having a natural right to it, and thereby be deprived of the opportunity and means to develop more fully as a human person.

4. Each Directly Responsible

In section 53 of *Divini Redemptoris*, Pius XI noted that individuals are frequently helpless when confronted with socially unjust situations. That being so, it would seem a bit much to insist that every one of us is personally responsible for the whole of the common good. That, however, is the "Fourth Law of Social Justice."[79]

This becomes clear once we consider our political nature and we realize we are not alone. When confronted with a situation that is impossible for the individual, the solution is first

---

[78]   Wojtyła, "Participation or Alienation?" *Person and Community*, 197–207.

[79]   Ferree, *Introduction to Social Justice*, 37.

to organize at that level of the common good. If that is ineffective, we get organized at the next level, and so on, all the way up to the whole of the common good itself, if that is what it takes to bring the proper forces to bear on the problem.

5. Higher Institutions Must Never Displace Lower Ones

The principle of subsidiarity is such an important principle in social justice that it is considered a "law." As Ferree explained, "Another law of Social Justice which stems from the institutional character of the Common Good is that no institution in the vast hierarchy which we have seen can take over the particular actions of an institution or person below it."[80]

Subsidiarity does not mean that individuals or the lower levels of the common good are always right and the higher individuals and groups are always wrong. Neither does it mean that the State does whatever an individual cannot do for himself.

Subsidiarity refers to action carried out by individuals and groups at the most appropriate level of the common good. This is the individual or group that is "closest" to the problem, and as insiders, the natural experts regarding the situation, or at least ordinarily the most knowledgeable.

After all, why should a Washington politician tell a farmer in Iowa how much acreage must be planted in corn, and how much in soybeans, or whether any should be planted at all? Why should government decide whether parents must educate their children in government schools instead of

---

[80]   Ibid.

permitting them to use the tax money collected for education to be used as the parents, not the State, see fit? Government may set minimum standards for education, but parents should have control over their children's education beyond that. Perhaps worst of all, why should authorities in charge of the new economy of the Great Reset decide what should be taken from those who produce and redistributed to those who do not produce?

6. Freedom of Association

"If every natural group of individuals has a right to its own common good and a duty towards the next highest common good,[81] it is evident that such a group has the right to organize itself formally in view of the common good."[82] This "liberty" or "freedom of association" is a natural right. It is so important that it is ranked with the triad of life, liberty, and private property as the means whereby each individual can pursue happiness—that is, become virtuous—fulfilling the purpose for which the social order exists.

Freedom of association has frequently been interpreted in economic and social justice as the right of labor to organize and demand higher fixed wages and more benefits. While certainly one legitimate application of liberty, and a critical one at that, it is far too limited and can even be counterproductive.

For example, a basic goal of organized labor (unions) has been to seek ever-increasing wages and retirement income

---

[81]   And, ultimately, with a view to the whole of the common good.
[82]   Ferree, *Introduction to Social Justice*, 38.

for its members. Raising costs of production without increasing production, however, increases prices to customers as well as the cost of doing business. Not surprisingly, this harms the poor it was intended to help and restricts global trade, decreasing the demand for labor. Ironically, workers and unions rarely organize for ownership, the recommended solution in Catholic social teaching to many of the social problems they attempt to address by raising wages and benefits.[83]

Other commentators assume that freedom of association refers to organizing for civil rights. This, too, is very important, but it can be a dead end if pursued without regard to the private property rights and powers of capital ownership. Even the most liberal interpretation and recognition of civil rights becomes meaningless without the economic rights to sustain it.

7. All Vital Interests Should Be Organized

All real and vital interests of life should be deliberately made to conform to the requirements of the common good. As Ferree noted, social justice "is a full-time job that never ends."[84] A caveat is in order here. "Organized" does not mean "regimented." This, along with their utter disregard for the fundamental human rights of every person in society, was a serious flaw in the Third Reich and Fascist Italy, as well as in the thought of Monsignor Ryan. As George Sabine noted:

---

[83]   *Rerum Novarum*, §§ 46–47.
[84]   Ferree, *Introduction to Social Justice*, 40.

> Totalitarianism undertook to organize and direct every
> phase of economic and social life to the exclusion of
> any area of permitted privacy or voluntary choice. But
> it is important to observe what this type of organi-
> zation concretely meant. First and foremost it meant
> the destruction of great numbers of organizations that
> had long existed and that provided agencies for eco-
> nomic and social activities. [Organizations] which had
> existed on a voluntary basis and were self-governing,
> were either wiped out or were taken over and restaffed.
> Membership became virtually or actually compulsory,
> . . . The result was a paradox. Though the individual
> was "organized" at every turn, he stood more alone
> than ever before.[85]

Admittedly, saying that "all vital interests should be organized"
sounds a little daunting. We must realize that as social justice is
the virtue directed at the common good, the bulk of the work
is done once we as individuals have internalized the basic precepts of the natural law that underpin the social order. These
can be summarized as "good is to be done, evil avoided."

After that, it is not a question of adding more tasks to
an already overloaded life but of doing what we are already
doing in a different manner; "old things in new ways." We
will simply be acting more effectively, as we might expect, and
certainly in a manner more consistent with our own nature.
They will, nevertheless, still be the same basic tasks directed
at becoming virtuous or maintaining us in that endeavor.

---

[85]   George H. Sabine, *A History of Political Theory, Third Edition*
(New York: Holt, Rinehart and Winston, 1961), 918–19.

From the perspective of social justice, then, we can only view the Great Reset and similar proposals as attempts to reach a desired goal by any means necessary. The end does not justify the means for a demonstrably just, even necessary end, much less one that results in the degradation of human dignity and the usurpation of the sovereignty of the human person under God.

5.5. The Characteristics of Social Justice

Social justice also has certain characteristics that help us distinguish true social justice from imitations or well-intentioned efforts that hide their ineffectiveness under the broad and forgiving umbrella of social justice. The principal characteristic of social justice is possibly the most difficult concept to grasp. It is based on the fact that all social virtue is truly *social*, not individual.

1. Only By Members of Groups

Social justice cannot be performed by an individual *as an individual* acting on his own behalf but only by an individual *as a member of a group* acting on behalf of the group. In philosophical terms, the "material cause" of the virtue—the agent that carries out an act of any social virtue—*must* be a member of an organized group.[86]

The agent is still an individual, but he is not in that case acting on his own behalf in a private capacity. He is, rather, acting instead as the representative of the group in a public or official capacity on the group's behalf.

---

[86]   Ferree, *Introduction to Social Justice*, 42–45.

This is like the case of someone who holds an office in government or religion. As a private person, Jane Smith cannot order a city employee to cut her grass or wash her car. As park commissioner, however, Jane can order a city employee to cut the grass on public land or wash park maintenance vehicles. The United States military has strict rules against "personal service"—that is, officers ordering enlisted personnel to perform duties or acts for the private benefit of the officer or his family.

Another aspect of the fact that only members of groups can carry out acts of social virtue is that social virtues are not substitutes or replacements for individual virtues, especially justice and charity. When individual justice or charity are not enough or simply are not working, the proper course of action is not to force virtues to work somehow or provide what is lacking from public or group resources.

Instead, the proper course of action is for people to organize with others. Then, as members of groups, they can work on correcting the institutions so that the institutions operate to allow the individual virtues to function properly once again.[87]

2. It Takes Time

All virtue involves the habit of doing good, and habits, especially social habits, take time to build, just as vice (the habit of doing evil), individual or social, is not something that occurs immediately. In social justice, time must be taken to

---

[87]   Louis O. Kelso and Mortimer J. Adler, *The Capitalist Manifesto* (New York: Random House, 1958), 161.

educate, persuade others, and organize with others to "fix the system."[88]

This characteristic of social justice is difficult for many people today to grasp. It is not because it is conceptually difficult, but because people have been trained to expect instant gratification. The fact that results take time may be the most frustrating part of social justice today.

Rather than patiently figure out a solution for people to have a basic income without redistribution, for example, they will demand what they want immediately, without seriously considering who is going to pay for it. This is the motivation behind the "Fight for Fifteen"[89] and universal basic income (UBI). Yet, as Ferree pointed out, that is precisely what social justice is not! As he explained in a key passage in *Introduction to Social Justice*:

> Let us give an example of how the Encyclical's [*Quadragesimo Anno*] great message can be misunderstood. In Paragraph 71, the Holy Father says: "Every effort must therefore be made that fathers of families receive a wage large enough to meet common domestic needs adequately. But if this cannot always be done under existing circumstances, Social Justice demands that changes be introduced into the system as soon as possible, whereby such a wage will be assured to every adult workingman."

---

[88] Ferree, *Introduction to Social Justice*, 45–47.
[89] The national campaign to raise the minimum hourly wage to fifteen dollars.

Now if we were to hand this quotation to a number of people, and ask each one of them what Social Justice *demands* in it, almost every one of them would answer, "A family wage."

They would all be wrong! Look again at the syntax of the sentence: the direct object of the predicate "demands" is the clause "that changes be introduced into the system." The Pope's teaching on the family wage is that it is due in commutative or strict justice to the individual worker;—what *Social* Justice demands is something specifically *social*: the *reorganization of the system*. For it is the whole system which is badly organized ("socially unjust") when it withholds from the human beings whose lives are bound up in it, the power to "meet common domestic needs adequately."[90]

Thus, something like Louis Kelso's "Second Income Plan" is closer to what Pius XI was talking about than the Fight for Fifteen or UBI. It could have provided people with a supplemental or base income, but it required persuading people to undertake the onerous tasks of enabling legislation, monetary reform, education, and so on. It is so much easier, as Ferree noted, to demand that somebody else do something, then go home with an immense feeling of virtue for having "done social justice."[91]

---

90   Ferree, *Introduction to Social Justice*, 11.
91   William J. Ferree, *Forty Years After . . . A Second Call to Battle*, incomplete ms., *cir.* 1985.

3. Nothing Is Impossible

An important characteristic especially today when social and economic problems seem overwhelming is that in terms of forming or reforming the social order, nothing is impossible. Strictly speaking, in social justice, there is never any such thing as helplessness. As Ferree stated, "No problem is ever too big or too complex, no field is ever too vast, for the methods of this social justice. Problems that were agonizing in the past and were simply dodged, even by serious and virtuous people, can now be solved with ease by any school child."[92]

This does not mean that something that is contradictory or not in accordance with nature can be done through social justice, regardless of the amount of coercion applied. It is, in fact, a fundamental principle of natural law that "with God all things are possible"[93] must be understood as meaning that God can do anything that is not contrary to His own nature; He would not otherwise be God. Contradiction is imperfection, and God is a Perfect Being. As Heinrich Rommen explained, "God's omnipotence is subordinated, humanly speaking of course, to the decrees of His wisdom. Absolute power is the power through which He can do everything that is not in itself contradictory. Hence God cannot cooperate in human sinning, and still less can He be its total cause. The Occamist question of whether God could will hatred of Himself involves an intrinsic impossibility."[94]

---

[92]   Ferree, *Introduction to Social Justice*, 47–49.
[93]   Matt. 19:26.
[94]   Rommen, *The Natural Law*, 55–56.

4. Eternal Vigilance

One point Pius XI stressed in his social doctrine is that the common good—that vast network of institutions, organizations, laws, rules, and other "social tools" that exists—is in a constant state of flux. As a human construct, there is always a tendency for the social order not merely to be imperfect *per se* but to become more imperfect over time as conditions change. As the pope noted, there is a radical instability inherent in human affairs.[95] Socially speaking, the situation is always changing. There may be nothing new under the sun, but the same old things constantly surprise us by manifesting themselves in new and different forms.

As a necessary corollary to the instability of human affairs, we realize that the work of social justice is never done. There is always something more to be done. As Ferree explained,

> The point is that human institutions are always changing, even the most fundamental ones, and these changes must always be directed to serve the Common Good. We, as human beings, cannot possibly foresee all the consequences of our actions. The inevitable result is that many of these consequences bring about unforeseen evil results; and as we go through life, acting always without ultimate realization of the consequences of our actions, these evil results pile up, one on top of the other, until many aspects of our social life are disorganized—have become unjust. When we

---

[95]   Discourse to Dioc. Congress of Catholic Youth, May 16, 1926; Cath. Action, 107–12, cited in Ferree, *The Act of Social Justice*, 219–23.

try to correct that injustice even by social action it is clear that our actions once more will have consequences which we cannot foresee, and that many of those new consequences will also be evil.

Besides that, there are a lot of other people who are not even trying to be good; and the evil consequences of their acts also are continually piling up in all the institutions of life. The result is that Social Justice is not only a full-time job as we have seen before, but it is also an *all-time* job.[96]

5. Effectiveness

This is one of the least attractive characteristics of social justice, especially for those hoping to be martyrs or who are trying to create them. The simple fact, however, is that working for the common good must be effective. You cannot just do something and hope it works. Also, a good intention benefiting the common good does not always translate into results.

We may gratify ourselves with a feeling of great accomplishment, but until we have organized and acted with others to correct a particular defect in the common good, we have yet to fulfill our responsibilities under social justice. Doing what is right without regard to the impact on the common good is not an option and may even be socially unjust. Perhaps Ferree explained it best in a manuscript that he unfortunately left incomplete at the time of his death.

---

[96]   Ferree, *Introduction to Social Justice*, 50.

Keep in mind that it was written four decades ago, and matters have not improved:

> The favorite "social technique" of our own time is the "peaceful" demonstration, especially when media coverage is likely or can be arranged. Subsidiary aspects of the demonstration are boycotts, sit-ins, organized lobbying pressures, single-issue "advocacy" and then—crossing an invisible line which is hard to define and harder still to hold—civil disobedience, violent demonstrations, and, ultimately, terrorism!
>
> Despite the social intent of all such techniques, and their almost universal arrogation to themselves of the terms "Social Justice" or "Justice and Peace," these techniques are all radically *individualistic*. There are several criteria which can be applied to test this:
>
> 1) They are directed immediately to some specific *solution* already determined in the mind of the "activist"; they are never a willingness to dialogue with other and differing opinions on what the *problem* really is.
>
> 2) They are always intensely concerned with the methodologies of *pressure*, not with those of *competence* in the matter in question.
>
> 3) They all require "*time out*" from the day-to-day social intercourse of *life*, and raise the question of how many objects one can juggle at any one time without dropping some or all.
>
> 4) Any "demonstration" is by definition a demand on *someone else* to *do something*. It takes for granted that whatever is wrong is the personal work of *someone*

else, not the common agony of all; and it always knows exactly who and where the *someone* is.

All this can be summed up in the observation that the "social activist" as we have seen them so far, is an earnest amateur by profession.

This is not to say that such "professional amateur-ism" is always wrong. It is wrong as a normal methodology. If it obeys the same principles which would permit a just war, or the insurrection against an entrenched tyrant, more power to it! But it is a hopeless and hence unjust substitute for the patient and full-time organization of every aspect of life which we have seen in the necessary implementation of Social Justice.[97]

6. You Cannot "Take It or Leave It"

As Ferree stated, social justice embraces a "rigid obligation." Each of us is individually responsible for our level or area of the common good, and we must organize with others to bring about necessary institutional reform.[98]

Social justice is not, however, something we add to the tasks of everyday life. Instead, it is a fundamental change in *how* we function as political animals—acting in an organized, social manner with others rather than ineffectually as isolated individuals.

Ferree summed it up best in his conclusion to *Introduction to Social Justice*. As he said:

---

[97]   Ferree, *Forty Years After*.
[98]   Ferree, *Introduction to Social Justice*, 52–53.

The completed doctrine of Social Justice places in our hands instruments of such power as to be inconceivable to former generations.

But let us be clear about what is new and what is old. None of the elements of this theory are new. Institutions, and institutional action, the idea of the Common Good, the relationship of individual to Common Good—all these things are as old as the human race itself. Moreover, much of the actual *application* of these principles to practical life is to be found in older writers under the heading "political prudence."

When all that is admitted, there is still something tremendously new and tremendously important in this work of Pope Pius XI. The power that we have now to change any institution of life, the grip that we have on the social order as a whole, was always *there* but we did not know it and we did not know how to use it.

Now we know.

That is the difference.[99]

It is evident that the Great Reset does not comply with the laws or conform to the characteristics of social justice. It should also be increasingly obvious that what many people call "social justice" is often neither very social nor particularly just or even charitable.

To reiterate the point made in the beginning of this book, it all begins with the human person, a special creation of

---

[99]   Ibid., 56.

God and the only reason for having a social order in the first place; society was made for man, not the other way around. That is why it is essential to incorporate a personalist orientation into our understanding of social justice. Personalism will allow us to avoid confusing individual justice and social justice, and demonstrate why it is imperative that whatever is done must respect the dignity and sovereignty of every single human person.

5.6. Personalism

The focus of Catholic social teaching—and of all natural law faiths and philosophies—is the dignity of the human person under God. In all such teaching, the human person is a special creation, differing both in degree and in kind from every other creature, sentient, animate, or inanimate.[100] By ignoring or dismissing essential human dignity, the Great Reset does not address this adequately, if at all.

The Reality of the Human Person

As developed by Karol Wojtyła within the framework of Aristotelian-Thomism and Catholic social teaching, personalism focuses on the reality of the human person and each person's unique dignity,[101] the "quality or state of being worthy, honored, or esteemed."[102] From the standpoint of

---

[100] *Ut Unum Sint*, § 28; Mortimer J. Adler, *Truth in Religion: The Plurality of Religions and the Unity of Truth* (New York: Macmillan Publishing Company, 1990), 154.

[101] Thomas D. Williams, "What is Thomistic Personalism?" *Alpha Omega* VII, no. 2 (2004): 164.

[102] "Dignity," *Meriam-Webster Dictionary*.

inalienable rights, dignity is the right of a person to be valued and respected for his own sake and to be treated with justice.[103] In Thomist philosophy, every single human being, because he is a human being, is automatically a person, and therefore "worthy, honored, or esteemed."

Respect for human dignity is realized through recognition and protection of the sovereignty of each person under the ultimate sovereignty of God. That in turn means recognition and protection of each person's fundamental rights and social status or place in society.[104] Limiting the discussion to Wojtyła's thought, there are five essential characteristics of personalism:

- **Binary Character**. All persons are distinct from things.[105]
- **Human Dignity**. All persons have rights by nature and are individually sovereign under the highest sovereignty of God.[106]
- **Determinable Instead of Determinate Nature**. All persons have determinable characteristics; all things have determinate characteristics.[107]
- **Self-Determination**. All persons have free will.[108]

---

[103]   Cf. "Person," *Black's Law Dictionary*.

[104]   Rufus Burrow Jr., *God and Human Dignity* (Notre Dame, Indiana: University of Notre Dame Press, 2006), 165.

[105]   Wojtyła, "The Dignity of the Human Person," *Person and Community*, 178–79.

[106]   Ibid., 177–80.

[107]   Wojtyła, "The Personal Structure of Self-Determination," *Person and Community*, 187–95.

[108]   Ibid. See also Karol Wojtyła, *The Acting Person* (Boston, Massachusetts: R. Reidel Publishing Company, 1979).

- **Political Animals**. All persons associate by nature within a consciously structured social order, being both individuals and members of society.[109]

Binary Character

According to the Aristotelian-Thomist natural law theory, personalism presupposes the existence of God, which can be known by reason.[110] Purely religious aspects of personalism are faith-based and are not directly relevant to this discussion.

Thus, personalism necessarily assigns a unique character to human beings, God's special creation, not to humanity, which is an abstraction created by man. Personalist thought therefore sees two types of relationships in society: relationships to other persons and relationships to things.[111]

Human beings are therefore *somebodies* instead of *somethings*, and we relate to one another by the interplay of rights and duties. A right is the power to do or not do some act or acts in relation to other persons, while a duty is the obligation to do or not do some act or acts in relation to other persons.[112]

Relations to things are not the same as they are to persons. Things have no rights, but persons have rights to and over things that define their relationships to other persons with

---

109   Wojtyła, "The Problem of the Theory of Morality," *Person and Community*, 146.
110   See Canon 2.1 of the First Vatican Council, the first article in the Oath Against Modernism, and § 2 of *Humani Generis*. N.B. This does not mean that God's existence has been proved by reason, only that it can be.
111   Cf. Wesley Hohfeld, *Fundamental Legal Conceptions* (1919).
112   Wojtyła, "Thomistic Personalism," *Person and Community*, 165.

respect to things.[113] Things, even artificial persons such as corporations and governments, are only objects. Objects can only act (in the philosophical sense) through human agents, and not on their own behalf.

Human Dignity

Thomist personalism divides reality into persons (which have dignity) and non-persons (which do not have dignity). Relations with persons therefore require a different ethical paradigm, an entirely different set of rules, than that which governs non-persons. Primarily, this means that persons are entitled to justice, defined as a rendering to each what each is due.[114]

Personalism accounts for the transcendent character of human actions and dignity as they relate to persons as both subject and object of actions—that is, as that which acts and that which is acted upon. This vests each human being in his capacity as either subject or object with an absolute character as a human person.[115]

Each human being is therefore not only required to act as a person (duty) but also entitled to be treated as such

---

[113]   A thing can be treated as a person, as with the legal fiction called a corporation. Conversely, a person can be treated as a thing called a slave. Aristotle described a slave as an animate tool without the capacity to acquire and develop virtue. *Politics*, 1253b; 1260b, 1-2. For the purposes of this discussion, we take as a given that chattel slavery is incompatible with personalist thought.

[114]   Wojtyła, "On the Dignity of the Human Person," *Person and Community*, 177–80.

[115]   Wojtyła, "The Will in the Analysis of the Ethical Act," *Person and Community*, 19–21; Wojtyła, "In Search of the Basis of Perfectionism in Ethics," *Person and Community*, 55.

(right). This implies there are moral absolutes that govern our relations with other persons, even in the so-called social sciences, such as economics, where norms have traditionally been considered arbitrary or merely expedient.

Determinable Instead of Determinate Nature

All *things* conform to their common nature with only minor variations. In contrast, human beings as *persons* make choices. As a result of conscious decisions, persons become virtuous or vicious, thereby becoming more fully or less fully human.

Self-Determination

Persons are responsible for their own acts. This is because the human person is a rational animal who when educated properly can distinguish truth and falsehood as well as good and evil. Further, because the human person has a spiritual nature, the motivation to act virtuously or viciously is internal instead of being imposed externally, even if we live in or inhabit "structures of sin."[116]

Political Animals

Human persons are naturally members of society, neither isolated individuals nor indistinguishable members of the collective.[117] We are beings who relate to others in a con-

---

[116]   *Evangelium Vitae*, § 24.
[117]   Wojtyła, "The Problem of the Theory of Morality," *Person and Community*, 146.

sciously structured moral manner as an essential aspect of what and who we are.[118]

Taking into consideration these characteristics of Thomist personalist thought, there is a paradox. Human persons belong to themselves as independent and sovereign beings under the highest sovereignty of God in a way that things cannot. At the same time, individual sovereignty and man's political nature imply that each person has the same dignity and status as all others. This allows one to give himself to all other persons in society, which could not happen if each person did not possess himself as a sovereign being in the first place.

Consequently, while all persons *have* rights absolutely, no one may *exercise* rights without limits, for that would infringe on the sovereignty of everyone else.[119] As Wojtyła made clear, there must be a give-and-take in social life if people are to develop more fully as persons. This would not be possible if human beings were isolated individuals or indistinguishable members of the collective.

Consequently, persons as political animals become most truly themselves by participating in the life of the community in a manner that benefits both themselves as persons and the common good as a thing, and thus other persons within the common good. By producing or creating moral acts, and even marketable goods and services, we realize our true nature as rational beings and persons.[120] As Wojtyła explained, "In

---

[118] Ibid.

[119] Cf. the discussion on the generic right of dominion and the universal destination of all goods in chapter 2, section 8.

[120] Wojtyła, "Thomistic Personalism," *Person and Community, op. cit.,*

creating, we also fill the external material world around us with our own thought and being. There is a certain similarity here between ourselves and God, for the whole of creation is an expression of God's own thought and being."[121]

The Gift of Self

Specifically, in personalist and economic terms (as opposed to mystical and religious), this "gift of self" is conveyed in two ways: one individual and one social. This understanding is inherent in Wojtyła's concept of person and gift, which he was responsible for inserting into *Gaudium et Spes*,[122] and can only be understood within the framework of his Thomistic personalism.

As Wojtyła stressed in all his lectures and essays on the subject, personality is based on the Thomist idea of natural law. This means that every human being is a person, and every person has the natural rights to life, liberty, and private property.

Thomistic personalism relies on persons exercising natural rights in a way that combines reason and action into an integrated, single "act." This integration of intellect and will is a key element in becoming more fully human—that is, virtuous—what Wojtyła called "the acting person."

Such "acting" by human beings—the exercise of rights, especially life, liberty, and private property—is irrefutable evidence of the human person as a moral being. As Wojtyła said in his book *The Acting Person*:

171.

[121]   Ibid., 171–72.

[122]   George Weigel, *Witness to Hope: The Biography of Pope John Paul II, 1920-2005* (New York: Harper Perennial, 2005), 166–69.

The title itself of this book, *The Acting Person*, shows it is not a discourse on action in which the person is presupposed. We have followed a different line of experience and understanding. For us action *reveals* the person, and we look at the person through his action. For it lies in the nature of the correlation inherent in experience, in the very nature of man's acting, that action constitutes the specific moment whereby the person is revealed. Action gives us the best insight into the inherent essence of the person and allows us to understand the person most fully. We experience man as a person, and we are convinced of it because he performs actions.[123]

In other words, we know that someone (or something!) is a person when he exercises rights because persons exercise rights. Anything that denies rights or renders rights ineffective is a denial of personality, and therefore of humanity. Anything that proposes or promotes the further erosion or even outright abolition of natural rights of life, liberty, and private property for a single human being without just cause and due process is anti-personalist and therefore anti-human.

Every person must first belong to himself before he can grow in virtue, thereby giving himself to God, then to others, which can only be by free choice. Each must determine, possess, and govern himself within the context of the natural law.[124]

---

[123]   Wojtyła, *The Acting Person*, 11.
[124]   Wojtyła, "The Personal Structure of Self-Determination," *Person and Community*, 192–93.

Wojtyła's analysis does not leave any room for reinterpreting the gift of self as abolishing private property and establishing an "economy of gift" to replace natural rights and the free market.[125] There is, in fact, no greater denial of someone as a person than to deprive him of the exercise of his natural rights, be it murder that deprives him of life, false accusations that deprive him of liberty, or taking what he created with his own labor or capital on the grounds that it does not really belong to him.[126]

Self-Giving Is Not Socialism

As is clear from *Centesimus Annus*, Wojtyła's gift of self presupposes the traditional understanding of private property without the distortions of the New Things of socialism and ultrasupernaturalism.[127] Given that, understanding the gift of self must consider man's political nature that Wojtyła stressed—that is, our individual and social nature in union, not in conflict.[128]

Individually, then, the gift of self consists of acting virtuously, doing good by and for one's self and specific others directly, but always with a concern for the common good, and thus for others in general. This means at least doing no harm to others or to the common good, and at most helping to create a culture of virtue by example within the common good.

125   Ibid., 187–95.
126   *Laborem Exercens*, §§ 5–10, 14–17, 20–21, 25–26; *Centesimus Annus*, §§ 4–8, 11, 13, 15, 19, 24, 29-33, 36, 41–43, 48.
127   *Centesimus Annus*, §§ 13, 19, 24, 29–31, 34, 39, 41–43, 48.
128   Wojtyła, "Thomistic Personalism," *Person and Community*, 173–74.

Socially, the gift of self consists of organizing with others and acting directly on the institutions of the common good to reform them to create structures of virtue.[129] The goal is to provide an environment suitable for the creation of a culture of virtue.

Thus, the gift of self consists, in the first place, of acts of individual virtue that benefit the person directly. This allows each person to become more fully himself and benefits the common good indirectly, giving to others by setting a good example. In the second place, the gift of self consists of acts of social virtue that benefit the common good directly. Acts of social virtue allow persons as members of organized groups to become more fully members of society. This benefits individuals indirectly by providing a suitable environment for human persons to become individually virtuous.

The Source of Power

Whether carrying out individual or social acts of virtue, the ordinary means of economically empowering persons both as individuals and as members of groups is private property in capital. Recognizing equal access to private property in productive capital as a universal human right is a crucial difference between economic personalism and both capitalism and socialism.[130]

- In **capitalism**, ownership of capital is concentrated in a relatively tiny elite. This limits the ability of persons to relate to others in society as persons of equal dignity.

---

[129] The Center for Social & Economic Justice calls this "social justice tithing."

[130] *Laborem Exercens*, §§ 14–15.

- In **socialism**, the collective owns or controls capital. This abolishes or controls the ability of persons to participate in society.
- In **economic personalism**, widespread capital ownership links every human being to the common good by securing all other rights and their status as free persons.

Thus, economic democracy provides the material foundation of political democracy. By enabling all persons to meet their most basic human needs through their own efforts, widespread capital ownership also provides the opportunity and means for each person to become virtuous, thereby becoming more fully human—the goal of personalism.

Wojtyła emphasized that personalism recognizes a radical distinction between persons and things, the latter category consisting of other beings and non-persons.[131] This is important, because the distinction between persons and things opposes what may be one of the modern age's most serious errors, and one that has inhibited or prevented many people from understanding Catholic social teaching. That is the failure to distinguish between actual human beings as persons and collective humanity or "the People," which is an abstraction—a thing.

At the same time, Wojtyła's Thomistic personalism does not contradict or present an alternative to Catholic social teaching, especially that of Leo XIII and Pius XI. Instead, Wojtyła's thought reaffirms the truth of natural law and

---

131   Wojtyła, "On the Dignity of the Human Person," *Person and Community*, 179.

thus of Catholic social teaching. His presumably innovative implementation of the reforms of Vatican II are a textbook example of the techniques and goals of Catholic Action, the organization that Pius XI reformed to be the primary vehicle to restructure the social order.[132]

Personalism and Social Virtue

Wojtyła's personalism reaffirms Catholic social teaching by making explicit what was implied, and by providing new insights into the profundity of Catholic social thought. This counters superficial and anti-personalist interpretations imposed by adherents of the New Things, especially all forms of socialism.

This is particularly the case regarding the correlation of personalism's gift of self with Pius XI's doctrine of social virtue. What Wojtyła called the gift or giving of one's self is not a slogan, poetic metaphor, platitude, or—as he made clear—a way of justifying any form of socialism or collectivism. Giving of one's self is a key element in Wojtyła's personalism. It is (and can only be) the act of organizing with others to benefit the common good that is the essence of Pius XI's social doctrine.

Using Ferree's analysis, then, we can easily draw the now-obvious correlation between the act of social charity and the gift of self. The act of social charity is loving our

---

[132]   "Catholic Action contributes . . . directly; by promoting and assisting all the organizations and enterprises that set out to apply Christian principles to politico-social life." Luigi Civardi, *A Manual of Catholic Action, A New and Enlarged Edition* (New York: Sheed and Ward, 1943), 33.

institutions as we love ourselves, and our neighbor as ourselves, while recognizing their flaws and seeking their perfection. Just as giving of one's self to others and to the whole
of the common good as an individual is the act of individual
charity, so giving of one's self and to the whole of the common good in an organized manner is the act of social charity.

How the gift of self makes each of us more fully human
is even more obvious once we realize the true character of
social justice. The act of social justice (as opposed to acts
of individual justice) does not consist of others providing
directly for our individual wants and needs.

Neither is social justice a mandate for us to provide
directly for the wants and needs of others. Instead, the act of
social justice consists of organizing and working with others
to make it possible for everyone to provide for his own wants
and needs through his own efforts.

This does not change in the case of dire emergencies, such
as natural disasters when public relief may be essential. As
Leo XIII explained, in extreme cases, the character of providing for others changes from charity to justice,[133] but it
does not change from individual to social virtue.

Public relief, welfare, etc., are directed to the good of individual persons. This is the case even if they number in the
millions and the State or international agency carries out the
action(s). It still only affects the common good indirectly.

Social virtue, however, is *by definition* not directed to individual good, even the good of millions of individuals. It is
directed to the common good—that is, the good, or right

---

[133]   *Rerum Novarum*, § 22.

structuring, of institutions. It only affects individual good indirectly. Thus, social justice does not consist of the direct relief to persons even in an emergency. It comes into the picture as organized efforts to change the system to prevent the emergency from happening again.

Social justice thereby assists each person in becoming more fully human by becoming more virtuous—but only if we have first given of ourselves to others through acts of social charity and of social justice. Pius XI's social doctrine recommends organizing with others for the common good. The goal is to remove barriers that prevent every person from having full access to the institutions of the common good.

The question then becomes how people can be empowered to participate in the common good when it is well-structured— and it is not by having their needs taken care of by others as the Great Reset proposes. This implies also that people must be able to organize with others to carry out acts of social justice to reform the system when it is flawed, not simply imposing changes by government fiat and enforced coercively.

CHAPTER 6

Economic Personalism

6.1. The Binary Perspective

"**P**ower," as Daniel Webster said, "naturally and necessarily follows property." Ironically, while most social
justice advocates demand "power to the people," they rarely
seem to get down to such specifics. As seen in the Great
Reset, demands for power often end up meaning consumption power (income) rather than production power (ownership), or mere political power without the economic power
to back it up.

The Final Debate

Nowhere was this more evident than in the near-legendary
final debate (for want of a better word) between G. K. Chesterton and George Bernard Shaw in November of 1927.
Immoderately moderated by Hilaire Belloc, who clearly
expected nothing substantive to come out of the evening's
festivities, the issue boiled down to which is more important, the power to produce and consume or the power to
consume alone.

Having already made it clear that he referred to the power to produce as well as to consume, Chesterton declared, "Mr. Bernard Shaw proposes to distribute wealth. We propose to distribute power." To this, Shaw responded, "My main activity as an economist of late has been to try to concentrate the attention of my party on the fact not only that they must distribute income, but that there is nothing else to distribute."

As was his habit, Shaw avoided the questions of the source of income and what income is supposed to be used to purchase if nothing is first produced. This may be why at the end of the debate, Belloc (as promised in his opening remarks) sneered and concluded by saying:

> I was told when I accepted this onerous office that I was to sum up. I shall do nothing of the sort. Neither of the two speakers pointed out that one of three things is going to happen. This industrial civilization will break down and therefore end from its monstrous wickedness, folly, ineptitude, leading to a restoration of sane, ordinary human affairs, complicated but based as a whole upon the freedom of the citizens. Or it will break down and lead to nothing but a desert. Or it will lead the mass of men to become contented slaves, with a few rich men controlling them. Take your choice.

The uniqueness of the personalist approach to economics as well as the whole of social life becomes evident when we look at exchanges like that between Chesterton and Shaw. Chesterton was obviously thinking in personalist terms. Whether he realized it, Chesterton's arguments tacitly acknowledged

Adam Smith's first principle of economics and Say's Law of Markets. These are, respectively, that "consumption is the sole end and purpose of all production"[1] and "production equals income, therefore supply generates its own demand, and demand, its own supply."

Shaw, on the other hand—not surprisingly for the chief spokesman of the Fabian Society—had a "one-track mind." Material well-being is the only goal that matters. Shaw's position and his attitude toward Christianity (especially Catholicism) are inherent in the first principle of the New Christianity as articulated by Henri de Saint-Simon, the early prophet of the Democratic Religion of socialism. In Saint-Simon's philosophy, material well-being is not merely the most important thing, it is the only thing, the sole purpose to which everyone must devote his life.

To Shaw, Henry George, Father McGlynn, Monsignor Ryan, R. H. Tawney, and a host of others, then, everyone must accept and *enthusiastically* support (in Monsignor Knox's sense) the New Christianity—that is, socialism. It does not matter what you call it. It can be the New Christianity, the Democratic Religion, Neo-Catholicism, Associationism, Fourierism, Georgism, Fabianism or any of its offshoots such as guild socialism[2] and social credit, the

---

[1]   Adam Smith, *The Wealth of Nations*, IV.8.49.

[2]   Guido "von" List imputed a *quasi*-mystical and socialist significance to the medieval guild to bolster his case against the Catholic Church and traditional forms of civil society, as did Theodore Fritsch, a major figure of pre-World War I anti-Semitism. Fritsch's influence on the organizations that eventually merged into the Nazi Party led to efforts to recruit Catholics to unite in a common struggle against the Jews, and the eventual creation of the myth

New Deal, the Great Society, democratic socialism, democratic, inclusive, or stakeholder capitalism, the gift economy,
localism, or the Great Reset. Make no mistake, anyone who
tries to follow the social doctrine of the Old Christianity, or
the natural law teachings of other faiths and philosophies,
is obviously a hypocrite, a liar, a deluded fool, and a traitor
to Christ—or to Moses, Muhammed, the Buddha, or the
Divine Society of the Religion of Humanity.

Ultimately, Chesterton refused to admit that distributism
is really socialism. He stubbornly insisted that there is more
to life than material well-being, and that even material
well-being is more than simply seeing that everyone has
enough goods and services and thinks the right thoughts.

The Meaning of Life

Chesterton acknowledged that production and consumption must go together; they are two halves of a whole. If
you want to consume, you must first have produced, and if
you produce, it must be for consumption. That is, you must
produce if you want to consume unless you receive charity

---

of Pius XII as "Hitler's Pope." Nicholas Goodrick-Clarke, *The Occult Roots of Nazism* (London, UK: Tauris Parke, 2004), 74–77,
82, 123–24, 126–27. Possibly in an effort to counter List's fanta-
sies, at least in part, Hilaire Belloc went to some pains to explain
the true social and economic significance of the medieval guilds,
although not entirely successfully. See Hilaire Belloc, *The Servile
State* (Indianapolis, Indiana: Liberty Fund, Inc., 1977), 78–79,
80; Hilaire Belloc, *An Essay on the Restoration of Property* (New
York: Sheed and Ward, Inc., 1936), 35, 88, 93, 136–38; Hilaire
Belloc, *The Crisis of Civilization* (Rockford, Illinois: TAN Books
and Publishers, 1992), 135, 185–90.

from others, redistribute the goods of others, or just steal what you need, which is not a rational, common sense way to run an economy.

There are a few difficulties with how Chesterton proposed to bring about a condition of society in which everyone can produce what he consumes and vice versa, such as not actually having a plan or a specific proposal. He had the right idea, however, and enough wisdom to know what he did not know. He maintained that it would be a far more human system if ownership of capital were widespread and if that ownership was sufficient to provide a living income for everyone.

For his part, Shaw knew exactly how to get what he wanted, or he thought he did, which amounts to the same thing. Institute socialism, and the Kingdom of God on Earth would be established, even though Shaw thought God is a fantasy. It was a minor detail, not even worth mentioning, that socialism of every size and shape ignores the demands of human dignity and denigrates the human person by reducing everything to material well-being, as does capitalism, for that matter.

To Chesterton, the meaning and purpose of life is to become more fully human—pursuing the good life, as Aristotle put it, achieving genuine happiness by becoming virtuous. As Chesterton genially remarked to Shaw on one occasion when Shaw accused him of living a life of hoggish, alcohol-swilling, meat-eating self-indulgence (that is, realizing his personal material well-being according to his own lights instead of Shaw's), there is more to life than just this life; "You can hardly expect us to accept your verdict . . . that man was not made to enjoy himself but to read Fabian tracts and listen to University Extension lectures."[3] For Chesterton, life is to be lived by adhering to your own standards, not enduring those imposed by others. Whether by politics, religion, or economics, forcing someone to conform to anything against nature or one's natural rights is wrong.

This binary aspect of human existence is inherent in personalism, as noted earlier. Life only makes sense if there is more to it than material well-being. There is a spiritual, fully human side that has needs and aspirations. Life is not limited to mere existence and meeting one's animal needs, as Shaw assumed with his narrow views.

Contradicting Shaw and other one-track-mind philosophers, personalism is inherently binary, as Wojtyła (John Paul II) explained in his Thomistic personalism. The universe is divided into persons and things. As persons, human beings are both material and spiritual, individuals and members of society, producers and consumers, owners of capital and owners of labor—the list is endless.

We cannot isolate one aspect of human existence as Shaw did and claim it constitutes the whole. That is the essence of heresy, which consists of "picking out" and exaggerating something true to the point where it becomes false. As Hilaire Belloc explained, "Heresy is the dislocation of some complete and self-supporting scheme by the introduction of a novel denial of some essential part therein. . . . Heresy means, then, the warping of a system by 'Exception': by

---

3   Louis Biancolli, ed., *The Book of Great Conversations* (New York: Simon and Schuster, 1948), 505.

'Picking out' one part of the structure and implies that the scheme is marred by taking away one part of it, denying one part of it, and either leaving the void unfilled or filling it with some new affirmation."[4]

Thus, despite efforts to present the Great Reset as some form of applied Christianity (or at least Christian principles), there is no direct or close connection to Catholic social teaching or natural law theory. It is the inevitable outcome of the New Christianity, the New Things of ultrasupernaturalism and socialism.

The point is, whether we are talking processes or people, there are two parts to many key aspects of life. We cannot say to *all* aspects of life, for then we would be making the binary aspect a single factor, which is a contradiction in terms and violates the first principle of reason!

Thus, for almost every action, there is an equal and opposite reaction, physically or socially. People and things tend to react in a manner consistent with which they are acted on. "For what things a man shall sow, those also shall he reap."[5] Water seeks its own level.

If you push someone, he usually pushes back. If you offer something in a transaction, he usually offers something of equal value in exchange. In social life as well as physics, all things not only pursue the good, as Aristotle noted in the *Nicomachean Ethics*, but also tend naturally to a balance. The "law of contradiction" and the "law of identity"—the negative and positive

---

4   Hilaire Belloc, *The Great Heresies* (Rockford, Illinois: TAN Books and Publishers, Inc., 1991), 2.

5   Galatians 6:8. There are sixty-one other passages in the Bible referring to such binary relationships.

statements of the first principle of reason, respectively—are based on this, as are Euclid's postulates of geometry.

Economic Personalism as Binary

As we might, and should, expect, the binary nature of personalism is also inherent in *economic* personalism. Economic personalism is an economic system centered on the dignity and economic empowerment of each person. It recognizes that life, dignity, and liberty require that each person should have the power and independent means to support and sustain one's own life, dignity, and liberty—that is, through one's natural absolute right to be an owner and the limited and socially determined bundle of rights that define how an owner may use what is owned. Economic personalism aims to diffuse economic power structurally by democratizing access to capital ownership to each and every human person.[6]

In other words, economic personalism is that aspect of the Just Third Way concerned with the production, distribution, and consumption of marketable goods and services in a way that respects the dignity of every human person as well as the demands of the common good. It requires that all persons participate as far as possible—if so desired—in all aspects of economic as well as social life to optimize the acquisition and development of virtue and become more fully human.

We qualify what we say by adding "if so desired" because no one should be forced to become more fully human or

---

6   Michael D. Greaney and Dawn K. Brohawn, *Economic Personalism: Property, Power and Justice for Every Person* (Arlington, Virginia: Justice University Press, 2020), iv.

virtuous if he does not want to be. If a free adult refuses to do more than the bare minimum necessary to survive and meet his material needs and refrains from harming others, no one else has anything to say about it.

Participation and Balance

Anyone can be prohibited or prevented from harming others or the common good. Why someone does as he ought, however, should be a matter of complete indifference to others. As Alexis de Tocqueville noted with respect to the true understanding of the separation of Church and State:

> The sects which exist in the United States are innumerable. They all differ in respect to the worship which is due from man to his Creator, but they all agree in respect to the duties which are due from man to man. Each sect adores the Deity in its own peculiar manner, but all the sects preach the same moral law in the name of God. If it be of the highest importance to man, as an individual, that his religion should be true, the case of society is not the same. Society has no future life to hope for or to fear; and provided the citizens profess a religion, the peculiar tenets of that religion are of very little importance to its interests. Moreover, almost all the sects of the United States are comprised within the great unity of Christianity, and Christian morality is everywhere the same.[7]

---

[7]   Alexis de Tocqueville, *Democracy in America*, I.xvii.

Updating what we think is de Tocqueville's meaning, the "moral law" to which he referred is not exclusive to Christianity, nor even to the Abrahamic faiths—that is, Judaism, Christianity, and Islam. As the natural law written in the heart of every human being, it is common to all faiths and philosophies, and is therefore valid for everyone, not just Christians.

The point remains the same. You cannot force anyone to become more fully human according to your lights, however much you may compel him to act within the constraints of the natural law and human positive law. By the same token, however, neither can you prevent anyone from participating in any institution of the common good—including (or especially) the economic common good—for which he is qualified and has the means. You do not permit a four-year-old child to drive a race car even if he knows how, but neither do you prevent a forty-year-old woman from purchasing a house in an exclusive neighborhood if she has the means, or from eating at a lunch counter if she is hungry and can pay.

Every person's participation in production as well as in consumption is not only an economic necessity per Say's Law of Markets but also a moral necessity for the development of human personality—another binary relationship. In binary terms, every natural right not only exists but also has its exercise. The rights *to* life, liberty, and private property are, in fact, meaningless without the rights *of* life, liberty, and private property. Similarly, the principles of *personalism* must be applied in *economic personalism*; both are necessarily two sides of the same equation.

Again, the binary aspect of personalism is inherent in Smith's first principle of economics as well as in Say's Law of Markets. In philosophy, strict, that is, commutative justice, the most fundamental type of justice, takes this into account and provides the basis for all other forms of justice.

Even in the mundane world of business, the "accounting equation"—Assets = Liabilities + Owners Equity—describes a binary relationship for every business enterprise. On the left side of the equation, you have what is owned (assets), and on the right side, you have who owns it (creditors and stockholders). This implies and thereby reaffirms the common sense, validity, and applicability of private property as a natural right.

We can therefore state as a fundamental principle of economic personalism that every human being is a person and, as such, should be both a producer or creator and a consumer.[8] While the right to consume is obvious, as a producer, each person should have access to the means of employing both labor and capital to be productive.

Every person should therefore be both an owner of labor and an owner of capital. By proposing to redistribute what some produce for the benefit of others who do not produce as a solution instead of as a temporary expedient, the Great Reset and similar proposals would throw the economic system further out of balance and offend against essential human dignity at the same time and by the same operation.

---

[8]   Karol Wojtyła, "Thomistic Personalism," *Person and Community: Selected Essays* (New York: Peter Lang, 2008), 171–72.

6.2. The Just Third Way

In contrast to the Great Reset, the holistic paradigm we call the Just Third Way is binary in character. By "binary," we mean the "interactive, interdependent, and balanced"—not exclusive or oppositional—"relationship between two essential elements such as labor and capital, people and things, supply and demand, production and consumption, etc."

With the goal of making it possible for every person to produce as well as to consume, the Just Third Way in the economic realm is a free market system that economically empowers all individuals and families. This is accomplished through the democratization of money and credit for new production and as the means for creating universal access to direct ownership of income-producing capital.

Is There a "Third Way"?

Some people might believe that the "third way" means no more than Madison Avenue's "new and improved" slogan so beloved of advertisers, politicians, and proponents of Great Resets. Admittedly, quite a few systems have been labeled third ways. Without exception, however, these have turned out to be variations on capitalism or socialism that either tend to Belloc's Servile State or differ from it only in name and unimportant details.

Clearly, third ways occur if people accept the same assumptions and distance themselves from capitalism or socialism, opening an entirely new range of possibilities. Nevertheless, convincing socialists, capitalists, and ultrasupernaturalists to question their basic assumptions is difficult. They tend to

turn absolutist when it comes to giving the binary character of personalism fair consideration. For them, something
tends to be either one thing or another, not both. From a
personalist viewpoint, this leads to the following errors:

- Production is due exclusively to labor; capital at best
  only enhances labor or (as Keynes asserted) merely
  provides the environment within which labor
  becomes productive. Workers do not own; owners
  do not work.
- Wages and welfare are the only legitimate forms of
  income.
- Only past reductions in consumption, never future
  increases in production, can be used to finance new
  capital formation and widespread ownership.
- Any arrangement other than capitalism, socialism,
  or the Servile State is impossible.

Thus, when Leo XIII proposed an alternative that was neither capitalist nor socialist but personalist, and Chesterton
and Belloc attempted to apply it, at least in theory, it fell
on deaf ears. Neither was Fulton Sheen any more successful
when he emphasized the importance of widespread ownership to Catholic social teaching:

> Presently, we are concerned with property in relation
> to freedom. Because the ownership of external things
> is the sign of freedom, the Church has made the wide
> distribution of private property the cornerstone of her
> social program. There are three possible solutions of
> the problem of property. One is to put all the eggs into

a few baskets, which is Capitalism; the other is to make an omelet out of them so that nobody owns, which is Communism; the other is to distribute the eggs in as many baskets as possible, which is the solution of the Catholic Church. Or to characterize them differently: selfish possession (Capitalism); personal dispossession with collective selfishness (Communism); diffused possession (Catholicism).[9]

We would say socialism instead of communism, and personalism instead of Catholicism, but that is mere semantics. It does not change Sheen's meaning—that widespread private property in capital is essential to a just society.

This was precisely what Leo XIII said in *Rerum Novarum* immediately after declaring that "as many as possible of the people [should be induced to] become owners."[10] Reiterating that "the right to possess private property is derived from nature, not from man,"[11] the pope listed three primary benefits of widespread capital ownership:

- Ownership will become more equitably divided, bringing together people now separated by disparities in wealth.[12]
- Because people pay more attention to what they own, production will increase, providing abundance for all.[13]

---

9   Fulton J. Sheen, *Freedom Under God* (Arlington, Virginia: Economic Justice Media, 2013), 33.
10 *Rerum Novarum*, § 46.
11 Ibid., § 47.
12 Ibid.
13 Ibid.

- People will no longer be forced to leave their own countries to seek a better life.[14]

Something Missing

There was still something missing, however. All these initiatives and others besides failed to address adequately the problem of financing widespread capital ownership. Take, for example, Abraham Lincoln's 1862 Homestead Act, and the efforts of Judge Peter Stenger Grosscup in the early twentieth century.

Tens of thousands of people took advantage of the Homestead Act. By its terms, anyone who was a US citizen or had the intention of becoming one and was over the age of twenty-one (and paid the six dollar filing fee) could claim 160 acres of land, build a nine by twelve structure, and develop the land for five years and then be granted title.

Although such programs and proposals as the New Deal, China's Belt and Road program, and, of course, the Great Reset have been described by supporters as the greatest economic initiative(s) in history, they all relied or will rely on taxation, massive government debt, or other forms of redistribution for funding. That, however, was precisely what Leo XIII warned against: "[The benefits of ownership] can be reckoned on only provided that a man's means be not drained and exhausted by excessive taxation. The right to possess private property is derived from nature, not from man; and the State has the right to control its use in the interests of the public good alone, but by no means to absorb

---

[14]   Ibid.

it altogether. The State would therefore be unjust and cruel if under the name of taxation it were to deprive the private owner of more than is fair."[15]

Setting aside the claims of Native Americans, the Homestead Act of 1862 did not rely on taxation or redistribution, at least of citizens or from taxpayers. The redistribution was from Native Americans and others, and often on questionable, if not unjust, grounds.

That, however, is not the point. If you want a program of expanded ownership to succeed—and a personalist liberal democracy to be sustained—you cannot rely on existing accumulations of savings for financing initial acquisition or ongoing operations, nor on a limited asset like land if everyone is to have the opportunity to be an owner.

Unfortunately, those who are generally most in need of a program of expanded capital ownership are usually those least likely to have existing accumulations of savings and the least likely to be able to save. Furthermore, if all the land is already owned by some people, there is nothing left for anyone else.

Lack of adequate financing inhibited the success of the Homestead Act, as it was during a period in which savings were being depleted and the currency deflated to restore the parity of the gold and silver currency with the paper currency. While the rich industrialists and railroads could create money through the commercial banks for capital expansion, small farmers and business operators were limited to the pool of rapidly shrinking existing accumulations of savings.

---

[15]   Ibid.

Homesteaders typically mortgaged their land to finance development and operations. They used "balloon financing," meaning they paid only interest during the period of the loan, with their debt principal due at the end. When the principal came due, they usually refinanced with another balloon mortgage.

In this way, people who ostensibly owned land or a business became de facto tenants-at-will. They could be evicted if they missed an interest payment, as the principal could be "called" (demanded immediately) when that happened.

Only the fact that most banks wanted their money and not the land kept foreclosures to a minimum, at least until the Great Depression and the inability of banks to continue carrying non-performing loans. Many institutions went bankrupt as the bulk of their loans were to people who could no longer make payments and the land or business had become worthless.

Thus, the "slavery of savings" is not merely an inconvenience. It is a disaster, both economically and politically. As Frederick Jackson Turner pointed out in his "frontier thesis," the end of "free land" under the Homestead Act meant the end of the uniquely American form of personalist liberal democracy.[16]

---

[16] Frederick Jackson Turner, "The Significance of the Frontier in American History," *Annual Report of the American Historical Association for the Year 1893* (Washington, DC: Government Printing Office, 1894), 200.

People-izing the Corporation

Judge Grosscup ran up against the same obstacle of past savings. As one of Theodore Roosevelt's "Trust Busters," Grosscup was deeply involved in the progressive movement when progressive meant something other than ultra-radical. He lobbied for reform of the 1890 Sherman Antitrust Act on the grounds that it was grossly inadequate to prevent corporate abuses, and he may have been instrumental in bringing about the Clayton Antitrust Act in 1914.[17]

As a "Lincoln Republican" concerned about ordinary people instead of the robber barons who, in common with today's super-rich, thought they were the only significant factor in the American economy, Grosscup wrote a series of articles in the early twentieth century. Published in American and British magazines, his pieces advocated widespread capital ownership to "people-ize" American industry.[18]

Given his international reputation and the fact that he was a friend of Roosevelt, it would not be astonishing to discover that Grosscup's ideas about expanded ownership influenced Chesterton's development of distributism. As Grosscup said in a lecture he delivered at the University of Nebraska law school, December 12, 1902, "A widespread withdrawal by the people at large from general ownership in the properties

[17]   "Judge Grosscup Talks on Trusts," *The Butte Inter Mountain*, December 13, 1902, 3; "Trouble for the Beef Trust," *Savannah Morning News*, February 21, 1903, 4; "Sherman Act Failure," *Richmond Times Dispatch*, December 27, 1907, 1; "Law of Economics Demands Combinations," *The River Press*, February 23, 1910, 8; "Grosscup Hits Sherman Act," *New York Sun*, June 25, 1911, 10.

[18]   "The Beef Trust Enjoined: Address by Judge Peter S.; Grosscup," *The Outlook*, February 28, 1903.

of the country cannot but be fraught with the gravest dangers. Such withdrawal will diminish if not destroy popular interest in national prosperity, for from those only who have a stake in prosperity can we expect great interests—the real strength of government; for government must be built on the interests as well as the affections of the people governed. An industrial system subject to such indictment is a rising menace to free government itself."[19]

Grosscup's articles were intensively researched. Virtually every aspect of his proposals was well-thought-out and would require only minor changes in corporate law. Primarily, he advocated a national law of corporations to replace the system of incorporation at the state level that still exists today. This avoided tying the proposal to finite land and opened the potentially unlimited frontier of commerce and industry to popular ownership.[20]

Unfortunately, Grosscup made the same mistake as Leo XIII, Chesterton and Belloc, and, later, Pius XI. He assumed that the only source of financing for broad-based capital ownership is past savings.[21]

When the Federal Reserve was finally established in 1914, Grosscup and Theodore Roosevelt might have realized that here was the desperately needed source of financing that could open ownership access of America's vast corporate

---

19   "Says Dangers Follow Growth of the Trusts," *The San Francisco Call*, December 14, 1902, 58.

20   Peter S. Grosscup, "How to Save the Corporation," *McClure's Magazine*, February 1905.

21   Ibid.

wealth without the necessity of past savings and without redistribution or taxation for all Americans.

Certainly, William Jennings Bryan and Carter Glass understood the need for financial reform. Had it not been for their support, it is likely that the Federal Reserve would never have come into being.[22]

Neither Bryan nor Glass, however, made the leap to using the commercial and central banking system to finance capital ownership for every citizen. As for Woodrow Wilson, he was an elitist in the pocket of Wall Street.[23] When he was president of Princeton, he instigated controversies that left "a deep scar on the University that did not heal for many years."[24]

Wilson's positivist philosophy of government was, like Keynes's economics, based on the theories of Walter Bagehot,[25] as revealed in his 1885 doctoral dissertation, *Congressional Government.*[26] He opposed anything that endangered what in a few years Pius XI would call a "despotic economic dictatorship."[27]

[22]   William Jennings Bryan, *The Memoirs of William Jennings Bryan* (Philadelphia, Pennsylvania: The United Publishers of America, 1925), 372; Arthur S. Link, *Woodrow Wilson and the Progressive Era*, 1910-1917 (New York: Harper & Row, Publishers, 1954), 53; Harold G. Moulton, ed., *Principles of Money and Banking: A Series of Selected Materials, with Explanatory Introductions* (Chicago, Illinois: The University of Chicago Press, 1916), II.261.
[23]   Link, *Woodrow Wilson and the Progressive Era*, 43–53.
[24]   Ibid., 9.
[25]   Ibid., 8.
[26]   Woodrow Wilson, *Congressional Government* (Boston, Massachusetts: Houghton, Mifflin and Company, 1885).
[27]   *Quadragesimo Anno.* §§ 105-106.

A fascinating sidebar to history is that Grosscup, although a Protestant, was acquainted with Archbishop John Ireland, America's acknowledged expert on *Rerum Novarum*, and even served with Ireland on a committee investigating trusts and corporations in 1907.[28] Grosscup frequently spoke before Catholic groups and thereby received a great deal of criticism from Nativists.[29]

Commemorating President Lincoln's birthday in 1907, Grosscup delivered one of his best talks to a Chicago Knights of Columbus Council.[30] He stressed the importance of the Great Emancipator for people of all faiths and philosophies. In particular, His Honor cited Lincoln's stand on the natural rights of life, liberty, and private property, contrasted with the attacks on the natural law in France at the time.[31]

A Systematic Diffusion of Power

What Lincoln did, and what Leo XIII, Grosscup, Chesterton and Belloc, Sheen, and others proposed, does not invalidate the idea of a Just Third Way. On the contrary, it clearly demonstrates not only the enormous potential for

---

[28] New York National Civic Federation, *Proceedings on the National Conference on Trusts and Combinations Under the Auspices of the National Civic Federation*, October 22-25, 1907 (New York: The McConnell Printing Company, 1908), 11, 221–31.

[29] "Editorial Potpouri," *Blue Grass Blade*, October 24, 1909, 11.

[30] "Address of the Hon. Peter S. Grosscup, Judge of the U.S. Circuit Court of Appeals, on 'Abraham Lincoln'," Celebration of Abraham Lincoln's Birthday and Second Anniversary of General James Shields Council No. 967 Knights of Columbus, February 12, 1907 (event program).

[31] "Federal Judge Speaks," *The Irish Standard*, February 23, 1907, 1.

improving today's broken system but also the great danger of
omitting, ignoring, or misconstruing the essential element
of where money comes from and who gets it. That is why
the Just Third Way of economic personalism is not merely a
development and fulfillment of what popes and others have
proposed, it is—so far as we know—the only morally sound
and financially feasible alternative to the Great Reset and
similar initiatives.

Based on the dignity of each person as a special creation of
God, the Just Third Way at the level of economic justice sup-
plies the omission that hampered the success of other personalist approaches. It combines the economic justice principles
discerned by Louis Kelso and Mortimer Adler in *The Capitalist Manifesto* and the financial techniques described in
The New Capitalists, with Pius XI's breakthrough in moral
philosophy described primarily in *Quadragesimo Anno* and
Divini Redemptoris[32] and Wojtyła's personalism.

As a free market system economically empowering every
human person within a realistic personalist framework, the
personalist Just Third Way offers a logical alternative to both
individualistic capitalism and collectivistic socialism. It does
this by promoting the reform of institutions of the common
good to encourage individual virtue.

This is accomplished by means of the systematic diffusion
of power and extension of equal capital ownership opportunities to every person, together with the institutional means
of acquiring and possessing private property in capital.

---

32   See William J. Ferree, *The Act of Social Justice* (Washington, DC:
        Catholic University of America Press, 1942), William J. Ferree,
        Introduction to Social Justice (New York: Paulist Press, 1948).

Promoting individual virtue by creating systems, structures, and processes that encourage habits of doing good, the Just Third Way conforms to the demands of personalism and respect for human dignity.

In contrast, the Great Reset and similar proposals assume that the goal of material well-being justifies any means used to achieve it and would impose desired results by fiat. Thus, while the Just Third Way encompasses more than economic personalism per se, it is fully compatible with respect for the dignity God gave every human person that is the essence of Thomist personalism as developed by Karol Wojtyła.

6.3. Binary Economics

One of the many paradoxes involved in the Great Reset has to do with human nature and the natural law. Despite centuries of failure, adherents insist that all we need to do is change human nature to remove private property as a natural right, try harder, and commit sufficient resources to the effort. Yet doing the exact things repeatedly and expecting different results is the definition of insanity.

At the same time, opponents of private property insist that despite millennia of alleged success, most (if not all) people are incapable of being owners and expanded ownership cannot work. They proclaim that advocates such as William Cobbett, Abraham Lincoln, Pope Leo XIII, Pope Pius XI, G. K. Chesterton, and Fulton Sheen did not really mean what they said. Instead, opponents of private property argue that human nature and Catholic social teaching has changed. They assert that the latter is no longer true and private property is no longer a natural right.

One omission alone has allowed these contradictions by the opponents of private property to stand. That is the lack of a feasible and just means by which non-owners can become owners without redistribution. That is why the work of Louis Kelso and Mortimer Adler is an important addition to the theory of personalism and a key element in its integration in economic personalism.

The Expanded Ownership Revolution

In 1958, Kelso and Adler published *The Capitalist Manifesto*. They followed this up in 1961 with *The New Capitalists*, the subtitle of which says far more than the main title: "A Proposal to Free Economic Growth From the Slavery of Savings."

Ironically, what Kelso and Adler advocated was not really capitalism, as that describes a system in which capital ownership is concentrated in the hands of a relatively tiny private sector elite. The titles were clever, though, and sound politics and marketing given that communism was still perceived as a serious threat.[33]

---

33   Kelso and Adler explain that they used the term "capitalist" to describe a "mature industrial economy . . . which produces the preponderant portion of its goods and services by capital instruments, and which is well enough equipped with such capital instruments to produce and enjoy a high standard of living." Louis O. Kelso and Mortimer J. Adler, *The Capitalist Manifesto* (New York: Random House, 1958), 11–12.

Although the Employee Stock Ownership Plan (ESOP) is what Kelso is most noted for, his work—like the ESOP itself—is more than it first appears, and is much more significant, even profound. Considered by many practitioners to be an elaborate employee benefit and tax gimmick, the ESOP is an application of principles of justice and finance Kelso developed in response to what he saw as a serious problem in today's technologically advanced economies. That is, how are people supposed to participate fully in economic life without access to the means to do so?

As a young man during the Great Depression of the 1930s, Kelso observed a paradox. In a country that had the demonstrated capacity to produce in superabundance, people were out of work, even starving. Every freight train seemed to carry a small army of men who had left home and family in desperate attempts to seek employment. He asked himself, "Why is this happening?"[34]

There are, after all, two factors of production: the human factor, labor, and the non-human factor, capital. That is, in personalist terms, there are persons and things. Both produce marketable goods and services, and production means the same whether by labor or by capital.

Further, consistent with the binary nature of personalism—and Say's Law of Markets—if you want to consume, you must produce. If you do not produce directly for your own needs, you must produce something to trade to someone else for what he produces that you want to consume.

---

[34]   Louis O. Kelso, "Labor's Untapped Wealth," The Kelso Institute, accessed May 26, 2021, http://kelsoinstitute.org/louiskelso/kelso -paradigm/lectures/.

The medium through which these exchanges are made, and the measurement thereof, is called "money."

Also consistent with Say's Law, as Kelso realized, if your labor is not sufficiently productive, you must acquire capital, and if your capital is not sufficiently productive, you use labor—or, better, more advanced capital! This, in essence, was what the popes had been saying.

At some point, it also occurred to Kelso to ask: If advancing technology makes such superabundance possible, why is it essential for people to have employers to pay them wages for labor that is not necessary for production? This led him finally to the key question: What keeps people from owning the technology that is carrying out the bulk of production and deriving their income from ownership of capital instead of being limited to wages and welfare? Not surprisingly, this is the same question addressed by the socialists and ultrasupernaturalists, as well as Leo XIII, Chesterton and Belloc, and others.

Abolishing Private Property

As we have seen, the socialist solution is to abolish private property. This does not necessarily mean that individuals are not permitted to have what some socialists insist to this day is "private property"—that is, title to and use of things. At times, this is even recognized as a right, but not an inalienable right by nature, at least as traditionally meant in the Aristotelian-Thomist understanding of natural law, and thus in personalism.

Socialism may *allow* private ownership, *but that is precisely the problem*. Ownership is not recognized as a right that every single human being has by nature itself, something God made an integral part of what it means to be a human person. Instead, it may be revoked at any time if the State, community, or collective so decides.

Capitalism is not much better. Rather than forbid private ownership of capital per se, capitalism restricts it to a private sector elite. Admittedly, this does have the advantage that an irredeemably "greedy and rapacious"[35] capitalist will often do what is good for other people by following his own personal advantage, just as Adam Smith pointed out in his "invisible hand" argument. At the same time, the completely altruistic socialist can destroy an economy trying to do what is good for others.

Why? Because the greedy capitalist is working with the system in a manner consistent with human nature, although his motives are completely selfish. Meanwhile, the generous socialist is going against the system and human nature, although his motives are charitable, even excessively or enthusiastically so.

This does not mean that greed is thereby transformed into a virtue, or charity into a substitute for justice or social justice, even when relabeled "social justice." What this demonstrates is the strength of institutions—even badly flawed or misused institutions—in influencing human behavior for good or ill.

---

[35]   Adam Smith, *The Theory of Moral Sentiments* (1759), IV.I.10; *The Wealth of Nations* (1776), IV.II.9. The illusion of injustice in Smith's theory is due to the fact that Smith did not allow for the increasing productiveness of capital, and thus the shift of income from production from owners of labor to owners of capital.

Money and Credit, the Key
to Widespread Ownership

Although Kelso was not familiar with Ferree's analysis of Pius XI's social doctrine, as an attorney and an economist, he understood the role of institutions, including the impact of laws on citizens. He was thereby able to identify the "problem behind the problem" that has led to alienating human persons from capital ownership and thus full participation in the common good: access to money and credit.

In this way—probably without intending to—Kelso removed the contradiction inherent in prevailing interpretations of Catholic social doctrine. Previously, both capitalists and socialists had been able to claim with a degree of credibility that Leo XIII and subsequent popes, as well as commentators such as Heinrich Pesch and Chesterton and Belloc, could not really have meant what they said about the importance, even sacredness, of private property for everyone, if only because the method suggested by the popes was not financially feasible.

That being the case, "of course" the demand for widespread capital ownership must mean socialist redistribution, capitalist prudential matter, or both. The most common interpretation in Catholic circles, therefore, was that it would be noble if current owners could be induced to sell or give away their property, but it is highly unlikely that they will do so. They may thereby be forced to redistribute, but only if it does not harm them too much. That this interpretation changed the basis of the natural law from reason to faith was conveniently ignored.

With his background as a corporate finance lawyer, Kelso changed all that. What he did, in hindsight, seems incredibly obvious. First, in common with the popes, he recognized that private property is essential to a just and well-ordered society. Kelso was quite clear that he did not mean ownership restricted to an elite few in the private sector or as an expedient permitted by the State or community that could be revoked at any time. Instead, his conclusion agreed with that of the early nineteenth-century English "radical" politician William Cobbett, whom Chesterton regarded as "the Apostle of Distributism": "Freedom is not an empty sound; it is not an abstract idea; it is not a thing that nobody can feel. It means,—and it means nothing else,—the full and quiet enjoyment of your own property. If you have not this, if this be not well secured to you, you may call yourself what you will, but you are a slave."[36]

In *The Capitalist Manifesto*, Kelso and Adler agreed with Aristotle's conclusion that a free person who owned nothing but his labor was, in effect, a "masterless slave." As such, although nominally an equal citizen and participant in the *pólis*, the organized community, he had less status than an actual slave who was respected as his owner's possession.

Kelso therefore addressed the problem of how to make it possible for everyone to own capital. In this way, everyone would have not merely nominal participation in society but actual and potentially full participation in the common good.

---

[36]   William Cobbett, *A History of the Protestant Reformation in England and Ireland* (1827), § 456.

First, Kelso made it clear that he did not refer to existing capital already owned by others. He referred primarily to the new, additional capital that, since it does not yet exist, is not yet owned by anyone. Ownership of new capital depends on who finances it and in what way it is financed.

Expecting the average wage worker to cut consumption and accumulate sufficient savings out of what was increasingly an inadequate income is clearly unrealistic. Kelso therefore proposed that everyone be empowered to use the same financing techniques that the big corporations and the rich have been using for centuries.

The "Magic" of Future Savings

Instead of saving by reducing consumption in the past or increasing wages in the present, it is possible—indeed, preferable—to save by increasing production in the future. An individual or business enterprise can start from a position of having no savings. By purchasing capital on credit, however, and promising to pay for the capital out of profits generated by the capital in the future, anyone can finance capital acquisition. That is, anyone who is "creditworthy," meaning his word is good and the capital he finances in this way is expected to be profitable.

The difficulty in financing by means of such "future savings" is that not everyone is either creditworthy or known throughout the community as such. Commercial and central banking, however, solved that problem centuries ago, but before Kelso came along, as a rule, only the rich and exceptional individuals were able to take advantage of classic banking techniques.

Contrary to popular belief, commercial and central banks do not simply create money out of nothing—or at least are not supposed to. When used as intended, commercial banks (also called "mercantile banks") only create money when a borrower brings a project to them for financing. If a borrower is creditworthy and the project is expected to generate a profit within a reasonable period, the bank temporarily "buys" the project by issuing a promissory note. The bank then creates new money backed by the promissory note—which is backed by the borrower's creditworthiness—and the borrower uses the money to finance the project.

If there is a central bank, the commercial bank can "sell" the project to the central bank. In that case, instead of the commercial bank creating money, the central bank creates money, hands it over to the commercial bank, and the commercial bank hands it over to the borrower. The borrower owes the commercial bank, and the commercial bank owes the central bank.

When the project makes a profit, the borrower repays the commercial bank plus a fee for the service—thereby buying back the project—and the bank cancels the money. If the commercial bank sells the loan to the central bank, then the borrower's loan payment passes through the commercial bank and goes to the central bank, which then sells back the project and cancels the money. In this way, there is always enough money to finance new capital to increase production in the future without having to cut consumption in the past.

There was, however, another problem. Paradoxically, the reason only the rich as a rule can use future savings is they have a virtual monopoly on past savings. That is, they have collateral the bank can seize if the capital project fails and the borrower defaults on the loan.

As Kelso reasoned, banks demand collateral for loans as a form of insurance and charge a premium for making loans with a higher risk of default. Why not take that risk premium by means of which banks self-insure and use it as the premium for an insurance policy that will then serve as collateral?

In this way, anyone can be creditworthy, because the risk shifts from the borrower to the project itself. It would no longer matter if someone was the wrong sex, age, race, religion, or anything else. Everything except the financial feasibility of the project would become a matter of complete indifference to the bank, and everyone, at least potentially, could become a capital owner.

Solidarism and the Just Third Way

Consistent with Catholic social teaching, Kelso's theories were integrated into the solidarity movement in Central and South America. In the late 1950s, Kelso corresponded with Señor Alberto Martén Chavarría, a student of the teachings of Heinrich Pesch and founder of *Solidarismo Costarricense*, the solidarity movement of Costa Rica.

"Don Alberto," named a national hero ("Benemérito de la Patria"[37]—a "Worthy of the People") by the Costa Rican

---

[37]   "Alberto Martén Chavarría," https://es.wikipedia.org/wiki/Al berto_Mart%C3%A9n_Chavarr%C3%ADa, accessed May 24,

legislature in 2009, realized that Kelso's theories had the potential to make Catholic social teaching a practical reality for everyone. He therefore incorporated many elements of Kelso's thought into his programs.

Rejecting recent interpretations of Pesch's work that have turned the German Jesuit into a socialist and an ultrasupernaturalist, Martén correlated Pesch's theories with those of Kelso, putting special emphasis on the principles of economic justice as articulated by Kelso and Adler.[38] These are 1) Participation,[39] 2) Distribution,[40] and 3) Limitation[41] (now "Social Justice"), and the "Four Pillars of an Economically Just Market Economy":

- **A limited economic role for the State**[42]
- **Free and open markets** within a strict juridical order as the best means of determining just wages, just prices, and just profits[43]
- **Restoration of the rights of private property**, especially in corporate equity and other forms of

---

[38] 2021; also Editorial Costa Rica, https://www.editorialcostarica.com/escritores.cfm?detalle=1184, accessed May 24, 2021.
Kelso and Adler, *The Capitalist Manifesto*, 52–86.
[39] Unión Soldiarista Costarricense (USC), *Solidarismo: A Tool for Democracy, Justice and Peace* (San Jose, Costa Rica: Unión Solidarista Costarricense, 1985), 3.
[40] Ibid.
[41] Ibid., 1.
[42] This is largely through meeting workers' needs through private sector initiatives instead of State action, and emphasizing popular support for democracy by integrating democratic procedures in corporate governance. USC, *Solidarismo*, 5.
[43] Ibid., 2.

business organization[44]
- **Widespread direct ownership of capital**[45]

As a result, *Solidarismo Costarricense* became a model for the Central American solidarity movement years before its success in Poland helped bring down the Soviet Union. Although little known outside of Central America, Martén's accomplishments and leadership were an integral, if largely unacknowledged, part of the efforts of President Ronald Reagan and Pope John Paul II to counter the threat of Marxism in Central and South America and the Caribbean Basin.

Later, there was an acknowledgment of the Just Third Way by *Solidarność*, the Polish solidarity union, in the 1980s. The new economic paradigm had the potential to fulfill the dream of Polish workers for real self-government and a just economic system that is neither capitalism nor socialism.

That, at least, is the opinion of Tomasz Pompowski. Tom served as one of the translators for Lech Wałęsa and Anna Walentynowicz ("Anny *Solidarność*") and later as a Vatican journalist during the pontificate of John Paul II.[46]

Given these circumstances, it may be time to take another look at authentic solidarism as an alternative to the Great Reset and similar proposals. This is especially the case in the lesser-developed countries or those suffering from the latest wave of neo-colonialism.

---

[44]   Ibid., 1.
[45]   Ibid., 1, 2.
[46]   Tom Pompowski, "30 Years of Nobel Peace Prize to *Solidarność* and Wałęsa Whose Dream Has Yet to Be Fulfilled," *The Epoch Times*, October 7, 2013.

6.4. The Principles of Economic Justice

Klaus Schwab and his supporters insist that the Great Reset is essential because nothing else can or will work. As we have seen in the previous section, however, that claim is simply not true. The techniques Louis Kelso applied to solving the problem of financing for expanded ownership have been proven to work. Are Kelso's techniques, however, consistent with the principles of natural law found in Catholic social doctrine and that of other faiths and philosophies?

Kelso, Adler, and Natural Law

Applying principles and methods of modern corporate finance to the problem of how to fund a program was Kelso's most obvious contribution to developing a more just social order. It is not, however, his most important contribution.

Many people today assume that Kelso first invented the Employee Stock Ownership Plan (ESOP) and then came up with a justification for it. The exact opposite is the case. Kelso first developed his principles of economic justice and then invented a way to apply them.

That is why the three principles of economic justice are an essential part of economic personalism and its correlation to natural law and thus to Catholic social doctrine. While these principles are implicit in all applications of the natural law theory to all faiths and philosophies, it is important to present them explicitly to ensure that the interconnection and correlation between them and the more generally expressed principles of the Church's social doctrine are evident.

Kelso and Adler articulated these principles in chapter 5 of *The Capitalist Manifesto*. It takes nothing away from Kelso's breakthrough to assume that Adler was primarily responsible for systematizing the principles and expressing them in a manner consistent with Aristotelian-Thomism. As Adler himself admitted, the ideas themselves were Kelso's; Adler "only" applied his vast expertise in philosophy to ensure their logical presentation.[47]

Later, the core group of the interfaith Center for Economic and Social Justice (CESJ), in Arlington, Virginia, refined Kelso's principles. They then integrated the principles into the social doctrine of Pius XI as analyzed by Father William Ferree, one of CESJ's co-founders.

Like the three legs of a tripod, the three principles of economic justice operate together, providing the framework for a just and stable economic order. If even one principle is missing or violated, then the structure collapses. As further developed by CESJ, the three essential principles of economic justice are:

- participative justice,
- distributive justice,
- and social justice.

All these principles are, as noted, equally important. Their immediacy and the order in which one logically follows the other, however, makes it more effective to explain them in the order given.

---

[47]   Kelso and Adler, *The Capitalist Manifesto*, ix.

Participative Justice

As "the input principle," participative justice defines how one contributes to the economic process in order to make a living. Among other requirements, participative justice mandates equal opportunity in gaining access to the means to acquire and possess private property (control over and enjoyment of the income from productive assets) as well as equality of opportunity to engage in productive work.

Participative justice does not guarantee equal results. It does, however, require that every person be guaranteed by society's institutions the equal human right to make a productive contribution to the economy, both through one's labor (as a worker) and through one's productive capital (as an owner). This principle rejects monopolies, special privileges, and other social barriers to economic self-reliance and personal freedom.

Participative justice correlates perfectly with, and is an application of, what Aquinas called "the analogy of being." As seen earlier, this means that every single human being is as human as all other human beings, and all human beings are human in the same way. This is an application of "the law of (non) contradiction," which is the first principle of reason on which both Aristotle and Aquinas built their entire philosophy.

That is why, for example, in the First Vatican Council, the Catholic Church defined the "Primacy of the Intellect" as infallibly true. If an article of faith is understood in a way that contradicts something that has been proven true by reason, there is a flaw either in faith or reason and it must be resolved, not dismissed or ignored.

All human beings therefore have the same access to the institutions of the common good, especially regarding the natural rights of life, liberty, and private property, or there is a de facto acceptance of the contradiction that not all human beings have the same rights in the same way. This does not mean, however, that someone who abuses his rights, violates those of others, or is demonstrably incapable of exercising his rights to the fullest manner as defined in a particular society should be permitted to do so. That would be individually unjust to others who are harmed, and socially unjust insofar as it harmed institutions.

It should be obvious why participative justice is listed first among the principles of economic justice. Like the natural rights of life, liberty, and private property where neither liberty nor private property is any use until and unless somebody is actually alive, neither distributive justice nor social justice has effective meaning until and unless someone is able to participate in what Aristotle called "the *politikos bios*"—the life of the citizen in the State.

According to Aristotle, to have a social identity, someone must own capital. He devoted the whole first part of the *Politics* to the importance of capital ownership to a free (at least for non-slaves) community. That is why the philosopher regarded nominally free men without capital ownership as "masterless slaves." They had the normally free status but not the effective status nor the means to take an active part in the life of the community.

Distributive Justice

Of the three principles of economic justice, distributive justice has suffered the most from the advent of the New Things. No one can really argue about participative justice, except perhaps to ask why, prior to Kelso and Adler, there has never been an explicit term given for something so obvious. As for social justice, the dispute about its true meaning has continued from the first appearance of the term in or about the 1830s.[48]

In binary economics, "the most classical form"[49] of distributive justice, the out-take principle, is based on the exchange or market value of one's economic contributions. This is the principle that all people have a right to receive a proportionate, market-determined share of the value of the marketable goods and services they produce with their labor contributions, their capital contributions, or both. This understanding of distributive justice respects human dignity by making every producer's and consumer's economic vote count.

Where strict or commutative justice is the justice of equality, distributive justice is the justice of proportionality. Anyone, for example, who contributes 10 percent of the value to some

---

[48]   "Social justice" was occasionally used prior to the 1840s but was of ambiguous import. It meant many things, such as common civility—that is, fair and impartial treatment of others outside of the legal system (*Constantine Republican*, February 21, 1838, 2), absorption into the collective in conformity with Fourier's blueprint for the "Divine Social Order" (A. Brisbane, "Association: Or, Plan for a Re-organization of Society," *New York Tribune*, September 30, 1842, 1), and even the administration of the legal system and the enforcement of the law in society, just or unjust ("Abolition of the Gallows," *New York Tribune*, February 7, 1844, 1).

[49]   *Compendium of the Social Doctrine of the Church*, § 201.

endeavor receives 10 percent of the gain or suffers 10 percent of the loss.[50] That is not, however, how many people today understand the term, and much of the confusion over distributive justice can be traced to the efforts of Msgr. John A. Ryan.

In 1916, Ryan published *Distributive Justice*, his magnum opus.[51] Where *A Living Wage*, Ryan's doctoral thesis, transformed what it means for something to be true by changing the basis of the natural law from reason to faith, *Distributive Justice* applied Ryan's principle of mutable truth to the virtue of justice.[52]

In *Distributive Justice*, Ryan ignored commutative justice, the justice that governs equality of exchange (the law of contracts)—that is, "equality of quantity."[53] Significantly, all forms of justice presuppose the validity of commutative justice;[54] "Without commutative justice, no other form of justice is possible."[55]

For over a century, commentators have assumed Ryan began with the classic Aristotelian-Thomist understanding of distributive justice and developed it in light of the social justice teachings of *Rerum Novarum*. Authorities have struggled in vain to reconcile the contradictions implicit in this assumption.

---

[50]   Aristotle, *Nicomachean Ethics*, 1130b30; Aquinas, *Commentary on the Nicomachean Ethics*, §§ 971–77.

[51]   John A. Ryan, *Distributive Justice* (New York: The Macmillan Company, 1916).

[52]   Ryan was not alone in this. E. F. Schumacher's popular *A Guide for the Perplexed* (1979) posits that truth changes at different levels of consciousness.

[53]   *Summa Theologiae* IIa IIae, q. 61, a. 2.

[54]   *Catechism of the Catholic Church*, § 1807.

[55]   Ibid., § 2411.

In reality, Ryan derived his concept of distributive justice and its equation with social justice not from *Rerum Novarum* but, via Henry George and Ignatius Donnelly, from the utopian and religious socialists of the early nineteenth century, notably the French socialist Charles Fourier as presented by Albert Brisbane. Distributive justice and social justice along with philanthropy[56] were used interchangeably as expressions of the principal doctrine of "the Church of the Future" as conceived by adherents of various "religions of humanity."[57]

Ryan's presumed development of doctrine amounted to rejecting the classical understanding of distributive justice and Monsignor Taparelli's principle of social justice, and replacing both with the meanings used by the utopian and religious socialists. Contradicting traditional Catholic teaching,[58] Ryan's version of social justice/distributive justice was therefore indistinguishable from the socialist understanding of the terms.

Ryan defined both distributive justice and social justice as distributing based on need rather than equality or proportionality of inputs, thereby adding distribution based on need to the traditional understanding of distributive justice.[59] When combined with a general intention for the

---

56   In general, social justice for the socialists referred broadly to all forms of meeting material needs. Philanthropy referred to voluntary redistribution, while distributive justice was the term when it was coercive.

57   Adam Morris, *American Messiahs: False Prophets of a Damned Nation* (New York: W.W. Norton and Company, 2019), 82–83.

58   *Compendium of the Social Doctrine of the Church*, § 201.

59   In section 22 of *Rerum Novarum*, Leo XIII admitted distribution on the basis of need under justice as an expedient in "extreme

common good (classical legal justice) and State control, Ryan claimed that distributive justice became "social justice."

To fund increased demands on State resources, Ryan expanded Henry George's single tax concept from land to all property income. The first part of *Distributive Justice*, however, has a detailed analysis of George's theory of title, ostensibly refuting George's rejection of a legitimate basis for private ownership of land. This has led many people to claim that Ryan repudiated his earlier enthusiasm for George's thought.[60]

Going into George's notions of title, however, was a diversion. Legal title was not an issue for George. Title, as far as he was concerned, is irrelevant. For George, real ownership resides in whoever has the right of disposal and enjoyment of the fruits: the income generated by what is owned. As he explained, "rent being taken by the State in taxes, land, no matter in whose name it stood . . . would be really common property."[61]

Social Justice

Our use of the term "social justice" for the third principle of economic justice requires some explanation. In chapter 5 of *The Capitalist Manifesto*, Kelso and Adler gave the third principle of economic justice as "limitation":

---

cases" under the principle of double effect. This was categorized by default under distributive justice (*Catechism*, § 2411), as such redistribution must be carried out by duly constituted authority.

60　Robert V. Andelson, "Monsignor John A. Ryan's Critique of Henry George," *American Journal of Economics and Sociology* 33, no. 3 (1974): 273–86.

61　Henry George, *Progress and Poverty* (New York: Robert Schalkenbach Foundation, 1992), 406.

3. THE PRINCIPLE OF LIMITATION

Since everyone has a right to property in the means of production sufficient for earning a living, no one has a right to so extensive an ownership of the means of production that it excludes others from the opportunity to participate in production to an extent capable of earning for themselves a viable income; and, consequently, the ownership of productive property by an individual or household must not be allowed to increase to the point where it can injure others by excluding them from the opportunity to earn a viable income.[62]

To those who developed the Just Third Way, however, it seemed that the principle of limitation (i.e., the anti-monopoly principle) was both too limited and limiting. It did not mesh well with Pius XI's general approach of persuasion rather than coercion; it could tend to impose desired results instead of making the desired results a matter of free choice within a justly structured system. The socially just goal is a system where virtuous people will ordinarily make the optimal choice for themselves and others.

Kelso and Adler's principle of limitation, however, left this third principle open to being misinterpreted as something akin to Huey Long's "Share Our Wealth" proposal in which all wealth over a predetermined amount would be confiscated and redistributed. It also calls to mind Belloc's proposals in

---

62   Kelso and Adler, *The Capitalist Manifesto*, 68.

The Restoration of Property that would impose disabilities on the rich instead of removing them from the poor.[63]

It was therefore decided to expand the principle of limitation to that of social justice, with the orientation that economic justice includes removing barriers to full participation and distribution instead of creating additional ones. As the feedback and corrective principle, therefore, social justice governs participative and distributive justice, enabling both to operate properly.

Within an economic system, social justice restores balance between overall production and consumption. It rebalances participative justice and distributive justice when the system violates either of these essential principles. Social justice includes, but is not limited to, a concept of limitation that discourages personal greed and prevents monopolies and barriers to participation.

In general, social justice embodies the principles of solidarity and subsidiarity: every person has a moral responsibility to organize with others to correct organizations, institutions, laws, and the social order itself at every level whenever the principles of participative or distributive justice are violated or are not operating properly. The application of social justice to the common good of specific economic institutions brings those institutions into conformity with the demands of the common good of all society.

Kelso's breakthrough in moral philosophy and its application to the problem of financing a program of expanded capital ownership renders the Great Reset and similar proposals

---

[63]   Belloc, *The Restoration of Property*, 133–44.

completely unnecessary as solutions. They are at best barely tolerable expedients in a dire emergency. Even that is only the case if people organize to implement a more just solution in conformity with the laws and characteristics of social justice and the principles of economic justice.

6.5. The Pillars of a Just Market Economy

The Great Reset and similar proposals violate human dignity at the most basic level by assuming as a given that most people cannot own capital. Louis Kelso's ideas upset the Great Reset and prove every socialist and capitalist in the world wrong by offering a just, free market-based theory of ownership with a practical means of applying this theoretical framework.

This is important because private property in capital is the chief support of human dignity within modern civil society.[64] Thus, as it is in Catholic social teaching, private property in capital is a key element in binary economics, a place it shares with the role of private property in the thought of Father Heinrich Pesch, SJ.

Pesch described private property as one of the "three institutional 'pillars' of economic society."[65] The others are "marriage and the family" and "the state as guardian of the positive legal order required by the value and rights of man."[66]

In Pesch's day as in ours, the insistence of the Austrian and German Catholic socialists that property was merely

---

[64]   Raphael Waters, "Freedom in the Political Order," *Social Justice Review* (November/December 2002): 165.

[65]   Gustav Gundlach, "Solidarist Economics, Philosophy and Socio-economic Theory in Pesch" *Social Order*, April 1951, 185.

[66]   Ibid.

prudential was simply a restatement of their traditional dogma that private property should be abolished. It was also, in part, a direct reaction to Pesch's adamantine stance on the sacredness of private property: "Because man was the center of the social system, he also was at the center of economic activity. Therefore, Pesch accepted the principle of wage labor and of the separation of labor and capital. (1, 17–18) He demanded, however, that the community, acting through the state, interfere to prevent capitalist excesses which might threaten the economic status of individuals, and especially their private property which they must have to be able to fulfill their function in society. (1, 188, 206–207)."[67]

Not surprisingly, private property in capital figures prominently in "the Four Pillars of a Just Market Economy" of binary economics and the Just Third Way of Economic Personalism. Based on natural law principles, binary economics recognizes a natural synergy, as opposed to an unavoidable trade-off, between economic justice and efficiency within a global free marketplace. Rejecting laissez-faire assumptions and the prescriptions of the Great Reset and similar proposals, binary economics holds that a truly free and just global market requires:

- expanded capital ownership,
- a limited economic role for the State,
- free and open markets, and
- and restoration of private property.

---

[67]   Alfred Diamant, *Austrian Catholics and the Social Question, 1918-1933* (Gainesville, Florida: University of Florida Press, 1959), 21. References in parentheses are to Pesch's *Lehrbuch der Nazionalökonomie* (1905).

Expanded Capital Ownership

Consistent with Article 17 of the United Nations' Universal Declaration of Human Rights supported by Pius XII, this refers to the right to own capital, individually or in free association with others. As Leo XIII said, "The law . . . should favor ownership, and its policy should be to induce as many as possible of the people to become owners."[68]

Mere income is not the goal of economic personalism. As noted above, the hallmark of an economically just society (and, more broadly, of social justice) is its systematic approach to balancing the demands of participative and distributive justice. This is done by lifting institutional barriers which have historically denied equal ownership opportunities—a natural right—to every citizen.[69]

A major problem in focusing on mere income is that it inevitably ends up treating people like permanent dependents. This inhibits or prevents them from becoming more fully human—that is, acquiring and developing virtue. Widespread private property in capital is key to personal empowerment and the "good life" of virtue.

Significantly, as auxiliary bishop of Kraków in April of 1960 in the suburb of Nowa Huta, Wojtyła brought about a peaceful resolution to days of rioting that threatened to spread throughout Poland by wresting concessions from the local communist political boss. Among these were an acknowledgement of the absolute rights to life, liberty, and

---

[68]   *Rerum Novarum*, § 46.
[69]   Cf. *Divini Redemptoris*, § 30.

access to the means of acquiring and possessing private property in capital that the regime had attempted to obliterate.[70]

As Wojtyła declared, private persons and non-State institutions such as organized religions have a natural right to own goods like the church they had received permission to build, but which the authorities had rescinded, touching off the riots. His talk that day was a de facto announcement that socialism had failed and is sometimes credited with igniting the spark that eventually led to the formation of *Solidarność* and the collapse of the Soviet Union.[71]

Making the dependent condition even worse is the fact that it is virtually impossible to guarantee income per se without government coercion or collective bargaining pressures backed up with the threat of State intervention.[72] This runs counter to the demands of personalism in general, and of an economically just society in particular, in which persons exercise free choice within a system of equal ownership opportunities and checks-and-balances to keep power spread to every person.

There has never been a society that, having redefined the institution of private property, avoided a similar redefinition of life and liberty, undermining the power and therefore the dignity of every human person. By abolishing private

[70] Gian Franco Svidercoschi, *Stories of Karol: The Unknown Life of John Paul II* (Liguori, Missouri: Liguori/Triumph, 2003), 130.

[71] Tomasz Pompowski, interviews with eye-witnesses and talks with His Eminence Cardinal Stanisław Dziwisz, aide to John Paul II.

[72] Goetz Briefs in *The Proletariat: A Challenge to Western Civilization* (New York: McGraw-Hill Book Company, 1937), 252.

property, socialists effectively redefine what it means to be human, as well as what it means to be alive or free.

There exists the problem of the fundamental principle of socialism: that meeting material needs relegates everything else, especially capital ownership, to unimportance; the end justifies the means. As Hilaire Belloc said of the various schemes such as social credit, they are not concerned with property—that is, with power—but with income.[73]

True, proposals such as the Great Reset would, in theory, solve the dilemma of how people meet their survival needs. It would, however, do nothing to assist them in becoming virtuous, which is (after all), the primary goal of Catholic social teaching, not the creation of permanent dependents.

A Limited Economic Role for the State

In *Rerum Novarum*, Leo XIII declared, "Man precedes the State, and possesses, prior to the formation of any State, the right of providing for the substance of his body."[74]

Limited economic power of the State is essential to economic personalism. It is too easy to "lead into temptation" world leaders who pass laws forcing people to act in ways the power elites view as desirable. Further, as a practical matter, when the State tries to take over control of everyday life, it becomes "overwhelmed and crushed by almost infinite tasks and duties."[75]

---

[73]   Belloc, *The Restoration of Property*, 9.
[74]   *Rerum Novarum*, § 7.
[75]   *Quadragesimo Anno*, § 78.

As a social tool, it is the nature of the State to be a monopoly. It controls coercion as a means of enforcing goals that society has accepted and internalized. Since monopolies ipso facto limit choice, the State should not own anything that could be owned and controlled directly and democratically by people.

In a personalist social order, God vests political sovereignty in persons who in turn delegate it to the State.[76] Since the State is the only legitimate civil monopoly, its power must therefore be subject to checks and balances and democratic accountability.

Ultimate sovereignty of every person can be maintained only if economic power is kept directly in the hands of the people, both as an inherent right and as a safeguard and protection against their own rulers. In general, the economic power of the State should be limited to encouraging private sector growth and policing abuses, ending economic monopolies and special privileges, removing barriers to equal ownership opportunities, and protecting property, enforcing contracts, and settling disputes.

There are also the equally important duties the State has in regard to supporting its proper function. These include preventing inflation and providing a stable and uniform reserve currency (a regulatory function distinct from creating money), promoting democratic unions to protect worker and ownership rights, protecting the environment, and promoting or (in extreme cases) providing social safety nets.

---

[76] This is the correct interpretation of § 19 of *Quas Primas*.

Free and Open Markets

Free, open, and non-monopolistic markets within an understandable and fair system of laws as the most objective and democratic means for determining just prices, just wages, and just profits.[77] A personalist economy is one in which everyone, not only a private sector or State elite, exercises economic power, which requires free and open markets in which everyone is free to participate.

Within a fair system of laws, the free market is the most objective and democratic means for determining just prices, just wages, and just profits as guided by the principles of justice, not someone else's idea of what (other) people need. As Leo XIII said, "Let the working man and the employer make free agreements, and in particular let them agree freely as to the wages; nevertheless, there underlies a dictate of natural justice more imperious and ancient than any bargain between man and man."[78]

When the market is restricted and controlled by a few, as proposed by promoters of the Great Reset, those who control the market for goods and services also control the marketplace of ideas. As can be seen in modern academia, economic freedom and intellectual honesty are inseparable.

When more people vote with their own economic power, the more objective and democratic the results. A free and open market, then, is one in which economic value judgments and choices are made by many people, not just a few.

---

[77]   *Centesimus Annus*, §§ 14–15, 42.

[78]   *Quadragesimo Anno*, § 45.

Where only a few people have the power to determine prices, wages, and profits, their judgments are necessarily more subjective and arbitrary. When anyone is in a position to dictate wages, prices, and profits, the result is a tyranny over the marketplace, and, eventually, control over people's subsistence.

Establishing a free, open, and non-monopolistic market, however, could be accomplished by eliminating all special privileges and monopolies created by the State, reducing all subsidies except for the neediest members of society, removing barriers to free trade and free labor, and ending all State-controlled or collectivist methods of determining prices, wages, and profits.

Restoration of Private Property

Restoration of private property, especially in corporate equity and other forms of business organization, is especially relevant today as ownership of corporations has become increasingly concentrated and minority owners deprived of their rights. Consistent with Catholic social teaching, people should control what is owned and enjoy the income it generates. They must own, not be owned. As Leo XIII declared, "A working man's little estate . . . should be as completely at his full disposal[79] as are the wages he receives for his labor. But it is precisely in such power of disposal that ownership obtains, whether the property consist of land or chattels."[80]

---

[79]   In context, "disposal" refers to control and enjoyment of the income.

[80]   *Rerum Novarum*, § 5.

To reiterate an important point, "property" is not the thing owned but the natural, inalienable absolute right to be an owner (i.e., "access"—the generic right of dominion) and the socially determined and limited rights of ownership (i.e., "use"—the universal destination of all goods). The limited and socially determined *rights of* property include the enjoyment of the fruits or profits of what is owned. As Kelso put it, "Property in everyday life, is the right of *control*"[81] as well as enjoyment of the income.

Illustrating the critical need to restore the rights of private property, especially in corporate equity—and not erode them further by expanding the concept of stakeholder to include non-owners as proposed in the Great Reset—is something called "the Business Judgment Rule." This is the principle that if the board of directors of a corporation decide something is in the best interests of the company (such as not paying dividends), minority shareholders have no recourse other than to sell their shares.

The only way minority shareholders can force a board of directors to pay dividends is to prove that the company will not need the money for other purposes. Since proving a negative is logically impossible—you cannot prove that something is *not*, only that something *is*—minority shareholders effectively have no legal rights under US law.

---

[81]   Louis O. Kelso, "Karl Marx: The Almost Capitalist," *American Bar Association Journal*, March 1957; Belloc, *The Restoration of Property*, 16–17. Cf. Matthew Habiger, *Papal Teachings on Private Property*, 1891-1981 (Lanham, Maryland: University Press of America, 1990).

Through the application of the Business Judgment Rule and similar principles, ownership and control have been separated in many instances throughout the world. That is why restoration of the rights of private property, especially in corporate equity, is essential for an economically just society.

Property secures personal choice, and, as John Locke observed, is the key safeguard of all other human rights. Where people want to de-monopolize access to ownership and profits in a nation's productive enterprises, it must also restore the original personal rights of property in the means of production, not erode them further. Private property is the individual's link to the economic process in the same way that voting is his link to the political process. When either is absent, the individual is disconnected or alienated from the process—from his milieu, his natural environment.

Restoring the idea as well as the fact of private property involves reforming laws that prohibit or inhibit acquisition and possession of private property. This would include ensuring that all owners, including shareholders, have their full rights to participate in control of their productive property, to hold management accountable through shareholder representatives on the corporate board of directors, and to receive profits in proportion to their ownership stakes.

Great Resets and similar proposals are completely unnecessary. Restoring owners' full rights in private property results in securing personal choices and economic self-determination for every citizen. It links income distribution to economic participation, not only by present owners of existing assets, but also by new owners of future wealth.

6.6. Vatican II and After

For many Catholics and even non-Catholics, Vatican II missed the mark, ultimately contributing to the Great Reset. The problem is that some people think that it was a disaster because it was not implemented, and others because it was. Paradoxically, both are partly right while being completely wrong.

Why Vatican II?

Contrary to popular myth, Pope John XXIII did not call the Second Vatican Council to institute ultrasupernaturalism and transform the Catholic Church into a socialist cabal.[82] His intent, in fact, was precisely the opposite: to restart efforts to counter the New Things.

In his inimitable fashion, Evelyn Waugh hinted that, as suggested by his selection of a pontifical name,[83] John XXIII might have planned the council from the moment of his election to bring order to what he saw as the havoc wreaked by the Fabian Society and their ilk. This was due to the Fabian takeover of the British government in the 1945 election and the usurpation of the interpretation of Catholic social teaching by Monsignor Ryan in the United States.[84] As a result, the world greatly needed a corrective to halt

---

[82] Ralph M. McInerny, *What Went Wrong with Vatican II: The Catholic Crisis Explained* (Manchester, New Hampshire: Sophia Institute Press, 1998), 7–8.

[83] Evelyn Waugh, *The Essays, Articles and Reviews of Evelyn Waugh* (London: Penguin Books, 1983), 616–17.

[84] Franz H. Mueller, *The Church and the Social Question* (Washington, DC: American Enterprise Institute for Policy Research, 1984), 117–18.

what Waugh viewed as a headlong plunge into a cesspool of socialism and ultrasupernaturalism.

Although hardly a prophet, Waugh predicted what would happen if the Catholic Church went with the collectivist version of liberal democracy on which the Fabians and Ryan based their theories, instead of the personalist version chronicled by Alexis de Tocqueville during his visit to the United States in the 1830s. From his vantage point in the mid-twentieth century, Waugh saw a grave danger to the whole of civilization as well as to the Church if the State continued to expand its role: "As the State, whether it consist of the will of the majority or the power of a clique, usurps more and more of the individual's 'private life', the more prominent become the discrepancies between the secular and the religious philosophies, for many things are convenient to the ruler which are not healthy for the soul."[85]

Waugh did not foresee that Americans would adopt the collectivist liberal version of democracy, "the tragic fate of Europe,"[86] and undermine their own Christianity. As he concluded his analysis, "There is a purely American 'way of life' led by every good American Christian that is point-for-point opposed to the publicized and largely fictitious 'way of life' dreaded in Europe and Asia. And that, by the grace of God, is the 'way of life' that will prevail."[87]

That the "purely American 'way of life'" did not prevail is evident by the flood of books and other commentary on the council blaming it for anything and everything. Not by

---

[85]   Waugh, *The Essays, Articles and Reviews of Evelyn Waugh*, 380.
[86]   Ibid.
[87]   Ibid., 388.

coincidence, that same American "way of life" is also the personalist "way of life" excoriated by adherents of the New Things and proposals such as the Great Reset.

A Hijacked Council

Unfortunately, the very forces that John XXIII opposed were able to influence in no small degree the deliberations of the council itself. This was particularly in the insertion of imprecise, yet perfectly orthodox language that could be reinterpreted according to the desires of less than orthodox commentators. For example, Karol Wojtyła and the other Polish bishops submitted an orthodox and precise draft for *Gaudium et Spes* which, while influential, was not adopted as the base text.

More importantly, following the council, the interpretation of the documents and the nebulous "Spirit of Vatican II" turned what should have been an orthodox, even somewhat innocuous event into a disastrous triumph for the New Things. With the contraception issue as a major distraction, adherents of the New Things took advantage of the climate of dissent fostered by Monsignor Ryan at the Catholic University of America. They were able to hijack the council to support a chaotic agenda seemingly custom-made to bring the visions of Félicité de Lemannais and other Neo-Catholic and New Christian prophets to fruition and overturn two thousand years of adherence to common sense concepts of natural law.

One of the more baffling omissions from the council deliberations was the work of Kelso and Adler. As we saw above, this has the potential to resolve what has appeared to be an otherwise devastating, even fatal paradox in Catholic social teaching: the lack of a feasible and just means to finance expanded capital ownership.

What came after the council is both too depressing and too lengthy to chronicle here, but truth and common sense can never be totally extinguished. Efforts to counter the New Things and their effects in both Church and State continued. In 1984, Father Ferree, Norman Kurland, and other concerned people formed the interfaith Center for Economic and Social Justice (CESJ) in Arlington, Virginia.

The Pastoral on the Economy

It was not long before CESJ came into conflict with the distorted version of Catholic teaching. This occurred when Ferree and Kurland spoke before the Catholic Lay Commission on the US Economy, a group of Catholic laity led by former US treasury secretary William Edward Simon.[88] The meeting was in preparation for a hearing to make recommendations for what would become *Economic Justice for All*, the US bishops' 1986 pastoral letter on the economy.

Concerned about the US bishops' competence in economic matters, the Lay Commission had decided to draft an alternative economic pastoral letter. This would, they believed, counter what they saw as the danger of the bishops

---

[88]   George A. Kelly, *Keeping the Church Catholic with John Paul II* (San Francisco, California: Ignatius Press, 1993), 137.

advocating an expansion of the Welfare State and increased government control of the economy.[89]

Ferree's opening remarks were not particularly tactful: "Your present dialogue with the Episcopal Committee is a 'dialogue of the deaf,' not really being heard by either party."[90] Kurland then presented a detailed outline of the Just Third Way, of which he was, and is, one of the world's leading proponents. At one point, the *New York Times* described him as "a one-man lobbying organization for Kelsonian ideas" in Washington.[91] *Business Week* called him "the resident philosopher of ESOPs in the capital."[92]

The first draft of *Economic Justice for All* was submitted to the bishops in November 1984. After two more iterations, in November 1985 and June 1986, the bishops approved the final document by majority vote in plenary assembly in Washington, DC in November 1986.

Kurland's inputs were ignored. Ferree, acknowledged as one of the world's leading experts in the social doctrine of Pius XI, was relegated to a footnote that misstated his position. It was lumped in as one of "several different but related ways in the Catholic ethical tradition."[93] Ferree's work was rejected

---

[89]   Ibid.

[90]   Typescript of Father Ferree's remarks, September 11, 1984.

[91]   Milton Moskowitz, "Lawyer Labors to Turn Workers Into Owners," *The New York Times*, § 3.6.

[92]   John Hoerr, "ESOPs: Revolution or Ripoff?" *Business Week*, April 15, 1985, 108.

[93]   National Conference of Catholic Bishops, Washington, DC, *Economic Justice for All: Pastoral Letter on Catholic Social Teaching* (Washington, D.C.: United States Catholic Conference, Inc., 1986), 37.27.

in favor of that of Ryan,[94] whom Ferree had characterized as dissenting from the social doctrine of Pius XI.[95] Incredibly, the pastoral letter favorably cited the work of Keynes's protégé, Fabian socialist and New Age guru E. F. Schumacher.

A few months later, in a talk given Sunday, February 10, 1985, in Butler, Pennsylvania, Ferree expressed serious reservations about the direction the draft pastoral letter was taking. As reported in the local newspaper, "Fr. Ferree . . . explored Employee Stock Ownership Plans (ESOPs) against the background of the Bishops' (draft) Letter on the Economy. He said the ESOP concept was presented to the bishops but they failed to give it any more than a 'throw-away' line in their draft letter. He indicated he hopes for better recognition in revision."[96]

Ferree's hopes for "better recognition" of expanded ownership were not realized, and he died before he could make a more effective protest. Even the "'throw-away' line" about ESOPs in the draft was deleted in favor of a general comment vaguely mentioning "several arrangements [for worker ownership] gaining increasing support in the United States."[97]

The Presidential Task Force

In 1985, CESJ members mobilized bipartisan political support for congressional legislation which established the

---

94   Ibid.
95   Ferree, *The Act of Social Justice*, 87.
96   "Bishops' Letter Faulted," *Butler Eagle*, February 14, 1985.
97   *Economic Justice for All*, § 300.

"Presidential Task Force for Project Economic Justice" under President Ronald Reagan. First conceived in a strategy paper by Kurland, the proposal offered a personalist alternative to military solutions to counter Marxism in Central America and the Caribbean.

Enacted as part of the International Security and Development Cooperation Act of 1985, the legislation created the first presidential task force funded entirely with private donations. It was supported by both the US Chamber of Commerce and the AFL-CIO. John William Middendorf II, former ambassador to the Organization of American States and the European Community, served as chairman. Kurland, CESJ's president, was deputy chairman.

High Road to Economic Justice, the task force's 1986 report, was America's first official endorsement of expanded capital ownership as a policy for achieving economic democracy, the essential precondition for reestablishing the natural law foundation of a stable political order. Some of the task force's recommendations were adopted into US foreign policy. They were also included as one of the World Bank's "market based" options for debt-equity conversions through ESOPs.

Just Third Way supporters throughout the world praised the initiative, including Don Alberto Martén Chavarría[98] of *Solidarismo Costarricense*, which also gave its endorsement.[99] Others included the controversial Jesuit Father Claudio

---

[98]   Letter to Norman G. Kurland, February 28, 1979.

[99]   Testimony Delivered by Arnoldo Nieto on Behalf of the Solidarista Movement of Costa Rica Before the Presidential Task Force on Project Economic Justice April 21, 1986.

Solano, founder of the John XXIII Social School in San José, Costa Rica.[100]

On August 3, 1987, when CESJ delivered the task force report at a White House ceremony, where President Reagan gave a speech honoring the work of the task force members. He made special mention of the program of La Perla coffee plantation in Guatemala, where workers had been offered part ownership by the owner in exchange for their defending the plantation. The workers swiftly took arms against communist insurgents to protect their lives, liberty, and property. In other plantations in the region, workers had either run away or joined the insurgents.

In addition to making a reference to Lincoln's Homestead Act, Reagan declared, "Freedom and opportunity are not just for the elite, but the birthright of every citizen, that property is not just something enjoyed by a few, but can be owned by any individual who works hard and makes correct decisions." He then said, "I've long believed that one of the mainsprings of our own liberty has been the widespread ownership of property among our people and the expectation that anyone's child (even from the humblest of families) could grow up to own a business or corporation."[101]

A copy of the task force report was later presented to His Holiness Pope John Paul II in a private audience at the Vatican in company with representatives of Polish *Solidarność*. It was on this occasion that the pope gave his personal

[100] Christopher Caldwell, "Organized Labor Without Unions," *Insight* magazine, February 12, 1990, 34–35.

[101] President Ronald Reagan, Speech on Project Economic Justice, delivered August 3, 1987, Washington, DC.

encouragement of the work of CESJ. An unconfirmed report asserted that John Paul II later recommended the proposal on three different occasions to visiting heads of state.

In 1988, CESJ members and friends funded a Polish translation of the task force orientation book, *Every Worker an Owner*. Forty thousand copies were distributed throughout *Solidarność* channels prior to the dismantling of the Soviet Union. Copies (in English) were sent under cover letter in May 1988 to every US Agency for International Development mission around the world.

Later Developments

In 1991, Kurland expanded the "Abraham Federation" concept from a paper he originally authored in 1978 to offer a just and lasting solution to the conflict between Israelis and Palestinians, as well as other conflict-torn areas in the world. Based on the sovereignty of each human person and the principle of universal access to capital ownership as a basic right of citizenship, the Abraham Federation offers a justice-based framework and sound economic approach that can be adapted for rebuilding nations.

November 1991 saw a CESJ delegation travel to Rome to present the English and Polish versions of *Every Worker an Owner* to John Paul II in a Vatican ceremony. At CESJ's all-day seminar at the Vatican presenting the Just Third Way to Church leaders and scholars, Achille Cardinal Silvestrini presented the first Global Awards for Value-Based

Management[102] to the heads of three worker-owned companies on behalf of CESJ.

As a result of the Rome conference, CESJ's collection of essays, *Curing World Poverty: The New Role of Property*, was compiled and published in 1994 by the *Social Justice Review*, the official journal of the Central Bureau of the Catholic Central Union of America in St. Louis, Missouri. Approximately five thousand copies were distributed, reaching high-level policy makers, business executives, labor officials, scholars, and religious leaders worldwide.

A grant to CESJ from the William H. Donner Foundation in February 2001 funded development of an expanded ownership strategy to address the crisis in the US Social Security system. The report was released in December 2002. This report was later expanded into *Capital Homesteading for Every Citizen: A Just Free Market Solution for Saving Social Security* (2004).

The book presented a comprehensive program of monetary, tax, and expanded ownership reforms to address the crisis in America's retirement income system. Laying out an "economic blueprint for the Just Third Way," the book proposed changes to the money and credit system that would stimulate higher rates of non-inflationary private sector growth while simultaneously creating new owners of newly created wealth.

Late in 2003, through the efforts of Father Cassian J. Yuhaus, CP, HED, past president of CARA, CESJ

---

[102] Subsequently changed to "Justice-Based Management" to reflect more accurately the principles of economic and social justice promoted by CESJ.

representatives met with then-Senator Rick Santorum and key staff. This was regarding the application of a Just Third Way strategy and Capital Homestead initiatives for building effective economic democracy in Iraq. The meeting led to another on CESJ's "Oil Shares for Every Iraqi" proposal at the Pentagon with officials of the Coalition Provisional Authority and a representative of the Joint Chiefs of Staff.

Although US officials ultimately took no action on the proposal, it received a positive response and was sent to Ambassador Paul Bremer, then head of the Provisional Authority in Iraq. Through independent Iraqi channels, the concept was presented to advisors close to the Grand Ayatollah Ali Sistani, receiving a favorable response.

With the input of Iraqi scholars, the original "Oil Shares for Every Iraqi Citizen" proposal was changed to give one equal, non-transferable, lifetime share to every person in Iraq. This modification led to the idea of a "Citizens Land Development Cooperative," which would provide a way for previously government-owned land and natural resources to be owned by citizens as shareholders of a professionally managed corporation.

Based on years of historical evidence, it is eminently reasonable to say that only natural-law based personalism has any hope of offering a more just and human future for all. Individualist capitalism, collectivist socialism, or any combination thereof, whether you call it the New Christianity, the Kingdom of God on Earth, the New Deal, the economy of gift, the Great Reset, or anything else, not only are incompatible with human dignity but also have failed. That is why we must become, as Fuller put it, "Architects of the future, not its victims."

Saint-Simon's principle of subordinating everything to creating a better material life, especially for the poor, has failed spectacularly in both Church and State. As Pope Saint John Paul II reminded the bishops of North and South America in 1999 in his post-synodal document *Ecclesia in America*, "love for the poor must be preferential, but not exclusive."[103]

The best, perhaps only way to ensure that everyone benefits from and participates in the common good is through a genuinely democratic program of expanded capital ownership that includes every child, woman, and man. This provides a built-in preferential option for the poor, but without harming the rich. Everyone must own, or be owned.

---

[103]   *Ecclesia in America*, § 67.

CHAPTER 7

A Personalist Proposal

If there is one conclusion that can be drawn from this study, it is that the Great Reset and similar proposals—and the problems they are intended to solve—are far from being a "Catholic issue." Instead, they are *catholic*—that is, universal—as are the natural law principles of personalism that must underpin a truly just solution to today's situation.

A Three-Part Teaching

To recap, there are three parts to Catholic social teaching. The first part is intended to meet the demands of charity but also buy time to implement the second part: making it possible for everyone to meet his own material needs and those of his dependents through his own efforts. This involves, third, restructuring the economic order. It can best be done within a society characterized by widespread ownership of capital as well as of labor.

Capital ownership vests people with the power essential to carry out the third part of the papal social program: reforming the institutions of the common good ("the system") to enable people to participate fully in the common good to develop his or her individual, personal good. The ultimate to restructure the entire social order to provide the proper environment within which every single human being can become more fully human—that is, virtuous.

Thus, the popes have made widespread capital ownership the indirect or secondary goal of Catholic social teaching. The primary or direct goal is to reform the system and remove barriers to participation through acts of social justice to make capital ownership, and thus personal empowerment, *possible* by every child, woman, and man. Then, with the economic freedom thereby attained, every person can become virtuous, or at least have access to the opportunity and means to do so.

The Act of Social Justice

Evidence indicates that families could be significantly strengthened, and systemic racism greatly diminished, by personal empowerment through expanded capital ownership. With respect to families, as the economic power of individuals and families has diminished, that of the State has increased. As a result, family members tend to look outside the family in times of difficulty and even in the ordinary course of events. This seriously weakens family bonds.

As for systemic racism, the underlying principles of socialism, ultrasupernaturalism, and New Age thought seem to lead inevitably to an "us versus them" mentality. Anyone who is different, seems to have something you lack, or whom you fear is transformed into a hated enemy, and to justify this is presumed to be inferior.

This is seen in exaggerated form in the obsession with racial purity found in Theosophy, *Armanenschaft*, Ariosophy, and Nazi ideology, but has spread throughout society as the influence of the New Things has become embedded in Western culture over the past two centuries. This suggests that if the influence of the New Things can be removed by all persons having equal access to the opportunity and the means to become capital owners, systemic racism and similar problems can be reduced, even eliminated.

A Specific Proposal

We are now able to put all of this together in a specific proposal that we will call "the Economic Democracy Act." As we are most familiar with the situation in the United States, we will frame the solution primarily within that legal, tax, social, and political system. Being based on principles of natural law, however, it should be obvious how this proposal can be adapted to virtually any country or region.

What we call the Economic Democracy Act, or "EDA," is a proposed legislative program of tax, monetary, and fiscal reforms for promoting sustainable economic growth while creating equal opportunity and access for every citizen annually from birth to death to become a shareholder in the technological frontier. It is designed to connect every person to the global economy as a fully empowered participant and owner of productive wealth by dismantling structural barriers in our basic institutions and by financing capital formation through ownership democratization vehicles.

The EDA embodies Article 17 of the Universal Declaration of Human Rights, which—as we noted in the introduction—states, "Everyone has the right to own property, alone as well as in association with others," and, "No one shall be arbitrarily deprived of his property." This economic agenda for the twenty-first century provides a blueprint for leaders committed to restructuring the legal and financial system to grow the economy at maximum rates with no inflation, in ways that build a Just Third Way version of economic democracy as the essential foundation for effective political democracy. The Economic Democracy Act promotes an "equal capital ownership opportunity" approach for financing a sustainable and just economy.

Among other objectives, this act offers a just, free market-oriented way to save the Social Security System as a national retirement income security plan. At the same time, however, the Economic Democracy Act provides a new national policy to foster life-long "capital income self-sufficiency" to achieve true economic independence for all citizens. If implemented, capital ownership would be systematically de-concentrated and made directly accessible to every person without reducing property rights of the wealthy.

Money and Credit

Through the Economic Democracy Act, access to asset-backed money and capital credit—which today helps make the rich richer—would be enshrined in law as a fundamental right of citizenship, like the right to vote.

Every central bank in the world has the power to supply local banks with the money needed by businesses to grow. New money and credit for private sector growth would, however, be "irrigated" through Economic Democracy Accounts (a.k.a., "Capital Ownership Accounts") and other economic empowerment vehicles.

Through a well-regulated central banking system and other safeguards (including capital credit insurance to cover the risk of bad loans), all citizens could purchase, with interest-free capital credit, newly issued shares representing newly added machines and structures. These purchases would be paid off with dividends of these companies that are tax-deductible by the corporation. Nothing would come out of past savings or reduce consumption income.

Dividends used to pay for shares would be treated as tax-deferred income, on which any taxes due would be paid when the shares were sold. Additional dividends used for consumption income would be treated as ordinary taxable income.

Tax Reforms

With respect to the tax system, Economic Democracy reforms would simplify today's overly complex and generally unfair tax system by substituting a single-rate tax on non-exempt personal incomes from all sources. Possible tax reforms in the United States would include paying all entitlements and other government spending from general revenues, eliminating the payroll tax on workers and employers, making dividend payouts deductible to corporations, and balancing the budget.

The Economic Democracy Act would rewrite and radically simplify existing tax systems to balance budgets automatically. Its tax reforms would keep more money in the pockets of taxpayers from their initial earnings to cover their own health, education, housing, and other basic household living expenses. The Economic Democracy Act tax reforms would make legislatures more directly accountable and responsive to all taxpayers.

While encouraging corporations to issue new shares to finance their growth and pay out all dividends on their shares, the Economic Democracy Act would eliminate all tax provisions, personal deductions, tax credits, and exemptions (except for basic exemptions for adults and dependents) that unjustly discriminate against or discourage property accumulations and investment incomes for poor and non-rich families.

A single tax rate on all sources of labor or capital income over exemptions would be automatically set to meet all government entitlement and other programs, and to pay down past deficits. To meet personal living costs, the basic incomes of all taxpayers up to $30,000 per adult and $20,000 per dependent (or $100,000 for a family of four) would be free from any income or payroll taxes. To increase taxable income for all citizens, corporations could escape from the multiple corporate tax by deducting dividend payouts.

In contrast to the Great Reset that takes the present convoluted and complex tax, financial, and welfare systems as a given, a single tax covering incomes from dividends, interest, rents, and inflation-indexed capital gains would enable over-burdened social welfare systems to be funded out of general revenues. The single tax rate would drop significantly with a broadening of the tax base, as all citizens begin to receive substantial dividend incomes through their Economic Democracy Accounts and as entitlements (constituting two-thirds of the current budget) can be radically reduced after keeping all current entitlement promises.

Inheritance

With respect to inheritance, under the Economic Democracy Act, the wealthy would be encouraged to break up the estates they leave to their heirs so that wealth would not keep concentrating from generation to generation. Rather than taxing the estate, the recipients of the estate would be taxed over a certain amount (say $5 million) on what they receive through inheritance.

Thus, wealthy individuals could avoid all estate and inheritance taxes if they leave the estate to many people, such as relatives, friends, employees, etc. Recipients could further shelter their portion of the inheritance from taxation if they roll the assets into their tax-sheltered Economic Democracy Accounts.

This raises the issue of money: where is it to come from? The goal of widespread capital ownership begs the question of how people without past savings or the capacity to reduce consumption to save are to finance it.

The answer is found in the science of finance. As Harold G. Moulton explained in *The Formation of Capital* and Kelso reiterated in *The New Capitalists*, no rational person invests in new capital unless it is reasonably expected to pay for itself out of its own profits in the future. This is called "financial feasibility."

Instead of using past reductions in consumption, it is possible—even preferable—to finance using commercial bank loans backed by future profits tied to future increases in production. This is available today for 100 percent worker-owned companies under current US law for Employee Stock Ownership Plans (ESOPs).

Social justice would promote laws to extend access to bank-financed capital credit to all citizens as a fundamental human right, like the right to vote. Thus, everyone would be able to purchase capital by promising to pay for the capital once it becomes profitable—assuming that the promise is good and the capital does, in fact, make a profit. To secure the lender against the risk of loss if the capital is not profitable, the borrower should also have collateral: other wealth to make good on the promise.

The problem is that most people simply do not have other wealth to use as collateral. Still, commercial and central banks were invented to turn creditworthy promises into money so that lack of liquid savings would not be a bar to production. Similarly, insurance was invented to spread the risk of loss from one to many.

Kelso realized that combining the money-creating powers of commercial and central banks with capital credit insurance to replace traditional forms of collateral would make it possible for people without savings ("the poor") to purchase capital on the same terms as people with savings ("the rich"). He demonstrated the feasibility of his idea with the ESOP.

Adherents of the Great Reset and similar proposals should therefore be in the forefront of demanding that people own capital, not insisting on redistribution and the abolition of private property. They have already dismissed the need to labor for income. Why not capital ownership?

The question now becomes how, specifically, are people without savings supposed to become capital owners? We answer that question by examining the financing logic behind Kelso's Employee Stock Ownership Plan (ESOP).

Employee Stock Ownership Plan

Established under the Employee Retirement Income Security Act of 1974 (ERISA), ESOPs provide widespread access to capital credit to each employee in a company. Technically, the ESOP uses a legal trust that is "qualified" under specific US tax laws encouraging employee ownership. Fortunately, these laws are extremely flexible so that each plan can be tailored to fit the circumstances and needs of each enterprise, and deficiencies in the design of an ESOP can easily be corrected.

An ESOP channels capital credit through a trust representing employees from the same sources and subject to the same feasibility standards and corporate guarantees as direct loans to the corporation. Loan proceeds are used to buy shares for the workers, who make no cash outlay from payroll deductions or their savings, and none of their present savings is at risk. Shares are allocated to the individual accounts of workers only as blocks of shares are "earned"; that is, the company contributes cash out of future pre-tax profits to the trust. The cash, which is treated as a tax-deductible employee benefit, is used to repay the stock acquisition loan.

While the ESOP is the only vehicle employing Kelso's techniques under current law in most countries, others have been proposed using "ESOP financing" to make it possible for everyone to own capital. Under an Economic Democracy Act, then, the ESOP would largely be superseded.

Economic Democracy Accounts

Under the proposed terms of the act, a tax-deferred individual wealth accumulation trust or account would be established that we have tentatively called an "Economic Democracy Account." Loosely analogous to the Individual Retirement Account (IRA) under current US law—except that it would provide current income—every citizen would set up an account at a bank or approved financial institution to finance new stock issuances by an enterprise that has a financially feasible capital project.

All citizens could thereby acquire diversified holdings of newly issued, full dividend payout and full voting corporate shares on credit repayable with future tax-deferred dividends. Citizens would use "no interest" credit and new money created by the banking system to purchase qualified shares. In addition to the Economic Democracy Accounts, other vehicles have been proposed to assist people in accumulating capital stakes and participating more fully in the economic life of the community. Citizens Land Development Cooperatives, Homeowners Equity Corporations, Consumer Stock Ownership Plans, and Ownership Unions would do what the Great Reset promises but more directly and efficiently in accordance with the principle of subsidiarity, and more respectful of human dignity.

Citizens Land Development
Cooperative (CLDC)

The CLDC was designed to serve as a for-profit land planner and private-sector developer geared to sustainable development and growth at the community level. The CLDC would plan land use and develop the land within designated urban and rural enterprise zones for industrial, commercial, agricultural, residential, and public purposes. It would lease the land and structures for public and private uses and impose charges for improvement and maintenance. To avoid restraints on competition, the CLDC would normally not own other businesses that choose to locate on CLDC developed land.

In this way, every person would automatically receive a single lifetime, non-transferable voting share in the CLDC as a fundamental right of citizenship. This share would be cancelled upon death or if the citizen changed his permanent residence to another community. As shareholders and through their representatives on the CLDC's board of directors, local citizens could hold land planners and CLDC managers accountable for local land use decisions.

Homeowners Equity Corporation (HEC)

As a for-profit corporation that purchases foreclosed residential properties in a local community, and through a "lease-to-equity" arrangement, the HEC would enable homeowners facing foreclosure to 1) remain in their residence, 2) pay off the market cost of the residence, and 3) build up equity as shareholders of the HEC.

A HEC would purchase foreclosed or other properties and would lease them to tenants (who might be previous owners of the foreclosed properties). Rental payments would be used to make payments on the acquisition loans, meet operating expenses, and a just profit. In return, tenants would be earning shares in the HEC to the value of the home they occupy. They would thereby not own their homes directly, but—having turned a consumer item into an investment—would own shares in the HEC.

A HEC could provide a means for those who cannot afford monthly mortgage payments on their home to participate in a lease-to-equity program. Vouchers could be provided to those who cannot afford the monthly lease fees. This is similar to a proposal made by Hilaire Belloc in 1936 in his *Essay on the Restoration of Property*: "As for the urban type [of land], there ought to be a simple rule: every lease should automatically contain the power of purchase by installment; any lease not containing such a clause should be void if it were a lease for more than a certain number of years. And, should this ordinance lead to a restriction of long leases, that should be met by forbidding the short lease without the renewal for a longer period."[1]

Consumer Stock Ownership Plan (CSOP)

A CSOP would allow customers to become the owners of corporations in the non-competitive, regulated segment of the economy, such as telephone companies, electric and

---

[1]   Hilaire Belloc, *An Essay on the Restoration of Property* (New York: Sheed and Ward, Inc., 1936), 108–9.

gas production and distribution utilities, mass transit, and cable-vision systems. The companies would gain opportunities to fund their expansion through new equity issuances sold to CSOPs and ESOPs, with low-interest credit provided from commercial lenders and repayable with future pre-tax profits.

For their patronage, regular users of the system would get back ownership rights, represented by shares released to their CSOP accounts as the CSOP's debt is repaid with pretax earnings paid in the form of tax-deductible dividends on CSOP-held shares. Released shares would be allocated among users according to their relative patronage of the system. Future dividends on CSOP stock would be used to offset each user's monthly bill.

Ownership Unions

An important goal of economic personalism is the transformation of *labor* unions into *ownership* unions. This would expand the mission of unions to reach out to and represent all shareholders, including worker-owners.

An ownership union would work collaboratively with management to secure financing of advanced technologies and other new capital investments through Economic Democracy Accounts for all citizens. It would represent a growing constituency of worker- and citizen-owners on governance rights issues as well as to help lower all barriers to accelerated and sustainable rates of green growth in a more democratically accountable corporate and financial sectors.

Ultimately, ownership unions would shift the source of worker incomes from wages to profit and equity incomes. This would enable companies to become more cost-competitive in global markets and reduce outsourcing of jobs.

Through these and other vehicles that could be designed, an Economic Democracy Act would gradually change the major institutions of an economy from those of a wage-welfare system to a universal citizen ownership system. In particular, commercial and central banking systems would replace existing government debt-backed reserve currencies, with private asset-backing in ways that expand ownership of capital as described in section 6.3.

To embed and continue this change, the broader culture would be restructured to allow citizens to participate in the economy as capital owners with full property rights. This would empower them to lead lives of virtue.

Where Do We Go From Here?

Given the widespread misunderstanding of Catholic social teaching today, there is a great need for an educational effort to clarify the meaning of "economic justice." Without this, many people will think that Klaus Schwab's Great Reset is "Christianity in action" and the answer to all our problems instead of a set of barely tolerable expedients presented as a permanent solution.

Any proposal must be assessed in terms of how it affects the dignity and empowerment of each person within the globalized and high-tech economies of the twenty-first century. With that principle in mind, perhaps now is the appropriate time for an encyclical to teach the principles of economic personalism, especially those of economic justice.

Many people outside the Church look to Catholic social teaching as a model for integrating moral values into economic and political life. An encyclical on economic justice would thus guide people everywhere in the challenge of redesigning their basic economic laws and institutions—especially monetary, financial, and tax systems that are today widening the gap between the richest few and most of humanity. The goal would be to extend universal and equal capital ownership opportunities in the future without harming property rights of existing owners—to raise up the 99 percent without pulling down the 1 percent.

The primary focus of such an encyclical would be the economic empowerment and full development of every person based on the three principles of economic justice: 1) participative justice, 2) distributive justice, and 3) social justice. To clarify further, the encyclical should explain fundamental principles of natural law, the difference between principle and application of principle, and the reconciliation of individual ethics and social ethics by means of the act of social justice.

This book seeks to re-awaken, not only for Catholics but for all people, an understanding of the universal principles of natural law. When enough people understand economic and social justice as expressed within the social encyclicals and by many architects of the personalist Just Third Way, we can work effectively to restructure all institutions to conform to natural law.

In this way, the entirety of the common good and all its institutions can be made equally accessible to each human person, thus enabling every person to pursue and develop his or her unique God given potential. Respect for each human being's dignity and sovereignty is the strongest antidote to the false allure of wage and welfare systems, whether of collectivist socialism or monopolistic capitalism.

The pause in human affairs imposed by the COVID-19 pandemic calls us to rethink and reestablish the common good of all humanity on a more solid footing, in accordance with the universal principles expressed within Catholic social doctrine and other natural law-based faiths and philosophies.

How we proceed forward must promote and support the dignity of every child, woman, and man, the needs of all other people as a group, and the rest of creation. This is the meaning and purpose of human existence itself.

If we as members of humanity can unite around this objective, we will be well on our way to meeting R. Buckminster Fuller's "Challenge" for the future: "Make the world work for 100% of humanity, in the shortest possible time, through spontaneous cooperation without ecological offense or disadvantage of anyone."

As Leo XIII said in *Rerum Novarum*, a great deal of good will result if our economic institutions are redesigned to enable "as many as possible of the people . . . to become owners" at the earliest opportunity. Without turning most people into permanent dependents, as in the Great Reset, the principles of economic justice, once understood and applied, would create that ownership opportunity and open the means for every human being to live with dignity and to work with others to build a society of truth, beauty, love, and justice for all.

Select Bibliography

Encyclicals and Church Documents

Ad Beatissimi Apostolorum (1914)
Catechism of the Catholic Church (1993)
Centesimus Annus (1991)
Compendium of the Social Doctrine of the Church (2004)
Divini Redemptoris (1937)
Ecclesia in America (1999)
Evangelii Praecones (1951)
Evangelium Vitae (1995)
Humani Generis (1950)
Laborem Exercens (1981)
Pascendi Dominici Gregis (1907)
Quadragesimo Anno (1931)
Quanto Conficiamur (1863)
Quas Primas (1925)
Rerum Novarum (1891)
Singulari Nos (1834)
Solicitudo Rei Socialis (1987)
Studiorum Ducem (1923)
Testem Benevolentiae Nostrae (1899)
Ubi Arcano (1922)

Ut Unum Sint (1995)

Articles

Andelson, Robert V. "Monsignor John A. Ryan's Critique of Henry George." *American Journal of Economics and Sociology* 33, no. 3 (1974): 273–86.

Anonymous. "Pius IX and the Revolutions at Rome." *The North American Review* 74, no. 154 (January 1852).

Anonymous. "The Beef Trust Enjoined: Address by Judge Peter S. Grosscup." *The Outlook* (February 28, 1903).

Anonymous, Unión Soldiarista Costarricense (USC). *Solidarismo: A Tool for Democracy, Justice and Peace.* San Jose, Costa Rica: Unión Solidarista Costarricense, 1985.

Brownson, Orestes. "Church Unity and Social Amelioration." *Brownson's Quarterly Review* (July 1844).

Caldwell, Christopher. "Organized Labor Without Unions." *Insight* magazine (February 12, 1990).

Dettloff, Dean. "The Catholic Case for Communism." *America* magazine (April July 23, 2019).

Farnam, Henry W. "Progress and Poverty in Politics." *The New Englander and Yale Review* 46, no. 205 (April 1887).

Gorren, Aline. "The Moral Revival in France." *The Atlantic Monthly* (September 1893).

Greaney, Michael D. "The Business Cycle: A Kelsonian Analysis." *American Journal of Economics and Sociology* (2015).

Grosscup, Peter S. "Address of the Hon. Peter S. Grosscup, Judge of the U.S. Circuit Court of Appeals, on 'Abraham Lincoln'," Celebration of Abraham Lincoln's Birthday and Second Anniversary of General James Shields Council No. 967 Knights of Columbus, February 12, 1907 (event program).

Grosscup, Peter S. "How to Save the Corporation." *McClure's Magazine* (February 1905).

Gundlach, Gustav. "Solidarist Economics, Philosophy and Socio-economic Theory in Pesch." *Social Order* (April 1951).

Hayek, F. A. "Reflection on the Pure Theory of Money of Mr. J. M. Keynes." *Economica* 11 (1931): 270–95.

Heinzle, J. U. "Galileo Galilei and Dr. McGlynn." *The Catholic World* 46, no. 271 (October 1887).

Hoerr, John. "ESOPs: Revolution or Ripoff?" *Business Week* (April 15, 1985).

Kelso, Louis O. "Karl Marx: The Almost Capitalist." *American Bar Association Journal* (March 1957).

Keynes, John Maynard. "The Works of Bagehot." *The Economic Journal* 25 (1915):369–75.

Kuligowski, Piotr. "Sword of Christ: Christian Inspirations of Polish Socialism Before the January Uprising." *Journal of Polish Education, Culture and Society* no. 1 (2012).

Kuligowski, Piotr. "The Utopian Impulse and Searching for the Kingdom of God: Ludwik Królikowski's (1799-1879) Romantic Utopianism in Transnational Perspective." *Slovêne* 7, no. 2 (2018).

Kurland, Norman G. "A New Look at Prices and Money: The Kelsonian Binary Model for Achieving Rapid Growth Without Inflation." *The Journal of Socio-Economics* 30 (2001).

McGlynn, Edward. "Lessons of the New York City Election." *The North American Review* 143, no. 361 (December 1886).

McGlynn, Edward. "The New Know-Nothingism and the Old." *The North American Review* 145, no. 369 (August 1887).

Michael Barr. "Lee Kuan Yew's Fabian Phase." *Australian Journal of Politics & History* 46, no. 1 (March 2000): 110–26.

Murray, Harry. "Dorothy Day, Welfare Reform, and Personal Responsibility." *St. John's Law Review* 73, no. 3 (Summer 1999).

Preston, Thomas S. "Socialism and the Church." *The Forum* 5, no. 2 (April 1888).

Rosen, Elliot A. "Roosevelt and the Brains Trust: An Historiographical Overview." *Political Science Quarterly* 87, no. 4 (1972).

Sada Mier y Terán, Alejandro. "The Legitimacy of Certitude in Newman's *Grammar of Assent.*" *Yearbook of the Irish Philosophical Society, 2014/15.* Edited by Angelo Bottone. Maynooth, Éire: Irish Philosophical Society (2015), 49–63.

Strube, Julian. "Contested Christianities: Communism and Religion in July Monarchy France." *Socialist Imaginations: Utopias, Myths, and the Masses.* New York: Routledge, 2018 (preprint).

Strube, Julian. "Socialism and Esotericism in July Monarchy France." *History of Religions* (July 2016).

Strube, Julian. "Socialist Religion and the Emergence of Occultism." *Religion* 46 (2016):3.

Turner, Frederick Jackson. "The Significance of the Frontier in American History." *Annual Report of the American Historical Association for the Year 1893.* Washington, DC: Government Printing Office, 1894.

Vogüé, Vicomte Eugène Melchior de. "The Neo-Christian Movement in France," *Harper's New Monthly Magazine* (January 1892).

Waters, Raphael. "Freedom in the Political Order." *Social Justice Review* (November/December 2002).

Williams, Thomas D. "What is Thomistic Personalism?" *Alpha Omega* VII, no. 2 (2004).

Books

Catholicism, the Popes, and Social Teaching

Brownson, Orestes A. *Essays and Reviews, Chiefly on Theology, Politics, and Socialism.* New York: D. & J. Sadlier & Co., 1852.

Civardi, Luigi. *A Manual of Catholic Action, A New and Enlarged Edition.* New York: Sheed and Ward, 1943.

Diamant, Alfred. *Austrian Catholics and the First Republic: Democracy, Capitalism, and the Social Order 1918-1934.* Princeton, New Jersey: Princeton University Press, 1960.

Diamant, Alfred. *Austrian Catholics and the Social Question, 1918-1933.* Gainesville, Florida: University of Florida Press, 1959.

Habiger, Matthew. *Papal Teachings on Private Property, 1891-1981.* Lanham, Maryland: University Press of America, 1990.

Kelly, George A. *Keeping the Church Catholic with John Paul II.* San Francisco, California: Ignatius Press, 1993.

McInerny, Ralph M. *What Went Wrong with Vatican II: The Catholic Crisis Explained.* Manchester, New Hampshire: Sophia Institute Press, 1998.

Mueller, Franz H. *The Church and the Social Question.* Washington, DC: American Enterprise Institute for Policy Research, 1984.

National Conference of Catholic Bishops, Washington, DC. *Economic Justice for All: Pastoral Letter on Catholic Social Teaching*. Washington, D.C.: United States Catholic Conference, Inc., 1986.

Newman, John Henry. *Essays Critical and Historical*. London: Longmans, Green, and Co., 1897.

Ratzinger, Joseph and Marcello Pera. *Without Roots: The West, Relativism, Christianity, Islam*. New York: Basic Books, 2006.

Ratzinger, Joseph. *Europe: Today and Tomorrow*. San Francisco, California: Ignatius Press, 2004.

Richey, Lance and Adam DeVille, eds. *Dorothy Day and the Church: Past, Present, and Future*. Valparaiso, Indiana: Solidarity Hall Press, 2016.

Sarah, Robert Cardinal. *God or Nothing: A Conversation on Faith with Nicolas Diat*. San Francisco, California: Ignatius Press, 2015.

Thorn, William, Phillip Runkel, and Susan Mountin, eds. *Dorothy Day and the Catholic Worker Movement: Centenary Essays*. Milwaukee, Wisconsin: Marquette University Press, 2001.

Weigel, George. *The Irony of Modern Catholic History: How the Church Rediscovered Itself and Challenged the Modern World to Reform*. New York: Basic Books, 2019.

Belloc, Chesterton, Knox, and Sheen

Belloc, Hilaire. *The Crisis of Civilization*. Rockford, Illinois: TAN Books and Publishers, 1992.

Belloc, Hilaire. *An Essay on the Restoration of Property*. New York: Sheed and Ward, Inc., 1936.

Belloc, Hilaire. *The Great Heresies*. Rockford, Illinois: TAN Books and Publishers, Inc., 1991.

Belloc, Hilaire. *The Servile State*. Indianapolis, Indiana: Liberty Fund, Inc., 1977.

Chesterton, G. K. *Orthodoxy: The Romance of Faith*. New York: Image Books, 1990.

Chesterton, G. K. *Saint Francis of Assisi*, London: Hodder and

Stoughton, Ltd., 1923.

Chesterton, G. K. *Saint Thomas Aquinas: "The Dumb Ox."* New York: Image Books, 1956.

Chesterton, G. K., *The Everlasting Man*. New York: Image Books, 1955.

Chesterton, G. K. *G.K. Chesterton, Collected Works, Vol. V*. San Francisco, California: Ignatius Press, 1987.

Chesterton, G. K. *G.K. Chesterton, Collected Works, Vol. VI*. San Francisco, California: Ignatius Press, 1991.

Knox, Ronald A. *Enthusiasm: A Chapter in the History of Religion*. New York: Oxford University Press, 1961.

Sheen Fulton J., *Communism and the Conscience of the West*. New York: The Bobbs-Merrill Company, 1948.

Sheen, Fulton J. *Freedom Under God*. Arlington, Virginia: Economic Justice Media, 2013.

Sheen, Fulton J. *God and Intelligence in Modern Philosophy*. New York: IBE Press, 2009.

Sheen, Fulton J. *Religion Without God*. New York: Garden City Books, 1954.

Biography

Bell, Stephen. *Rebel, Priest and Prophet: A Biography of Dr. Edward McGlynn*. New York: The Devin-Adair Company, 1937.

Broderick, Francis L. *Right Reverend New Dealer: John A. Ryan*. New York: The Macmillan Company, 1963.

Carey, Patrick W. *Orestes A. Brownson: American Religious Weathervane*. Grand Rapids, Michigan: William B. Eerdmans Publishing Company, 2004.

Coren, Michael. *Gilbert: The Man Who Was G.K. Chesterton*. New York: Paragon House, 1990.

Dale, Alzina Stone. *The Outline of Sanity: A Life of G.K. Chesterton*. Grand Rapids, Michigan: William B. Eerdman's Publishing Company, 1982.

Day, Dorothy. *The Long Loneliness: The Autobiography of the Leg-*

endary Catholic Social Activist. San Francisco, California: HarperOne, 2009.

Farley, James A. *Jim Farley's Story: The Roosevelt Years*. New York: McGraw-Hill Book Company, Inc., 1948.

Ffinch, Michael. *G.K. Chesterton*. San Francisco, California: Harper and Row, Publishers, 1986.

Gilhooley, Leonard. *Contradiction and Dilemma: Orestes Brownson and the American Idea*. New York: Fordham University Press, 1972.

Goldman, Lawrence. *The Life of R.H. Tawney: Socialism and History*. London: Bloomsbury, 2014.

Kelly, J. N. D. *The Oxford Dictionary of Popes*. New York: Oxford University Press, 1986.

Malone, Sylvester L. *Dr. Edward McGlynn*. New York: Dr. McGlynn Monument Association, 1918.

Reeves, Thomas C. *America's Bishop: The Life and Times of Fulton J. Sheen*. San Francisco, California: Encounter Books, 2001.

Riley, Kathleen L. *Fulton J. Sheen: An American Catholic Response to the Twentieth Century*. New York: Society of St. Paul, 2004.

Sheen, Fulton J. *Treasure in Clay: The Autobiography of Fulton J. Sheen*. Garden City, New York: Doubleday & Company, Inc., 1979.

Sheppard, Lancelot C. *Lacordaire: A Biographical Essay*. New York: The Macmillan Company, 1964.

Stearns, Peter N. *Priest and Revolutionary: Lamennais and the Dilemma of French Catholicism*. New York: Harper and Row, Publishers, 1967.

Svidercoschi, Gian Franco. *Stories of Karol: The Unknown Life of John Paul II*. Liguori, Missouri: Liguori/Triumph, 2003.

Ward, Maisie. *Gilbert Keith Chesterton*. New York: Sheed & Ward, 1943.

Ward, Wilfred. *Life of John Henry Cardinal Newman*. London: Longmans, Green, and Co., 1913.

Weigel, George. *Witness to Hope: The Biography of Pope John Paul II, 1920-2005*. New York: Harper Perennial, 2005.

History

Burrow, J. W. *The Crisis of Reason: European Thought, 1848-1914*. New Haven, Connecticut: Yale University Press, 2000.

Corrigan, Michael A. *Private Record of the Case of Rev. Edward McGlynn*, ms. *cir.* 1895.

Davies, Norman. *God's Playground: A History of Poland, Volumes I and II*. New York: Columbia University Press, 1984.

Davies, Norman. *Heart of Europe: A Short History of Poland*. Oxford, UK: Oxford University Press, 1984.

Goodrick-Clarke, Nicholas. *The Occult Roots of Nazism*. London, UK: Tauris Parke, 2004.

Dickey, J. D. *American Demagogue: The Great Awakening and the Rise and Fall of Populism*. New York: Pegasus Books, 2019.

Harrison, John F. C. *Quest for the New Moral World: Robert Owen and the Owenites in Britain and America*. New York: Charles Scribner's Sons, 1969.

Jennings, Chris. *Paradise Now: The Story of American Utopianism*. New York: Random House, 2016.

Johnson, Oakley C. *Robert Owen in the United States*. New York: Humanities Press for the American Institute for Marxist Studies, 1970.

McLoughlin, William G. *Revivals, Awakenings, and Reform: An Essay on Religion and Social Change in America, 1607-1977*. Chicago, Illinois: University of Chicago Press, 1978.

Morris, Adam. *American Messiahs: False Prophets of a Damned Nation*. New York: W.W. Norton and Company, 2019.

O'Sullivan, John. *The President, the Pope, and the Prime Minister: Three Who Changed the World*. Washington, DC: The Regnery Publishing Company, Inc., 2006.

Pease, Edward R. *A History of the Fabian Society*. Lincoln, U.K.: Frank Cass & Co., Ltd., 1963.

Roe, W. G. *Lamennais and England: The Reception of Lamennais's Religious Ideas in England in the Nineteenth Century*. London: Oxford University Press, 1966.

Zamoyski, Adam. *The Polish Way: A Thousand-Year History of the Poles and Their Culture*. New York: Hippocrene Books, 1994.

Philosophy and Theology

Adler, Mortimer J. *How to Think About God: A Guide for the Twentieth Century Pagan*. New York: Collier Books, 1980.

Adler, Mortimer J. *Six Great Ideas*. New York: Macmillan Publishing Company, 1981.

Adler, Mortimer J. *Truth in Religion: The Plurality of Religions and the Unity of Truth*. New York: Macmillan Publishing Company, 1990.

Aquinas, Thomas. *Commentary on Aristotle's Politics*. Indianapolis, Indiana: Hackett Publishing Company, Inc., 2007.

Aquinas, Thomas. *Summa Theologica*. Westminster, Maryland: Christian Classics, 1948.

Aristotle. *The Nicomachean Ethics*. Buffalo, New York: Prometheus Books, 1987.

Aristotle. *The Politics*. London: Penguin Books, 1981.

Bocheński, J. M. *The Methods of Contemporary Thought*. New York: Harper and Row, Publishers, 1968.

Burrow, Rufus, Jr. *God and Human Dignity*. Notre Dame, Indiana: University of Notre Dame Press, 2006.

Ferree, William J. *Social Charity*. Arlington, Virginia: Center for Economic and Social Justice, 2003.

Ferree, William J. *Forty Years After . . . A Second Call to Battle*, incomplete ms., *cir.* 1985.

Ferree, William J. *Introduction to Social Justice*. New York: Paulist Press, 1948.

Ferree, William J. *The Act of Social Justice*. Washington, DC: Catholic University of America Press, 1942, ©1943.

Ryan, John A. *A Living Wage*. New York: Grosset and Dunlap, Publishers, 1906.

Ryan, John A. *Distributive Justice*. New York: The Macmillan Company, 1916.

Ryan, John A. *Social Doctrine in Action: A Personal History*. New York: Harper & Brothers, Publishers, 1941.

Wojtyła, Karol. *Person and Community: Selected Essays*. New York: Peter Lang, 2008.

Wojtyła, Karol. *The Acting Person*. Boston, Massachusetts: D. Reidel Publishing Company, 1979.

Politics, Law, and Sociology

Bagehot, Walter. *The English Constitution*. Portland, Oregon: Sussex Academic Press, 1997.

Bokenkotter, Thomas. *Church and Revolution: Catholics in the Struggle for Democracy and Social Justice*. New York: Doubleday, 1998.

Cahill, E. *The Framework of a Christian State*. Dublin, Éire: M.H. Gill and Son, Ltd., 1932.

Goldman, Eric F. *Rendezvous with Destiny: A History of Modern American Reform*. New York: Vintage Books, 1956.

Hales, E. E. Y. *Pio Nono: A Study in European Politics and Religion in the Nineteenth Century*. New York: P.J. Kenedy & Sons, 1954.

Heineman, Kenneth J. *A Catholic New Deal: Religion and Reform in Depression Pittsburgh*. University Park, Pennsylvania: The Pennsylvania State University Press, 1999.

Marlin, George J. *The American Catholic Voter: 200 Years of Political Impact*. South Bend, Indiana: St. Augustine's Press, 2006.

Masterman, C. F. G. *The Condition of England*. London: Methuen and Co., 1909.

Rauch, R. William, Jr. *Politics and Belief in Contemporary France: Emmanuel Mounier and Christian Democracy, 1932-1950*. The Hague: Martinus Nijhoff, 1972.

Rommen, Heinrich A. *The Natural Law: A Study in Legal and Social History and Philosophy*. Indianapolis, Indiana: Liberty Fund, Inc., 1998.

Rommen, Heinrich A. *The State in Catholic Thought*. St. Louis,

Missouri: B. Herder Book Company, 1947.

Sabine, George H. *A History of Political Theory, Third Edition.* New York: Holt, Rinehart and Winston, 1961.

Spencer, Philip. *Politics of Belief in Nineteenth-Century France.* London: Faber and Faber Limited, 1954.

Tocqueville, Alexis de. *Democracy in America.* New York: Alfred A. Knopf, 1994.

Tocqueville, Alexis de. *The Recollections of Alexis de Tocqueville.* Cleveland, Ohio: The World Publishing Company, 1959.

Economics and Finance

Ashford, Robert and Rodney Shakespeare. *Binary Economics: The New Paradigm.* Lanham, Maryland: University Press of America, Inc., 1999.

Briefs, Goetz. *The Proletariat: A Challenge to Western Civilization.* New York: McGraw-Hill Book Company, 1937.

George, Henry. *Progress and Poverty.* New York: Robert Schalkenbach Foundation, 1992.

George, Henry. *The Condition of Labor: An Open Letter to Pope Leo XIII.* New York: Doubleday & McClure Co., 1891.

Greaney, Michael D. and Dawn K. Brohawn. *Economic Personalism: Property, Power and Justice for Every Person.* Arlington, Virginia: Justice University Press, 2020.

Harrington, Brooke. *Capital without Borders: Wealth Managers and the One Percent.* Cambridge, Massachusetts: Harvard University Press, 2016.

Kaufmann, M. *Christian Socialism.* London: Kegan Paul, Trench & Co, 1888.

Kelso, Louis O. and Mortimer J. Adler. *The Capitalist Manifesto.* New York: Random House, 1958.

Kelso, Louis O. and Mortimer J. Adler. *The New Capitalists: A Proposal to Free Economic Growth from the Slavery of Savings.* New York: Random House, 1961.

Keynes, John Maynard. *A Treatise on Money, Vol. I and II*. New York: Harcourt, Brace and Company, 1930.

Keynes, John Maynard. *The Economic Consequences of the Peace*. London: Penguin Books, 1988.

Keynes, John Maynard. *The General Theory of Employment, Interest, and Money*. New York: Harcourt, Brace & World, Inc., 1965.

Moulton, Harold G., ed. *Principles of Money and Banking: A Series of Selected Materials, with Explanatory Introductions*. Chicago, Illinois: The University of Chicago Press, 1916.

Moulton, Harold G. *The Formation of Capital*. Washington, DC: The Brookings Institution, 1935.

Moulton, Harold G. *The New Philosophy of Public Debt*. Washington, DC: The Brookings Institution, 1943.

Moulton, Harold G. *The Recovery Problem in the United States*. Washington, DC: The Brookings Institution, 1936.

Mulcahy, Richard E. *The Economics of Heinrich Pesch*. New York: Henry Holt and Company, 1952.

O'Brien, George. *An Essay on Medieval Economic Teaching*. London: Longmans, Green & Co, 1920.

Perkins, John. *Confessions of an Economic Hit Man*. San Francisco, California: Berrett-Koehler Publishers, Inc., 2004.

Schwab, Klaus and Nicholas Davis. *Shaping the Future of the Fourth Industrial Revolution*. New York: Currency Books, 2018.

Schwab, Klaus and Thierry Malleret. *COVID-19: The Great Reset*. Geneva, Switzerland: World Economic Forum, 2020.

Schwab, Klaus and Peter Vanham. *Stakeholder Capitalism: A Global Economy that Works for Progress, People and Planet*. Hoboken, New Jersey: John Wiley and Sons, Inc., 2021.

Index